DEMOCRATIC TRANSFORMATION AND SOCIAL CHANGE IN NIGERIA

(A Personal Journey from Intellectual Conscience to Praxis)

Vol. One

DEMOCRATIC TRANSFORMATION AND SOCIAL CHANGE IN NIGERIA

(A Personal Journey from Intellectual Conscience to Praxis)

Vol. One

Udenta O. Udenta

KRAFT BOOKS LIMITED

Published by

Kraft Books Limited
6A Polytechnic Road, Sango, Ibadan
Box 22084, University of Ibadan Post Office
Ibadan, Oyo State, Nigeria
✆ +234 (0)803 348 2474, +234 (0)805 129 1191
E-mail: kraftbooks@yahoo.com
Website: www.kraftbookslimited.com

First published 2015

ISBN   978–978–918–234–3 (Paperback)
ISBN   978–978–918–287–9 (Hardback)

First printing, May 2015

Dedication

Dr Arthur Agwuncha Nwankwo, mentor, teacher, guide
&
Dr Nuel Ojei, greatness is a state of being; in you have all
its fine elements found a true home

Acknowledgements

There are two sets of people worthy of thanks in the course of preparing a work of this nature. The first are those individuals who played a part in realizing my set objective in constructing this vision, while the second category is made up of those who played and have continued to play a crucial role in my life in more broad terms. Because of the specific nature of this enterprise, apart from my deep love and profound appreciation for my parents, the late Chief B. I. Udenta, my mother, Madam Paulina Ijeabalu Udenta and my siblings, Fidel Chinelo Nkire (nee Udenta), Okey Maurice and Ben Ikeneche Jr for our distinctly unique family moments and abiding values, a greater number of individuals worthy of mention bestride the different historical and cultural moments captured in this narrative.

My formative and archetypal growing up years in my native community of Mgbowo would have been devoid of those inscrutable and elemental forces of peer group joys, pains, laughter, mischief and occasional social excesses that combine to form all-round personalities without the solidarity and camaraderie of the following: Chijioke Okibe, Johannes Okibe, Charles Okibe, Basil Eze, Charles Eze, Charlie Kama, Jude Kama, Jude Azionu, Tony Ude, Romanus Onyanta, Bony Ikerionwu, Charles Onuigbo, Ikechukwu Urulor, Humphrey Ezenta, Arobath Eze, Jude Azide, and so many others whose passion and enthusiasm for life remains ever fresh in my imagination.

My high school experiences were enriched by the creative energy, joyful competition and scholarly and athletic pursuits of an incredible array of school mates and friends, some of whom I celebrated in the General Introduction to my Six-Volume Collected Boyhood Works. They include Simon Agu (Asa Si Agu), Patrick Isiogwu, Emma Akpa, Richard Uwakwe, Augustine Umahi, the late Peter Chike, the late Christopher Aju, Bernard Ugwu, Emmanuel Chukwuma Nwobodo (Sinbad), William Ochife, Victor Ochi, Emma Onuorah, Job (Onuorah) Ude, Martin Okonkwo and so many other worthy companions whose names I cannot currently recollect.

My undergraduate studies at the University of Nigeria, Nsukka (1980-1984), defined my identity, crystallized my deeply held moral and ideological principles and loyalties and laid a secure foundation for my future intellectual development and critical social practice. All these would have been impossible without the fraternal fellowship of my comrades in the Marxist Youth Movement such as Femi Ahmed, Alex Ayatulumou (Ayatolla), Nkem Abonta, Alex Anemaku, Innocent Akenuwa, Antifon R., Mobolade Omonijo, Emma Ezeazu, Chris Uyot, and Sunday Udeze, among several others; our principal Staff Adviser, Prof. Uzodinma Nwala, and other inspiring lecturer-comrades like the late Prof. Ikenna Nzimiro, the late Prof. Inyang Eteng, Prof. Obasi Igwe, the late Prof. Nduba Echezona, Prof. Okwudiba Nnoli and Prof. Chidi; my classmates such as Emeka Onuorah, S.B.C. (Simon Boniface) Nwankwo, Joan Chinegbundu, Ozioma Ezeifedi, Emeka Okeke (Warhead), Chibuzo Asomugha, Stanley Armah, Azubuike Okoro, Alvan Ewuzie, Chinenye Ukwuagu and Imelda Emeribe, among several others; some of the members of the class immediately ahead of us, like the late Esiaba Irobi and Chuma Ezenyirioha, and the class or two immediately below us, like Chijioke Edoga; and my fellow activists in the Student Union Movement, like Charles Chukwuma Soludo, Johnny (Chinua) Asuzu, Paulinus O. Attah, Matthew (Ozonnia) Ojeilo, Uche Anioke, Emeka Nwosu, the late Iyke Oji, Tony Ezebuiro, Charles Agbo, the late Chima Ubani and Olu Oguibe. The likes of Ndu Nwanke, Tony Mgbeahurike, C.O.C

Egumgbe and Osita Okechukwu were a class or two ahead of us but interacted with and deeply influenced my set in large measure.

My profound sense of gratitude also goes to the teachers who opened my eyes and alerted my ears to new ideas even when their ideological affinity clashed with mine; my colleagues with whom I engaged in ceaseless debates and series of rational inter-subjective dialogic; and my students who sometimes managed to push my intellect to its limit in their spirited quest for knowledge. Top on the list of my teachers will be the late Professor Emmanuel Obiechina, the late Professor Donatus Ibe Nwoga, Professor Juliet Okonkwo, Professor Kalu Uka, Professor Romanus Egudu, Professor Chidi Nelson Okonkwo, Professor Obi Maduakor, Professor Chimalum Nwankwo, Professor Emeka Nwabueze, the late Professor Ossie Enekwe, Professor Virginia Uzoma Ola, Professor Emeka Okeke-Ezigbo, Professor Odun Balogun, Professor Okpure Obuke, Professor Tony Afejioku and Professor S. E. Ogude.

I extend warm thanks to the following colleagues of mine, some older in age who acted as a bridge between two generational intellectual forces and currents, especially in our individual and collective exploration of the place of the humanities in general, and literature and aesthetics in particular, in human transformation: Professor Tess Onwueme, the late Professor Ezenwa Ohaeto, Professor E. B. Uwatt, Dr Segun Agbaje, Elo Lesso, Professor G. N. Uzoigwe, Professor Afam Ebeogu, Rev Fr (Professor) Jude Aguwa, Rev Fr (Professor) J.I. Okonkwo, Professor Innocent Okoye, Ikem Nwosu, Dr O. U. Emele, Professor Osita Nwosu, Engr Emma Nwankwo, Arc Chika Eni, Professor J. O.J. Nwachukwu Agbada, Professor E. Chukwu, Professor U. D. Anyanwu, Professor Isidor Diala, Uzo Nwokocha, Bar Patrick Ugochukwu, Professor Emmanuel Inyama, Professor Okey Okeke, Professor Okey Okechukwu, Professor Ogbonna Onuoha, Professor Ezike Ojiaku and Barr Nnamdi Obiareri.

I owe a debt of thanks to my students between 1988 and 1998 who contributed significantly in enriching my knowledge of literature and cultural studies and who, in turn, repaid my efforts with academic devotion and a stringent application of their intellectual abilities in the course of their studies. I will specifically mention the likes of the late Nnamdi Abara, Vivien Jonathan, Emeka Obiakonwa, Chris Abani, Obinna Uruakpa, Lenin Chigbundu, Nkiru Okere, Chinyere Nwagbara, Christy Otuka, Uchenna Abadom, the late Emma Opara (aka Echeruo), Kelechi Akubueze, Gabriel Okorie, Azubuike Erinugha, Stella Nwankwo, Oby Udogu, Margaret Orji, Ifeoma Ume and a host of others.

The narrative in this volume covers the historical space up to 1996, from my formative years to my encounter with the Fourth Dimension Institution; and from the collapse of the Soviet Union/the retreat of Euro-Communism/the birth of a new, substantially deideologized New World Order to the formation and rapid growth of the Eastern Mandate Union (EMU). I will thus limit my appreciation to the Nigerian political elite whose politics I became heavily involved with during this historical period and who opened my eyes to the currents, mechanics, dynamics and contradictions inherent in bourgeois politics even when some of them subscribe to its radical, left-leaning variant.

My profound thanks go to the following; Dr Arthur Agwuncha Nwankwo, Ambassador Dr Patrick Dele Cole, the late Senator Francis Ellah, the late Dr Chuba Okadigbo, Hon Dubem Onyia, the late Prof. Chike Obi, the late Chief Clement Akpamgbo, the late Chief Philip Umeadi, Sen. Liyel Imoke, Sen. Aniete Okon, the late Edidem Bassey Ekpo Bassey, the late Sen. Paul Ukpo, the late Chief Jerry Okoro, the late Engr Victor Nwankwo, Chief Kingsley Ikpe, Sen. Dr Jim Nwobodo, Chief Chuba Egolum, Dr Jimmy Imo, Dr Inno Chima, Prof. Eddy Oparaoji, Tochukwu Ezukanma, Chief Emmanuel Iwuanyanwu, Prof. A. B. C. Nwosu, Sen. Ben Obi, Senator Uche Chukwumerije, Dr Walter Ofonagoro, Amb Professor George Obiozor, the late Dr Stanley Macebuh, Sen. Ken Nnamani, Hon Ejike Nwankwo, Chief Onwuka Ukwa, Chief Sampho Nwankwo, the late Sen. Abraham Adesanya, the late Chief Bola Ige, the late Chief Pa Solanke Onasanya, Chief Ayo Adebanjo, Chief Olu Falae, Chief Ayo Opadokun, Sen. Kofo Akerele-Bucknor, the late Chief Ganiyu Dawodu, Chief Mrs Ayoka Lawani, the late Chief Gani Fawehinmi, Chief Ebenezer Babatope, Alhaji Balarabe Musa, and the late Dr Bala Usman,

Many thanks to the members of the Abuja Circle of Illumination for the ideas we have shared on countless occasions, the spirit of Enlightenment that characterizes our thoughts and the liberation of the mind we urge for all of humanity: Dr Umar Ardo, Ambassador Yusuf Mammam, Dr Yima, Sen. Dr Kelechi Akubueze, Ambassador F. O. Iheme, Kunle Fagbemi, Max Gbanite, Dr Godwin Udibe, Law Mefor, Tunde Akpeju, and Sunny Agollo.

To the members of the Abuja "Pentagon", most particularly the chairman, Toyin, Mariam, Shehu, Kazeem, Umar, Dan and F, true democratic spirit will never perish in Nigeria as long as your ideas live.

To my secretaries, Blessing and Lilian, thanks for the hard work, diligence and dedication that saw this work through.

Most importantly, to the two most precious people in my life, my wife Vivian, for her unconditional love, patience, sacrifice, understanding, support and perseverance as she endured for upwards of over seven years as I retire to bed 4 am every day in the course of preparing this work and the 19 others that are part of an integral writing and publishing project, and my son, Chidera, who, at 11 years, can predict Dad's every move, whim, mood and temperament and will adjust and behave accordingly. You are my all.

Preface

I have thought long and hard about constructing a narrative about the place of my growing intellectual consciousness and critical social practice in the context of the different historical, political and cultural turns the postcolonial Nigerian state took from the mid-1970s to the end of the 20th century. I was initially reluctant to create this three volume study on the realization that the charge of self-advertisement could be hauled in my direction, especially having not done any extraordinary or spectacular deed capable of altering and significantly re-ordering the character and direction of the polity. Since the philosophical construct of the Cartesian principle that locates the subject at the epicenter of human transformation beginning from the European Enlightenment, bourgeois historiography has been seduced by the specter of greatness as an individual claim rather than as the evolution of historical and class consciousness reposed in the souls of social imaginaries. I am, however, persuaded that the mediation of reality is an individual and collective human habit in the perpetual search for different portals and pathways of this affirmation of possibilities in life's multivalent spheres.

While the record of my conscience as an intellectual and social practice as an active member of my generation may not contain watersheds in the evolution of Nigeria's postcolonial spaces, it is by recording those realities and nuances of a normal life, that signposts may be marked for the appreciation of the momentous, history-changing acts that define a milieu. Our individual and collective acts of remembrances, of memories that may be lost forever, and of the unbroken pieces and tissues of recognition of the dialectics and dynamics of an era transforming into new historical and cultural quantities and qualities, should still occupy a special place in the imaginings of those still faithful to the teleological foundation of knowledge, of the sacrament of objective reality, and of fidelity to the linearity of our historical progression. These should constitute the bulwark of active resistance to the anti-totalizing and anti-metanarrative logic of the postmodern traps of historical and cultural discontinuities, broken memories and ambiguities of identity, irrecoverable lost historical spaces and moments and the prescient maladies of life's assumed depthless, contingent and ephemeral qualities.

Let me quickly add that this three volume study, beginning with the present effort, is not an autobiographical narrative in the classic sense of the term. There is no attempt to recreate and evoke atmosphere, nor a desire on my part to give an account of personal history in any systematic fashion. I have consistently tried to locate personal situations, events, incidents and occurrences as backdrops to the changing canvass and tide of history, to situate them as signposts of wider social encounters as a mind consciously and instinctually mediates its intellectual and social identity in relation to the logic of bourgeois liberal democratic ethos and quantum social transformation that undergird the essence of its age. This work is thus more the reconstruction of the historical, ideological, political, social and cultural forces embedded in the ethic of a generation and their impact on the intellect and social awareness of an individual than an attempt at personal story-making aimed at self-legitimation.

Nevertheless, a peep into a number of historical substances of a decidedly personal nature may help in explaining the design of this project and locating the context of its significance as both a personal journey as well as a tribute to the life force of a generation. My liberal upbringing in a family that may be classed as belonging to the rural elite exposed me early in life to social, cultural and intellectual situations that might have been far ahead of its time. Before I turned 15, I had written over 17 pieces of prose, poetic, dramatic, quasi-philosophical and social commentary works, in addition to a near comprehensive recollection of life in a village high school. These works have been compiled into a six volume studies titled *Boyhood Works*. Also, before I left high school at 16 years I had read some of the essential classics of Philosophy, Greek mythology and political thought, apart from virtually all the canonical works of African literature, stopped attending masses as an act of intellectual rebellion against the highly rigidified doctrines of the Catholic Church, experimented with mystical philosophy, became a Marxist, and led a highly successful student resistance to oppressive school living conditions that brought instant positive results.

In 1981 when I was in the second year in university, at 17, I helped organize the resistance of Higher Institutions Students Association in my community of Mgbowo against what we construed as a decadent, oppressive elite political order, and wrote and widely circulated a pungent document calling on students and peasants to arms that heralded the unpalatable consequence of seeing the community occupied for two days by heavily armed policemen with full complement of Armoured Personnel Carriers (APCs). As a student Marxist, first as the Secretary of Publicity of the Marxist Youth Movement, and subsequently as the Secretary General of the Politbro of its central committee, I spent more time writing and pasting the weekly "Revolutionary Path" mass conscientization track all over the campus, traversing the length and breadth of the country clutching what the authorities classified as "subversive literature" and attending clandestine and mostly nocturnal revolutionary cell meetings rather than a rigorous pursuit of a degree in English and Literary Studies that I assured my parents I was undertaking.

At 23 I had finished the draft of *Revolutionary Aesthetics and the African Literary Process* and by 25 had completed the draft of three additional scholarly works on African literature from the perspective of Marxist aesthetics. My teaching and research career between that age and 34 was periodically interrupted by my involvement in pro-democracy and human rights activism and stints in detention, culminating in my abandonment of academia in 1998 due to a long spell in detention. Between 1997 and 1998, when I was in and out of detention, and before I assumed the position of the National Secretary of one out of the three main political parties in Nigeria with the death of Gen. Sani Abacha and the commencement of a new wave of democratization process, I had completed the draft of *Autonomy of Values: Determinations, Affirmations and Mediations*, my principal philosophical work, if it meets the most basic philosophic criteria.

The present effort is the first of a three-volume work that mediates the nexus between my intellectual consciousness and critical social practice and the overarching political and social forces that undergird Nigeria's democratic transformation within periodized historical spaces. Volume one maps the contours of the momentous late 1970s to the mid-1990s; a period that witnessed the construction of Nigeria's Second Bourgeois Democratic Republic with the negotiated withdrawal of the Praetorian Junta regime in 1979, the abortion of that Republic by another set of military despots in December 1983, and a series of military coup d' etat and counter coup d' etat that created and rapidly dissolved the Third Bourgeois Democratic Republic in November, 1993. The narrative also covers the deepening of the unequal and exploitative ties between a contradiction-ridden postcolonial state and the postmodern, post-imperial nations of the West through the injection of calamitous IMF and World Bank formulated Structural Adjustment Programme that dislocated the structural coherence of the Nigerian economy while emasculating not only its productive forces but ensured the retreat of the state from its social obligations to the people,

The period also was defined by the annulment of the June

14

12, 1993 presidential election won by the late Chief M. K. O. Abiola and the emergence of Gen. Sani Abacha as the most ruthless face of an oppressive neo-colonial military formation, and finally the rise of pro-democracy and human rights agitational groups such as the Eastern Mandate Union (EMU), the National Democratic Coalition (NADECO), the Campaign for Democracy (CD), the Committee for the Defence of Human Rights (CDHR), and the United Action for Democracy (UAD), that began to wage a life and death struggle against repressive junta hegemony. This first volume ends with the dissolution of the Soviet Union and the obsolescence of the Eurocommunist moment, and at the domestic Nigerian theatre the emergence of the Eastern Mandate Union (EMU) and its re-drawing of the Nigerian geo-strategic and ideological map.

At a personal level, this historical period coincided with my 'coming of age', for want of a better term, some of whose key ingredients include my passage from high school to university study, my involvement with radical student unionism and Marxist revolutionary agitation, my graduate studies and tenured appointment as a university scholar, teacher and researcher, my first creative and scholarly writings, and my wholesome participation in the pro-democracy and human rights projects aimed at restoring democracy in Nigeria. The only additional comment worth making here is that while till date I remain unquestionably an intellectual Marxist, critical environmental forces compelled my vicarious participation in the left-leaning bourgeois political programmes of the period, a situation that became more complicated in the next decade and half as the volumes two and three of this narrative will make abundantly clear.

Udenta O. Udenta
Abuja
September, 2014

Contents

Chapter

1

INTRODUCTION

On 1st October, 1960, 46 years after the British colonial imperialists defiled the organic developmental pattern of the autonomous and semi-autonomous social formations constituted by various ethnic nationalities and constructed a political and economic colonial polity they named Nigeria, the nation crossed into the threshold of postcoloniality as a sovereign state. The symbolic gesture of lowering an old flag and hoisting a new one was declarative, at least, on one score: a rite of passage was deemed complete on the sphere of the ritualization of the immanent transcendence of authority visibly transferred, as well as the dramatization of the positive omens and portents of a fresh dawn.

Those who were deceived by this rite were the many that hungered deeply for genuine political freedom, economic liberty, cultural emancipation and social inclusion. They were seduced by the flowery rhetoric and soaring oratory of the emergent political leaders whose eventual underwhelming performance stemmed as much from the deeply etched Greco-Roman, Post-Enlightenment capitalist brand they were weaned on and which was at odds with the concrete needs of their people as from naivety and inexperience in the complex art of statecraft. Once the initial euphoria of 'Uhuru' wore thin the contradictions embedded in the structural and institutional design of the Nigerian postcolonial state began to rapidly unravel its coherence and self-ascribed legitimacy. Implicated in this crisis of consciousness, national dissociation of sensibility and cultural dissonance were the conflation of political and economic forces that defined the dominant material relations in an increasingly spatialized postcolonial polity.

If the high assumption of postcolonialism was the inauguration of an egalitarian democratic state with all its solemn testaments of positive social transformation and cultural renewal, then Nigeria's seeming 50 plus years perpetual search for positive national direction on the stupendous weight of an integral national ideology and philosophy of being is a concrete indication of the near normativization of the steady abortion of the idea of the state as a cohesive force and the exhaustion of the historicist spirit that undergirds its existentialist formation. In metaphysical terms, therefore, the ontology of postcolonialism as a re-humanizing agency with deep institutional purchase into the birth of a new social order that negates the deformities of colonialism has been substantially desacralized and deconstructed by the truths of political instability and economic dislocation, failures of several democratization projects, grave poverty trap that has ensnared millions, collapse of state institutions and the moribundcy of social infrastructure, existence of multiple criminal platforms, low-level insurgencies by terrorists and extremist groups and the factor of institutionalized corruption as the high watermark of the state's political economy of power.

In periodizing Nigeria's postcolonial history, especially in the context of constructing democratic instruments and building democratic institutions, the 1960s witnessed the comprehensive desubstantialization and disaggregation of the emancipatory spirit of the anti-colonial, national liberation struggle forged by the alliance between the people through their mass political, labour, youth and women platforms and the emergent political and intellectual elite. The decentring and evacuation of the ontology of popular resistance occurred when ethnic supremacist political ideology, a dominant comprador bourgeois elite mentality, grossly unequal material relations of production, the political economy of corruption and graft and a fraudulent electoral process were emplaced at the epicenter of the nascent postcolonial social formation. The postcolonial democratic state, overburdened by the spatialization of social and cultural spaces on the weight of the already mentioned counterproductive political and economic dynamics, began to unravel rapidly.

The mapping of the dissolution of what one can classify as national political, social and cultural totalities, in addition to the fragmentation of its moral geography and spiritual architecture, began with the factionalization of the Action Group (AG) in 1962 and the subsequent treason trial and imprisonment of its leading lights, including its highly influential and charismatic founder, Chief Obafemi Awolowo; the 1962 national census debacle and the negotiated census results of 1963; the flagrant abuse of the electoral process in the 1964 General Elections that threatened to transform the multiform political pluralities of the early 1960s federalist philosophy of governance into a dominant one-party hegemony; and the inexorable descent into the nadir of political perdition, bloodletting, chaos and disorder in the Western region on the heels of the 1965 regional elections. The obliteration of the instruments, infrastructure and institutions of democratic governance occurred on 15th January, 1966, when a group of young military officers carried out a coup d' etat against the civilian regime. The basic contradiction of that history-altering event is located at the point of disalignment between its putative nationalist orientation and ethos, which was declared as its objective intention, and the ethnicist consequences of its actualized intent.

The breakdown of the liberationist ontology of postcoloniality which had already occurred at the political, social and cultural planes was completed at the sphere of the military and security apparatus of the state as different factions of the squabbling elite mobilized partisan loyalties from the various military formations to ground obscurantist ethnic ideologies. The result was the breakdown of law and order within the command structure and among the rank and file of the military–an institution the postcolonial state had touted as its last line of defence against narrow, sectarian, irredentist, insular and centripetal forces, apart from its primary responsibility of maintaining the coherence and legitimacy of society's unequal material relations. The counter-coup d' etat of July-August, 1966, the pogroms of May through September of the same year, the failure of the political and military elite to reach consensus after several peace initiatives, the re-structuring of the country into a 12-state administrative arrangement and the declaration of the Republic of Biafra and the war the Nigerian State levied against it led to the 30-month fratricidal bloodbath that took nearly 3 million lives, dislocated economic and social life and ended the key episteme of national unity as a metaphysical category.

Aside the varying narratives of the Nigerian-Biafran war as either a struggle for national liberation against the genocidal policies of ethnic supremacist and hegemonic North/West power structures or a fight to restore Nigeria's inviolate national unity against a bellicose irredentist agenda, its end in January 1970 ushered a decade of high expectations and broken promises, of the deepening of contradictions among factions of the ruling military elite, of coups and counter-coups, and eventually the re-democratization of the state in 1979 on the basis of a commandist, anti-federalist Presidential constitutional inheritance. However, in establishing the terms of its departure, the negotiating military formation inserted sufficient debilitating political and economic illogic into the structural and institutional transition framework as to make its leisurely re-entry into power a foregone conclusion.

The Second Bourgeois Republic of 1979-1983 was a cooptative democratic project on various fronts. It reconfigured the ethnic and class alliances of the First Bourgeois Republic while dispensing with its initial radical postcolonial spirit and ethos. It absorbed the elemental features of Federalism at the normative level but contradicted, negated and subverted it at the level of performativity; that is, the application of power derived from an anti-federalist constitution. It mouthed slogans and phrases about social justice, egalitarianism, economic inclusion and the construction of a compassionate social order but strengthened and consolidated the ties between the postcolonial state and the late, postmodern and post-imperial capitalist polis with all its prescient oppressive and exploitative structures and mechanics. It promoted the paradigm of ethical revolution as the key instrument of its moral authority and political legitimacy while being comprehensively implicated in the near absolute transgression against the moral and spiritual foundation of the liberal democratic state in the spheres of institutionalized corruption and graft, economic banditry and electoral fraud. Just as the First Republic, the Second was unable to exist and operate beyond the limits set by its inherited and self-created contradictions and ultimately yielded space to the military high command, who initially constructed the conditions of its self-implosion, on December 31st, 1983.

Antonio Gramsci's historicizing method of inventory is adequate in mapping the construction of a dominant military-civil hegemony and in locating the sites of political and social contestations in the democratic process in Nigeria of the 1980s and 1990s. The Gen. Muhammad Buhari's dictatorship of 1983-1985 was marked by a near absence of a well structured political transition arrangement, was defined by the rigidification of the commandist-authoritarian military power structure, was characterized by the subordination of the Ideological State Apparatuses (ISAs) to the Repressive State Apparatuses (RSAs), and promoted the philosophy of moral piety in a non-liberal social space as the existentialist site of its legitimacy. The regime's alienation of the influential elements in its core constituency, the hatred directed towards it by the displaced and disgraced political elite and the indifference of the masses towards its fate as a consequence of its totalitarian appropriation of all available social spaces without an ameliorating egalitarian economic programme sealed its fate and made the Gen. Ibrahim Babangida takeover of power in August 1985 one of the easiest in Nigerian history.

Gen. Babangida was fully conscious of the terrible political fate that befell his predecessor and unfolded an 8-year democratization process that exhausted the mental and intellectual capacity of the Nigerian elite, constructed a complex political, economic and governing bureaucracy that sucked virtually the elite of all ideological hue into its cavernous and capacious fold, legislated the existence of two political parties that leaned slightly to the right and left of the ideological spectrum, empowered these political formations with ready-made constitutions and manifestoes and built physical infrastructure for their organizational and administrative operations. However, the regime became overwhelmed by its inherited and self-created contradictions, succumbed to the limits set by the ontological identity of a dependent postcolonial capitalist state in relation to the genuine democratic yearnings and economic freedom demands of the people and imploded on the weight of the annulment of the June 12, 1993 presidential election as the organic logic and dialectical end result of its ahistorical nature and essence.

The Gen. Sani Abacha years (1993-1998) marked a new low in the application of oppressive authoritarian policies by the hegemonic military establishment. Independent media platforms were muzzled and journalists critical of the regime were either killed or thrown into detention or forced into exile. The regime also declared a total war against the nation's labour, pro-democracy and human rights civil society groups by unleashing maximum Repressive State Apparatuses to murder, maim, jail or force into exile some of its leading lights, including political activists, intellectuals, artists and cultural workers. The minimal liberal political space which existed under Gen. Babangida's dictatorship was effectively shut down in an aggressive exclusionary process that weeded out the bulk of the political elite from political participation. Political parties constructed by them were de-legitimated and disbanded to be replaced by apologist and collaborationist political contraptions that eventually adopted Gen. Abacha as their joint Presidential candidate in the 1998 Presidential election. Externally, while the imperialist countries of the West isolated Nigeria politically and diplomatically, the pace of economic co-operation and unequal business and trade partnership remained very robust. Gen. Abacha's sudden death in June 1998 provided yet another opportunity for the re-formulation of a democratization programme that led eventually to the procreation of the Fourth Bourgeois Republic on 29th May, 1999.

In an organic sense, the crisis of Nigerian democratic transformation and positive social change stems from the dissociation of ontological identity, consciousness and sensibility that operates at several levels. For a start, is there an aggregated unity of ontological identity among the ethnic nationalities in whose social spaces are constructed the idea and reality of the Nigerian state? In essence, does there exist concrete proof that the cosmological and metaphysical conditioning of these entities have transformed over periodized historical time, in the context of the production and reproduction of knowledge, into values that are normativized as essentially Nigerian in character and content? What are the cultural tensions, if not outright disconnect, between the identities formulated by ancestral kinship and faith and the colonial and postcolonial construction of identity that transgresses both?

There are two other levels this ontological contradiction resides in. The ontological crisis spawned by colonialism is located in the insertion of polymorphous syncretic metaphysics into the tenuous historical and cultural totality it constructed. By partially displacing the foundational linearity associated with the historical progression and ontological presence of the ethnic nationalities the colonial state is composed of, it created sufficient space for the implantation of the post-Enlightenment dialectic of rationalism, empiricism and logical positivism as well as the more practical attributes of mercantile capitalism, political control and cultural imperialism into the colonial social formation. The ontological crisis engendered by colonialism is not only explained by the subversion of the multiple ontologies of the pre-colonial era but the erection on their substantive remnants a new alien and ahistorical ontological identity it legitimated. In more practical terms, the political systems, modes of material production, transcendental beliefs and cultural, ethical and spiritual values and norms of the colonial national groups, in their singularity and totality, must cohere with or rather inhere in the ontological graph drawn up by the colonial moment.

If the spatialization of culture under intense pressure from late, postmodern capitalism captures the essential spirit of postmodernism in the words of Fredric Jameson, then colonialism may be construed as the disaggregation of the ontology of the social and cultural imaginaries of colonial subjects in the postcolonial moment. The contamination of the ethos of postcoloniality by the ontological crisis unleashed by colonialism is further complicated by the struggle for space in the postcolonial moment by the complex articulation of pre-colonial ontological formations. Thus, in enunciating the categoric paradigms of the Nigerian postcolonial state in the spheres of democracy building and economic transformation, inclusive growth and self-sufficiency the operators of the state apparatus must confront the prescient postcolonial ontological reality, transgress and subvert the ontology of colonialism and accommodate the cosmologic totality of the pre-colonial era. It is by problematizing this complicated relationships that would be grounded the difficulty in constructing the relevant architecture of thought and knowledge essential to the institutionalization of a coherent postcolonial social order either in the sphere of democratic statecraft or in the field of aesthetics, literature and cultural production.

Most crucially, the logic of 'non-recognition' of the imperative cosmology and ontology of postcoloniality as a product of the configuration and re-configuration of the various ontological formations already identified can be expressed in metaphysical terms. If we unconceal the sequence of filiations and affiliations that the material properties of metaphysics embody–in an epistemic sense–it will be possible to map the contours of the distance and nexus between immanent transcendentalism, transcendental materialism and material transcendence. If we achieve this state of illumination, it will be quite possible to bridge the cognitive disconnect that separates the different levels of signification of the ontology of the Nigerian state and thus locate more cogently the crisis of its democratic transformation. Embedded in these three regions of transcendence is the acuity of being and becoming; a process that flows from the production of values to their affirmation, mediation and reinvention. While immanent transcendentalism appears as the spiritual ontology of pre-coloniality, transcendental materialism expresses the ontology of colonialism and material transcendence, the critical episteme of postcoloniality.

The graph of Nigeria's democratic transformation can never be plotted in the dark, in the sphere of 'unknowing' where recognition is concealed. Historical, material, cultural and spiritual spaces must not just exist and cohere but must achieve a state of coherence to unconceal the force of recognition. Thus, the design of Nigeria's democratic instruments should grow out of this recognition, especially as the expression of ontological formations periodized in historical progression marked with metanarrative linearity. In the same vein the building of democratic institutions should be organically aligned to the key terms normativized by democratic instruments. Finally, the Nigerian democratic process should express a totality, not merely in the act of performance; that is, the constant animation of instruments and institutions, but most importantly the realization of cosmological possibilities–at the ontological, epistemic, cultural and ideological levels–in social production and the reproducibility of values.

The force of recognition which unconceals the idea of the Nigerian State as a constructed ontology has been consistently missed by the postcolonial 'cultural dominant.' In essence, the non-recognition of the nation's ontological status has always led to the persistent concealment of its key metaphysical attributes and thereby inaugurating the impossibility of crafting a wholesome democratic tradition that reflects the totality of postcoloniality.

How then can the Nigerian State overcome this dilemma? Principally by excavating the layering of the constituent units of each ontological formation and inserting and grounding the materiality of transcendence in the notion of being, so as to determine the primary and secondary elevations in the scale of causality. History is the key agency of mapping and measuring the contours of social formations, so long as it embodies the following attributes: metanarrative logic, linearity and materiality. Every ontological formation expresses its material episteme through modes of concealment and revelation. Even in categoric structuralist cognition of the force of 'overdetermination' as a complex web of multiple articulation of causes and effects, the material foundation of history and the successive dialectical formations that grow out of it, and which transgress and sometimes subvert it, are all fused to its cosmological totality. It is thus by scrutinizing the mode of production and material relations embodied in the ontology of the social formations of pre-coloniality, coloniality and postcoloniality on the substantive grounds of what constitutes oppressive hegemonic forces at each historical turn, and what also constitutes liberationist counterhegemonic forces, that a Nigerian democratic compass can emerge capable of pointing the way to the nature and essence of the key instruments and institutions critical to positive social transformation.

In mediating material relations and configuring the ontological totality adequate for the construction of its democratic system (on the basis of historical, cultural and spiritual evidence), the postcolonial Nigerian State must harness and integrate those ingredients of material transcendence not completely exhausted by secular translation into the Marxist philosophical and ideological world outlook that reposes the essential counterhegemonic quality critical to human transformation. By transforming the ontological particulars of material transcendence from its subjective location as an ideological formation, as an apparatus of false consciousness, into a more secular domain through the transgression and spatialization of its integral cognitive context, it necessarily combines with Marxist conception of material history to recuperate and re-animate the radical spirit of Nigerian postcoloniality.

In stressing this point it must be noted that while the universality of materiality in the philosophy of history and the comprehension of the principle of historical specification remain the dominant ontological foundation of postmetaphysical and postsecular societies, its claim of legitimacy has been tempered and mediated in human regions that harbor and express the totality of reality and cultural experience in the broadest context of materiality. Thus, while harnessing the gift of material history as a product of the singularity of continuous archetypes in realizing the democratic organism of the postcolonial Nigerian State material transcendence, now transformed as a form of the 'materiality of ideology', should be reinscribed into its domain in contexts that are not merely marginal in nature. However, in reinstating material transcendence, even in its radicalization as a 'materiality of ideology' in working out the ontology of Nigerian postcoloniality, we must also problematize the limits set by three related terms that share a putative solidarity with it. How to overcome the contradictions inherent in the cognitive-perceptual space objectification, reification and hypostatization occupy in relation to material transcendence is not a matter I can theorize in this introduction. It is, nevertheless, an issue I am currently working on in constructing a totalizing material history and material relations in Nigerian postcoloniality that harnesses the possibilities of material transcendence reanimated as 'materiality of ideology' in an essentially Marxist project.

The generation of Nigerians who were born after 1960; that is, my generation, has a unique historical responsibility of helping to draw the graph of the nation's postcolonial trajectory and map the contours of its contemporary evolution. That uniqueness flows from, at least, three distinct sources. Absolved of any blame in the omissions and deficiencies of the anti-colonial struggle, and excluded from the obscurantist performances of the 1960s that spatialized, decentred and ultimately subverted the political, economic and cultural promises of postcoloniality, including but not limited to the fratricidal bloodbath of 1967-1970, it has become the nation's receptacle, the embodiment of all the forces worked into its ontological formation across periodized historical spaces. In a way, its modernist spirit and sensibility has the advantage of a coherent metaphysics:

historical and cultural recognition and awareness of identity constructed around an ontology that is clothed with a metanarrative and teleological aura.

Moreover, it is a generation that has been substantially spared from the scepter of postmodernism with its logic of historical depthlessness, cultural discontinuities, and the contingency, ephemerality and temporality of identity-formation that is now creeping into the nation's social and cultural spaces, in music, literature and the entertainment industry. This cosmologic malady or epistemic crisis does not only emanate from the anti-totalizing, deterritorialized, translocational, transcultural and hybridized mindset of Nigeria's lost Diasporic children but is also increasingly defining the consciousness of their peers within the national frontiers. This generation can thus empower a vision of new democratic direction built on a constructed postcolonial ontology that is undergirded by the nation's material history and the integral cognitive context of material transcendence now radicalized as 'materiality of ideology'. The insertion of material transcendence into the totality of material history does not entail the complete exhaustion and evacuation of its spirituality but rather the despiritualization of its aspects that negate and are inconsistent with the substantive secularity of materialist dialectics.

Chapter

2

THE HISTORICAL, IDEOLOGICAL AND CULTURAL CONTEXT OF AN AGE

A reading of the introduction to my collected boyhood creative works will offer adequate insight into the psychosocial and cultural setting of my formative years in the 1970s.[1] The piece contains a little dose of family history; the archetypal growing up sequences of reminiscences and episodic remembrances, the awakening of artistic consciousness; and the foundation of moral belief and political ideology.[2] That introduction also illuminated the forces and currents that eventually shaped my intellectual and creative tradition, which are profoundly located in the existence of a vibrant family reading and dialogical culture; the existence of a well-stocked family library, the emergence and sustenance of a dynamic popular music culture between the 1970s and the early 1980s; my exposure to world and

African intellectual and literary productions in the crucial year of 1977 (when I first began to write) up to 1980 when I finished high school; my first encounter with Marxism by reading several critiques of V.I. Lenin's viewpoints on political issues; and eventually my reading of the original works by the exponents of the ideology in book and magazine formats.[3]

However, this chapter will investigate, in a greater, all-encompassing detail, the tissues of reality already alluded to, and lay a wider canvas of the mosaic of history, interlocking consciousness and growth in social perception between 1977 and 1984, when I graduated from the Department of English and Literary Studies, University of Nigeria, Nsukka. In apprehending the changing contexts and patterns of historical evolution, it will be necessary to encounter both the generalized dialectics of social, cultural and ideological transformation of an epoch with self-in-grained ethos and *weltanschauung*, as well as the individualized specificities of experience that condition intellectual and ideological growth, and in which are inhered, the substances of social practice.

The 1970s particularly could be defined as a momentous period in Nigerian historical experience. Internationally, the decade was defined by the intensification of the global ideological struggle which readily found expression in the pursuit of grand strategic ideological, political and economic interests by communist and capitalist imperialist forces, usually in the Third World theatres. The decade also witnessed an increasingly militant phase in the struggle for the decolonization of portions of the African continent (Angola, Mozambique, Namibia and South Africa), and the unqualified support provided it by a nationalist, and increasingly populist regime of Murtala Mohammed, and subsequently by the successor regime of Olusegun Obasanjo. Another defining image of the decade was the rise of Arab/ Muslim militancy in the Middle East, the emergence of crude oil and petro-dollar as a bargaining chip in international and geo-strategic relations, and ultimately in the direction and fortunes of the global capitalist economy.[4]

Specifically in Nigeria, the 1970s became a site for the contestation of the legitimacy and authenticity of several historical and social ideals and assumptions. The civil war which ended in January 1970 on the twin humanistic parlance of "No victor, No vanquished", and the implementation of the 3Rs of Reconciliation, Rehabilitation and Reintegration provided an additional impetus for a new national beginning, with the harrowing, traumatic and disquieting events of the late 1960s as a tragic backdrop. Yet the pursuit of a happy national future, and the renewal of hope on humanism, brotherhood and fraternity, paid lip-service to the colossal damage the war inflicted on the Igbo psyche, the collapse of corporate identity and group structures of meaning and affirmation with the attendant rise of an atavistic variant of individualism as a mode of "Surviving the Peace"[5]; an idea and reality that has haunted the Igbo ethnic and cultural base ever since. In essence, this social dysfunctionalism which was never attended to adequately led, today, to the collapse of elite consensus, the unraveling of group political identity and, in combination with both institutional and structural marginalization, has eroded the humanity, dignity, pride and substance of a once great nation and people.

Historically speaking, few people now remember that while the rest of the nation began to engage, master and control the opportunities and possibilities that opened up with the indigenization of the command and control structures of national social and economic assets which coincided with the oil boycott/oil boom of 1973, in the Igbo heartland, both within the ranks of the dispossessed business and corporate elite, and among the general populace, a different kind of struggle was in play. It is on record that, apart from fixing the infrastructural facilities on which daily life is organized (homes, schools, hospitals, markets, etc), and undertaking different manners of group counseling and therapy, and psycho-social reorientation of mangled lives and souls, a great number of Igbo corporate players readily hawked and battered wives and daughters and sisters over executive tables in several ministries and extra-ministerial agencies in Lagos for the securing of basic licenses, instruments and LPOs to re-start their businesses which were destroyed during the years of war.[6]

Yet, this spectre of corporate dissonance and dissociation of moral sensibility, and the emergence of an extreme form of self-preservation was not altogether a new phenomenon. The application, during the civil war, of "hunger as a legitimate instrument of warfare", gave rise to the phenomenon of "Afia Attack", a subterranean, shadowy smuggling market system that developed in the war man's land, and made popular by roving bands of women into defied tradition, honour and family values, and prospered as providers for their families, and self-sustaining business and commercial entrepreneurs. It was obvious that the phenomenon was facilitated through the support provided such "rebel" women groups by the Nigerian Military High Command who befriended and protected them and helped in implanting into them the notion of "Di Gbakwaa Oku" (husband can go to blazes), an idea that the late Tony Ubesie depicted with so much wit, irony and sarcasm in one of his Igbo novels.[7]

Inevitably, "Afia Attack" women became transformed in the later part of the war into "bunker women" – that legion of female comforters to the Nigerian officer corps in their luxurious war bunkers; a women group that crossed the battle divide, pursued by hunger and poverty, and in search of better fortune, irrespective of their marital and other social and cultural affiliations. It has indeed been speculated that the civil war did not end with the official Biafran surrender; this was merely an outward manifestation of defeat. The war ended, in the eyes and imagination of many, when Biafran women defied husband, father and brother and the love of their children, and crossed over to the "enemy" side.

The futility of sustaining a struggle in the context in which many men could no longer fend for or cater for their families, and in which they even became dependent on and accepted the food and other essential supplies, including occasional emotional comfort, by the "Afia Attack" and "bunker women", would have become obvious to many.[8]

In the midst of these hopes and uncertainties; in the threshold of disbelief and faithlessness, but still with a poignant and stubborn insistence on the meaningfulness of life, the later 1970s threw up its own peculiar aura of political promise on the agenda of a democratization process vigorously prosecuted by the Obasanjo regime. Of the five political parties which were registered, only the Nigerian People's Party, (NPP) had an Igbo core, soul and conscience. Led by Dr Nnamdi Azikiwe, the party ultimately became a response to the need to re-integrate "Ndigbo" into the political mainstream, to reincarnate the glory days of the 1960s and to restore some sort of hope and identity to a drifting and psychologically wounded people.

Azikiwe's presidential aspiration should thus be seen in this light; less an attempt to win the presidency, and more an eloquent statement that barely nine years after the disaster of the civil war that the Igbo can more than "bounce back", hold their own with their ethnic rivals, and demand and secure recognition at the political negotiating table when the national question is placed for consideration.[9]

However, the collapse of elite consensus in Igboland as a consequence of the Biafran tragedy, and which had been taken to an absurd level in the contemporary epoch, was already asserting its instinctual impetus as the logic of intra-group relations. Zik was uncomfortable with re-engaging the services of his old allies in the NCNC; he rather settled for the grooming and induction into the political elite class new entrants, chief among which was the earthy late Chief Sam Mbakwe, a courageous defender of public causes and the champion of the "abandoned property" saga, and who became elected as the civilian governor of old Imo State, and Chief Jim Nwobodo, a charismatic, flamboyant and wealthy young businessman who emerged as the governor of old Anambra State.

Opposed to Zik's political assumptions were members of the old NCNC apparatchik like Dr K. O. Mbadiwe, Chief Collins Obi, Dr Nwafor Orizu, Prof. Godwin Odenigwe, and newer political strategists and activists like Dr Chuba Okadigbo and Dr Alex Ekwueme. When Chief Emeka Ojukwu was granted amnesty and returned to Nigeria in 1982, he strengthened the profile, stature and historical relevance of this group. Yet, a third force was established by the radical, left-leaning members of the elite who anchored their political faith on ideological parameters and found accommodation in the most leftist of the five parties – the People's Redemption Party (PRP). Worthy of mention as espousers of this radical alternative are the late Chief Sam Ikoku who was the Secretary General of the party (he was also the Secretary General of AG in the 1960s); Dr Arthur Agwuncha Nwankwo, the founder of Fourth Dimension Publishers and a radical, Marxist-leaning intellectual and entrepreneur, who became the party's governorship candidate in old Anambra State in 1983; Senator Uche Chukwumerije, a radical Marxist – oriented economist and scholar, and the late Chief Mokwugo Okoye of the fabled Zikist Movement, who emerged as one of the most forceful and towering ideologues of the third force in Igbo elite politics.

There is little doubt that the traumas and tragedies of the civil war created alternative patterns of sublimation and overcompensation especially in the field of sports and popular music culture. Contradistinctionally, while the Igbo world drifted, virtually unanchored on any coherent social and political base; and while the Igbo elite squabbled about their place in the polity, the Rangers International Football club, based in Enugu, and made up of young men who were either demobilized Biafran soldiers and "Youth Soldiers", or were in secondary schools during the war, took the Nigerian soccer scene by storm, as it were. Enjoying a cult following in the whole of the 1970s, and the beginning of the 1980s, the team dominated the domestic soccer scene and made giant strides at the continental soccer level.[10] The team's followership was truly a cultural phenomenon, as they came to embody the indomitable spirit of courage in adversity, heroism and social and cultural assertion. If truly sport has the capacity of rallying a people, and infusing in them the unquenchable feeling of group solidarity and corporate identity, the Rangers International fulfilled that yearning and need. It became the standard bearer of a resurgimenting ethnic urge for excellence, battered mercilessly by the defeat of Biafra, and led to the belief about the possibility of conquests of other fields in the face of the haunting failure of the secessionist enterprise. Almanacs, calendar, pictures, posters, and music compositions celebrated the heroism of the team. Its triumphs became the triumph of an entire people; its setbacks, the reversal of their collective fortunes.

The remarkable feat achieved by Rangers International was replicated at the popular music level in the whole of the 1970s and early 1980s, to the extent that with the possible exception of Fela Anikulapo-Kuti, Sunny Okosun (who had his educational and music roots in IMT, Enugu), Ofege, Bongos Ikwue and BLO, virtually all the artistically endowed pop groups who sustained the vibrant pop music culture of the era were either of Igbo origin or were based in Eastern Nigeria.[11] Groups worth mentioning in this regard include The Wings which was led by Spud Nathans (Jonathan Udensi), and easily the best pop vocalist in the history of Nigerian popular music culture, as I observed elsewhere[12]; Jerry Biofraind who led the Super Wings when Nathan died, and who later pursued a successful solo career with such hits as "Shooting star"; Manfred Best who led the other faction of the wings called The Original Wings, after the death of Nathan, and whose hit tribute to Spud Nathan remains a pop music classic till date; Wrinkers Experience with their hit number, "Fuel for Love"; The Doves with such hits as "The Sky", "Rhythm Bullet" and "The Lord is my Shepherd"; Semicolon with such hits as "Ready, Steady, Go" and "Slim Fit Maggie"; Black Children with their hot, sonorous "The World is Changing"; The Aktions with "Show me Baby" and " I Don't Have to Cry"; the Rock of Ages; Tony Grey, based in Warri; and The Apostles with "She's a Drop Out", etc. There was also the Founders Fifteen, which was made up of mostly soldiers serving at the Obinze Owerri Military base with their immortal ballad, "Be My Own"; and of course such eternal numbers from The Wings as "Catch that Love"; "You Will Really Want Me Back"; "Someone Else Will"; "But Why...", etc.

While the endnote 11 of this chapter will provide further insight into this tradition and its culturally empowering thematic for a psychologically disembodied generation, mention is also worth making of such later groups as the Sweet Breeze, a group of students at IMT, Enugu, who defined the Pop scene of the late 1970s with such hits as "She's My Choice", "She is Cooler Than You", And "Palm wine Tapper"; Christy-Essien-Igbokwe who gained prominence in the 1970s sit-comedy soap opera, "The Masquerade" as Akpeno, and who made significant contribution to the Pop music scene between 1978 and 1986, and subsequently Jide Obi and Chris Okotie (trained at the University of Nigeria, Enugu Campus), who is arguably the most popular, successful and charismatic Pop musician of all time in Nigeria.

At the traditional genre of popular music, the sense of cultural awakening and social renaissance (a fitting name for the East Central State owned newspaper), was sustained by Osita Osadebe who reinvented the idiom, style, theme and format of "Highlife Music", especially with his masterpiece, "Osadebe 75", Celestine Ukwu, whose philosophical insights and moral musings enriched the ethical content of a troubled age; Gentleman Mike Ejiagha whose ballads and folk tales, rendered in an innovative musical style known as *Akuko n'egwu* – story and song –

captivated audience and listeners; and the Oriental Brothers, led by Kabaka and Sir Dr Warrior (who later pursued a successful solo career), whose combination of the rich resonance of highlife with an energetic, fast-paced, rhythmical instrumental base and overlay, made it the most dynamic force in social and cultural arenas, at public and private levels, and ensured for it a pride of place as one of Nigeria's most successful traditional pop music groups of all time.

Thus, in a way the 1970s and the early 1980s, at least in Eastern Nigeria was a time of intense social scrutiny and cultural experimentation; of the inexorable disavowal of group identity on the heels of the civil war and the reconstruction of cultural and social identity at other levels[13]; the search for political direction in the absence of a secure political power base; and the gradual, very incremental process of re-building shattered hopes and lives, at the entrepreneurial and intellectual planes – the last occasioned substantially by the establishment of the Fourth Dimension Publishers by Arthur Agwuncha Nwankwo in 1976.[14]

I completed elementary school in 1975 and entered high school the same year, as yet unaware of and unaffected by these momentous, and contradictory patterns of social and cultural transformations. That was to come much later. Indeed my elementary education started about 1969 at Utu, Nnewi, and continued after the war at St. John's Elementary School, Mgbowo, in Awgu LGA of Enugu State. I have, elsewhere, given a succinct account of my school days and the forces and currents that shaped my destiny.[15] The same piece under reference is also a necessary reading to fully grasp the range of forces that helped the growth of my intellectual consciousness, the development of passion for art and other creative impulses, a sheer obsession with reading (at various times in my Akanu Ibiam hostel bed, I will lay open close to eight or so books, and read them at the same time), and the deepening of my ideological belief. It will therefore not serve any useful purpose replicating those situations here – including the range of books I literally consumed, as that introduction did justice to all that.

Nevertheless, two things stand out from the recollection of my high school days. This is apart from the wide range of artistic genres I experimented on, and which I have collected into six fairly readable volumes.[16] The first is that I never undertook any systematic study of Marxism as a philosophy or political ideology in my high school days. While I was exposed to Marxism-Leninism through the reading of both original works on the subject, and Western critical evaluation of its universal significance, I never attempted any structured understanding of that science nor was I aware of the existence of any Marxist movement in Nigeria. In retrospect, it may be stated that the appeal of the subject to me, and my ready absorption of its core message, during my initial encounter with it, was occasioned by my emerging intellectual rebelliousness, spirit of enquiry and mental agitation, disputation with established orthodoxy and compassion for the weak, the marginalized and the down trodden. It had to await my entering into the University of Nsukka in 1980 for me to encounter a fledging though vibrant and dynamic Marxist Youth Movement, and became immediately part of the process of raising student awareness to the prospect, vitality, legitimacy and authenticity of an alternative political cause, and probably helping in the dawning of a proletarian revolution in Nigeria.

The second point is that there never was any doubt in my mind that I was going to study English and Literature in the university, and pursue a career as a university teacher. I was fortunate to have parents who rarely interfered with their children's life choices, and who would do everything in their power to support and encourage the flowering of whatever potential or possibility one might have, no matter the direction, so long as it was within the bounds of law and social convention. I recall collecting money from my father to purchase the JAMB form, and to have filled the form without letting them into what course I wanted to study. Apart from literature, my next passion is philosophy, history and religious studies (it endures to this very day). So philosophy and religious studies were my second choice of course of study. I never gave Law, Political Science and Sociology a second glance (these were hugely popular courses of study for high school students). I also recollected that my high school principal, Mr Umekeje was astounded at a SCOBA[17] meeting hosted by my father, when he learnt that I was reading English and not Law. He felt truly let down, charging that I was wasting my talent, probably because of the trouble I caused him during my final year in high school.[18]

I took the University Matriculation Examination in the second term of my final year, shortly after the WASC mock examination in which I scored A1 in all but one subject. This was in Enugu on a day that was preceded by high drama as we chased "leaked" question papers all over the town. Though I was fully prepared for the examination I did not want to be left out of the chase, and ended up assembling about three versions of the examination question papers. At the examination hall, I compared the initial five answers I made (and I was fully sure to those answers) to the answers in all the leaked question papers. None matched, whereupon I tore them all, and proceeded to answer the questions on my own.

Back in school, and to the anxious questions and intense expectations of my classmates who did not take the exam about how I fared, I only surmised that if those awaiting their results, as against those who wrote the exam after passing their WASC examinations, will be judged equally, that I was already in the university. When I heard that the results had come out while attending a party somewhere in my village, I left the scene and came home, moody for no justifiable reason. The following day, I collected my fare to Enugu from my mother (my father had left for work early in the morning) with scarcely a word, and took off. Though

I saw my name as No.2 on the list of those admitted to read English at UNN, I had to check it with my other particulars (exam and registration numbers) several times, sometimes going as far as 200 metres, and coming back to cross-check it.

Later in the day, when I came back, my mother complained to my father that I had been behaving strangely since the previous day, whereupon I told them that "I have passed JAMB". Their joy was instantaneous and rapturous and did a world of good to me in seeing them feeling so fulfilled and rewarded, given their labour and sacrifices on me, and my siblings since we were born. I was already two months old in the university, about November 1980, when the WASC result came out, in which I made Division 1 and thus confirmed my status as a matriculable student, having passed all the subjects with mostly A pass level.

The University of Nigeria, Nsukka, was established by the government of the then Eastern Region in 1960, though its history dated considerably further back down the historical timeline. It emerged as an inevitable consequence of a deterministic historical dialectic: the explosion of desire for higher education by a populace thirsting for "the white man's" knowledge, and the lack of tertiary education opportunities for the mass of the people. It was painfully obvious that the University College, Ibadan, was incapable of absorbing qualified students desiring university education and the Eastern region was, educationally speaking, assimilating faster this thirst, given its relatively newer exposure to the tradition of Western education.[19]

The university was thus established in response to this agitation for learning, and was designed by its founding father, Dr Nnamdi Azikiwe, as a centre of learning that would incorporate the tradition of British liberal education with the more utilitarian and functionalist educational philosophy of the USA. Thus, while the University of Ibadan represented the best example of British liberal education with the pride of place occupied by classics and the liberal arts disciplines, the UNN espoused the American predilection to practicality and utilitarianism. It gave a pride of place to the professional disciplines in the Management Sciences and Environmental Studies and Law, and was the first to institute the inter-disciplinary, cross-cutting General Studies Programme that afforded opportunities to students of all disciplines to acquire knowledge in fields of study other than their major. Thus, as a student of English I took over 12 credits each in Social and Natural Sciences sufficient for me to fully grapple with the key issues, theories and concepts developed in these fields of study.

My journey from high school to UNN could be described as migration from a rustic rural setting to a semi-urban environment with a provincialist ethos. My expectations were high, because for the first time, I would be encountering, as a young adult, those sets of notions, philosophies, ideologies and intellectual currents that baffled me as a youngster. And because I was an enthusiastic and over-willing student I was fully psychologically prepared for the challenges and requirements of university life.

However, the account of my UNN days: 1980-1984, will start with my life as a student revolutionary; the explication of my encounter with literature and literary scholars and theorists will follow this account. The reason for this was that as a student I lived a dual life or more properly speaking, I had a double existence, a near schizophrenic behavioural pattern that produced virtually two mutually exclusive identities. I was Lawrence Onwuamaeze Udenta in the Department of English; obscure, apparently an adequate but not too gifted student, well mannered, a departmental librarian, and self-effacing. But to the student population I was Udenta O. Udenta, (a name I adopted in 1981 when I was about to contest as a member of the Student Union Parliament), boisterous, noisy, argumentative, charismatic, a fervent revolutionary and Secretary General of the Marxist Youth Movement. These two identities were to converge in my final year when, as one of the leaders of a student uprising,[20] I incurred the wrath of the university and departmental authorities, whereupon my lecturers then knew for the very first time that a turbulent revolutionary had been in their midst all this while.

I cannot now recollect precisely how and when I got to know about the existence of a Marxist Youth Movement in the university, but I do recall that shortly after I lost an election into the Student Union Parliament in 1981, when I was in second year,[21] I plunged wholeheartedly into informal debate and argumentation, and intensified my appearances at public squares, newspaper stands, cafeterias and open grounds where I, together with other "hotheads", held audiences spellbound with our smattering of word affairs and ideologies. Later, my profound involvement with Marxism and my deep immersion into its linguistic properties and usage would make me a devastatingly effective debater and public speaker that few could match. It must have been in one such unstructured but ebullient public outing that I must have run into Femi Ahmed, a third year student of Political Science, one of the leading student Marxist theoreticians in the country, and who was to exercise a considerable and lasting influence on me as an ideological mentor and revolutionary guide.[22]

The moment that contact was made, I plunged headlong into what was to become a heady, passionate, and deeply spiritual involvement with Marxism. The excitement Marxism had for me would endure till the emergence of Mikhail Gorbachev as the leader of the then Soviet Union, and whose twin ideo-paraxial platforms of *Perestroika* and *Glasnost* was to deconstruct Soviet Communism, ensured the disintegration of the union and inevitably led to the retreat of Euro-communism. But in retrospect, I have always strived to create a balance between my commitment to Marxism, and my fidelity to the authenticity of other social and cultural theories and processes that lie outside of its terms of reference. Though I was not an "intellectual" Marxist but a "practising" one, I was emotionally substantially distantiated from its spiritual appeal–a category that can lead to fanaticism and idolatry – to the degree that today while I accept the authenticity of dialectical materialism as the most scientific and reliable method of social enquiry and historical investigation of the behaviour, relationships and interconnectedness of phenomena, my subscription to historical materialism as the only coherent thesis of mankind's social transformation in this contemporary age is substantially qualified.

My enthusiasm in having embraced the "Fraternity" after my heart was soon challenged by the knowledge that the student Marxist Youth Movement was riddled by factionalism, intense squabbling, existence of cliques and ideological sloganeering. I was soon sucked into the vortex of a complex situation and emerged as a strong voice in the panel of enquiry that was established.[23] The end of that process was the emergence of a new leadership of the movement with Femi Ahmed as the Secretary General and myself as the Secretary of Publicity. It was much more than the passing of the baton of leadership by an old guard to younger revolutionary elements, it was more a shift in focus from a loose, largely uncoordinated movement to a tight, mobile, highly disciplined revolutionary cadre-oriented structure virtually in line with the need of the emergence of a professional revolutionary class to lead the proletarian movement, and in strict compliance with the organizational structure of the Bolshevik party.

My initial disquiet over the turbulent occurrences in the movement was adequately compensated by the knowledge that a student Marxist belongs to the "in-crowd", a category of individuals set apart from the rest of the mass of the people. In the 1980s Marxism was very attractive in Third World Universities, and to be a scholar other than a Marxist one, was to be bourgeois, conservative, reactionary and anti-people; appellations that many scholars worked very hard to avoid. Moreover, the raging fires of the anti-colonial, anti-imperialist struggle in Zimbabwe, Namibia and South Africa compelled attention and demanded total support and such support only lay within the frontiers and boundaries of Marxism. The impetus in creating a formidable Marxist intellectual and political tradition in Nigerian universities was vigorously filled by the writings of Franz Fanon and Walter Rodney, particularly, for apart from the classical works on Marxism by Marx, Engels and Lenin, and the writings of Chairman Mao, Ho Chi Mih, Kim IL Sung, Fidel Castro and Che Guevara; and apart from the life, work and writings of Nkrumah, Sekou Toure, Amil Cabral and Augustino Neto, the most formidable weapon available to Nigerian Marxists were Frantz Fanon's *The Wretched of the Earth* and Walter Rodney's *How Europe Underdeveloped Africa,* two largely influential and canonical works that became the instant bibles of the movement. Another distinguished work which was immensely popular with students, though it is non-Marxist on some of its handling of key theoretical issues, was Chinweizu's *The West and the Rest of Us.*

The Marxist tradition in scholarship, intellectual guidance and political and ideological leadership in UNN, was provided by Prof. Uzodimma Nwala, the Staff Adviser to the movement, quiet, subtle, self-contained and self-effacing. He exercised a moderating influence on us but was also firm on principle and passionate about ideological causes. His style was to gently guide us through the complex pathways of mastering the intricate facts of the science, in a participatory approach (this calls to mind Paulo Freire's method in *The Pedagogy of the Oppressed* – (another hugely popular revolutionary work) that was devoid of tendentiousness, illustrationism, condensation and paternalism. Other worthy champions of the movement then included Prof. Inyang Eteng, Prof. Okwudiba Nnoli (whose *Ethnic Politics in Nigeria* influenced a generation of Marxist scholars and students), Prof. Emmanuel Obiechina, and close to us in age, the late Nduba Echezona and Prof. Obasi Igwe (whose G.S103 Social Science lecture was the most electrifying lecture on campus).

Within the fairly crowded student Marxist scene, apart

from Femi Ahmed, the other committed members of the movement I could still remember included Alex Ayatulamo (Ayotolla), Alex Anemaku, Innocent Akenuwa, Antifon R, (they must have been in their final year when I joined the movement), Emma Ezeazu, Mobolade Omonijo, Chris Uyot, and Sunday Udeze.[24] When I became the Secretary General of the movement in 1982, the position that Femi Ahmed occupied and which he was reluctant to relinquish even after graduating (because of his suspicion that though fully committed to the movement and having made tremendous sacrifices towards it, I was too close to the "petty bourgeois"[25] student union leaders, and may not be able to sustain the near puritanical discipline and ideological passion he had established), I set about expanding its membership base. My desire was to build and lead a movement that is faithful to its core ideological identity, which is politically empowered, which would be led by a vanguard of tested revolutionaries, but which will break out of its narrow ideological and social terrain as a near cultic circle, and embrace and influence a wider student audience. I wanted the movement to be in the mainstream of the Student Union Movement and feel very proud that in my final year, I had positioned it as the most progressive, popular and charismatic student movement with an intimidating array of followership, so much so that it began to influence and even determine the composition of the Student Union Government.

To achieve this objective I had to expand the membership base of the movement by positioning its cadres in core leadership positions, including making provision for substantial positions to be awarded to powerful new members. I organized a systematic membership drive, increased the circulation of the movement's leaflets in all nooks and crannies of the campus and encouraged key members to participate in Student Union activities and other extra-curricular ventures, as a way of popularizing it. All these ploys worked because within a very short space of time I had registered as members, most of the dominant personalities that defined and dominated the Student Union Movement, such as Chukwuma C. Soludo, Ozonnia Ojeilo, Attah P. D. Attah, Chinua (Johnny) Asuzu C. D. Nwosu, and Uche Anioke, to mention the ones I can recall now.[26] Another noteworthy achievement of my leadership of the Marxist Youth Movement was the production of a successor class of committed ideologues in the likes of the late Chima Ubani, Olu Oguibe and Chijioke Edoga[27].

A student revolutionary, of necessity, lived a double life. He or she may be something different to his lecturers and classmates, and completely another thing to the rest of the student population. The movement was not a social club with widely spaced out activities that one may voluntarily be part of. The movement was life as we knew it, from dawn till dusk, on the expectation that we were working towards the inevitable triumph of a socialist revolution in Nigeria in as short a time as possible. We fervently believed in this dawning of a socialist era and will ruthlessly mow down our implacable ideological opponents who hold totally different views with the relentless unleashing of irresistible high-sounding Marxist terminologies.

Activities in the movement were mainly organized around ideological classes which were coordinated by the Secretary for Ideological Classes; Political Education Programme, which was coordinated by the Secretary for Political Education; and the mass dissemination of the weekly "Revolutionary Path" leaflet and other movement's publications. Every member of the movement was expected to attend the ideological and political instruction, and made to present discussion papers at such fora. Ideologically mature members were expected to contribute to the writing of the "Revolutionary Path", though in the end very few dedicated members sustained such an effort.

The movement also established deep, strategic linkages with other such structures in the leading universities at the time, especially at Obafemi Awolowo University, Ile Ife; University of Ibadan; University of Lagos; Ahmadu Bello

University; University of Ilorin, University of Sokoto; University of Port Harcourt and University of Calabar. Together, these movements formed the Patriotic Youth Movement of Nigeria (PYMN), which became the ideological backbone of the National Association of Nigerian Students (NANS) and ensured that the core leadership of NANS was drawn from the ranks of committed Marxists for years to come. The PYMN always met in rotation, at different locations, usually in the night and after participants had traveled from all over the country, over laden with "subversive" revolutionary literature. I recollect that it was at one of such major meetings at UNIFE during the Ife-Modakeke conflict of 1981 or 1982, that I met for the first time such distinguished student Marxists as Femi Falana, Owei Lekamfa, Tony Ayeni, Kayode Komolafe, Chris Mamma, Chris Abashi and Chom Bagu. We were to go on, later in life, to meet in different contexts and established warm, fraternal relationships at other levels.

As a postscript, it was during my discussion with Prof. Uzodimma Nwala in April 2007 that he reminded one of the fact that we were all "Stalinists" in our approach to organizational and philosophical matters; in our world view; and in our ideological rigidity and inflexible belief and faith in an imminent revolutionary rupturing of Nigeria. He also reminded me that as social practitioners who should link theory and practice and if we had investigated deep enough we would have seen, through a scrupulous application of the science of dialectical materialism, that the seeds of Soviet disintegration and retreat of Euro-Communism had already ripened in the 1980s, and we would have made adequate analytic/theoretical preparation for it. Alas, we never heeded these signs, so that when Gorbachev, Perestroika and Glasnost came calling some of us were caught napping, insisting in their analysis that the reality of the New World Order, the threat of globalization, the de-ideologization of interstate transactions and geo-strategic international relations in favour of practical economic and strategic benefits, and a narcissistic-nationalist ethos and paradigm as the defining impulses of the new age, are nothing but mere illusion.

However, I can safely say that the seeds of my ideological commitment to Marxism which was sown in my high school days, and which matured as a university student, still stand me in good stead till today. The Marxist intellectual and ideological tradition prepared me for the greater challenges I later faced, especially as a pro-democracy activist and human rights crusader during the tyranny and despotism of the late General Sani Abacha, and as the founding national Secretary of such an ideologically rooted party as the Alliance for Democracy (AD). It strengthened my faith in humanity and humanism. It toughened my fiber and made me more daring, resolute, confident and secure, and contributed in no mean way in ensuring that I remain disciplined even in the face of the most extreme form of provocation and deprivation. This is apart from deepening and strengthening my analytic, strategic and linguistic capacities, both as a public speaker, a writer, and a public intellectual.

CHAPTER TWO
NOTES AND REFERENCES

1. See "The General Introduction" to Volume One of Collected Boyhood Works of Udenta O. Udenta

2. *Ibid*, p. 2-5.

3. *Ibid*, p. 8-11.

4. The deep-seated historical, political and geo-strategic conflict between the Jews and the Arabs boiled over in 1973 in the Yom Kippor war. The Arab nations leveraged on their "Oil Power" by imposing a boycott of oil supplies to leading Western nations who were in strategic partnership with Israel. The economic consequences of this decision was far-reaching, the least not being the rise of petro-dollar, the use of petroleum resources as a strategic bargaining weapon in international politics and interstate relations, and the tremendous revenue and wealth that accrued to oil-producing nations, including Nigeria, as a result of escalated price of petroleum products which the boom heralded. However, the boom years of the 1970s turned into the burst years of the 1980s occasioned, in part by poor political governance (corruption, graft, non-accountability, etc,) faulty fiscal and monetary policies and the consumerist orientation of economic blueprints and national strategic economic planning.

5. Cyprian Ekwensi's *Survive the Peace* is a poignant examination of post-civil war traumas and psychological disorientation and an eloquent thesis that the challenges of re-building shattered lives, hopes and communities; and of engaging in sustainable and rewarding productive ventures and re-enacting meaningful social relations; of

rebuilding trust and confidence and restoring harmony, balance and ordered rhythm to the social, cultural and psychological space are as daunting, if not more, than those witnessed during the war years.

6.   While historians and social researchers point at great battles and military campaigns that marked great and strategic turning points in wars; a sort of fundamental and irreversible shift in the balance of forces, there are other determining non combat, human situations and social relations that equally capture the direction and fortunes of a war. Regarding the Nigerian civil war, one only need read Tony Ubesie's haunting narrative about the gradual collapse of the Biafran war resistance mirrored in the gradual disintegration and collapse of family values, family ties and spousal social responsibilities in his highly acclaimed Igbo novels (*Ukwa Ruo Oge ya Odaa*–Bread Fruit Falls When its Time Comes; that is, when it ripens, and Isi *Akwu Dara Na Ala (Emetula Aja)* – A Palm Fruit Bunch that Falls on the Ground has Touched the Sand).

From a close examination of Ubesie's brilliant works, and a detailed study of existing civil war records-historical, factual and imaginative-three strands or tissues of reality have emerged: the phenomenon of *Di Gba Kwa Oku* (Husband can go to blazes); *Ndi Afia Attack* (Women who trade within the no-man's land of shifting control between the two opposing force), a smugglers' den of flexible moral bargains, elastic and shifting loyalties and indeterminate moral, ethical and social responsibility; and the concept of "Bunker Women"; those breed of Biafran women who threw overboard the notion of spousal obligations and family ties and, propelled by the compelling need for economic survival and material empowerment, crossed over the enemy lines to dwell with the Nigerian Army officers, literally inside their bunkers.

Indeed, the numerous discussions I held with individuals who are knowledgeable about these situations point in one clear direction: the civil war ended with defeat for Biafra not when her forces were overrun and she surrendered on the battle field. No, the war ended when some of her women abandoned husbands, children, parents, siblings and friends and decided to cast their lot with the commanding officers of the advancing Nigerian army columns. By shattering the social and moral communion that bound the community together, through what might have been for some of them a traumatic self-preservative quest, they made an eloquent statement about the hopelessness of the Biafran condition, the futility of the war effort and the inevitability of her military and political collapse.

The end of the war signposted another harrowing moral dilemma: how to re-construct and re-build lives fundamentally diminished during the war years. Effort in this direction took many men and women through several life-directions: honest and diligent labour that entailed the picking up of the pieces of existence, material and social, prostitution, highway robbery and other anti-social and counter-cultural conducts, and in some cases having economically empowering deals sealed over the naked bodies of many a wife in executive offices as the expectant husband waited in the reception hall nearby, because the officers in charge demanded such as the sole condition of granting an award of a contract.

7.   See note 6 above

8.   See note 6 above

9.   During the 1979 General Elections that restored civil rule after 13 years of unbroken military dictatorship (1966-1979), none of the five registered political parties was able to gain a commanding governing majority in the two chambers of the National Assembly: the upper chamber or the Senate and the lower chamber or the House of Representatives. This compelled the National Party of Nigeria (NPN), the majority party, to enter into a working legislative alliance with the Nigeria Peoples Party (NPP), led by the late Rt. Hon. Dr Nnamdi Azikiwe.

In retrospect, it is apparent that though Dr Azikiwe knew he stood little chance of winning the 1979 Presidential election, he however used that process to make a potent statement about the humanity of the Igbo barely nine years after the civil war. He sought, through this political enterprise and his presidential quest, to rehabilitate them into the nation's political mainstream, to restore their sense of worth, being and dignity, and to attenuate the disequilibrating and alienating socio-psychological traumas, angst and ennui spawned by their recent historical tragedy. He succeeded to an extent because the NPN-NPP pact yielded for the Igbo elite, nine years after the civil war, the office of the nation's Vice-President (NPN) and Speaker of the House of Representatives (NPP), as well as key cabinet positions. However, the accord collapsed between 1981 and 1982. In 1983, the NPN decided to go for a clean electoral sweep; a then unprecedented electoral fortune that was difficult to understand and explain, given the nation's parlous economic, social and political condition and which became the immediate trigger for the military re-entry into the nation's politics on 31st December, 1983, a mere two months after the new government was sworn into office.

10. The Rangers International Football Club, based in Enugu, Nigeria, and made up of young men most of whom saw war between 1967-1970 dominate the domestic football league in the 1970s and the early 1980s. The team had a cult followership in the Igbo heartland, with many seeing in them the people's indestructible and unconquerable spirit. They also saw in the several triumphs of that club the people's resurrectional capacity, their resilience in the face of overwhelming odds, and ultimately their pre-eminent position among Nigeria's cast of nationalities.

11. The flowering of pop music culture in Igbo land in the 1970s and 1980s was an incredible phenomenon. In the midst of a grim struggle to survive the peace and re-build shattered lives arose, Prometheus-like, a burgeoning music exposition of unrivaled passion, lyricism, instant social communicability and connection to mass impulses, desires, needs and interests. It was a music cultural phenomenon that threw up geniuses in the areas of singing, songwriting, multi-instrumentality expertise and music production. From the Wrinkers Experience with their "Fuel for Love" to the Sweet Breeze with such eternal ballads as "She's My Choice", "Palm wine Tapper" and "Igbaka Iba Inum", the period witnessed the explosion of such pop rock groups with their powerful melodies as Black Children, "The World is Changing"; Wings, "Catch that love", "You Will Really, Really Want Me Back", "Someone Else Will" and "But Why", all sung by arguably Nigeria's greatest pop singer,

Spud Nathan (Jonathan Udensi); Apostles with their "She is a Drop Out"; Founders Fifteen based at Owerri with their "Be My Own", The Doves with such hit as "Rhythm Bullet", "The Sky is the Limit of Everything" (A Man Gotta Do): and "The Lord is My Shepherd"; the Semi- colon with such eternal numbers as "Ready, Steady, Go" and "Slim Fit Magi"; and The Aktions with their "Show me, Baby" and "I Won't Cry." Equally, names of such performers like Jerry Boifraind, Harry Mosco, and Manford best, to mentioned but a few of the pop exponents of the period, will always remain fresh in the minds of pop musical experts and lay listeners alike.

The entrance of the Oriental Brothers led by Sir Warrior, Kabaka and Dan Satch reinvigorated the traditional music scene and complemented the established repertoire of such high life masters as Osita Osadebe, Celestine Ukwu and the Ogene International Band. Mike Ejiagha and Okonkwo Asa (Seven, Seven) grounded the story and song genre powerfully into the soil of the land and held millions spellbound with their soulful ballads and eternal tales of right and wrong, wit and cunning, good and evil. Other notable artistes of the period worth mentioning are the Peacocks International Band with their potent and exhilarating rendition of high life music in a funky, groovy manner that powerfully summoned the energy, vitality and exuberance of the young, as well as making social commentary on different strands of moral and social conducts, and Nelly Uchedu, the quintessential lady of melodious tunes, lyrical passion and soulful traditional piety.

12. The age of ferment of ideas and talents which underpinned the awakening of a people struggling

to survive the post-war peace also permeated the entertainment and media industry. It was thus not strange that arguably, the most successful, long-running soap-opera which attained a cult-like status with millions of devotees was the hilarious comedy vignettes called the "Masquerade", based in Enugu. It dominated the Nigerian television drama industry in the 1970s up to the early 1980s and made instant megastars of the likes of Chika Okpala (Chief Zebrudaya Okoro Igwe Mogbo – the principal character); the late Chief Mrs Christy Essien-Igbokwe (Akpeno – Jegede's irascible, garrulous and quarrelsome wife); ....
(Chief Jegede Sokoya – Zebrudaya's bombastic and boastful friend); and Clarus (   ) and Giringori (The late James Iroha– the series creative engine), Zebrudaya's mischievous and bumbling house helps. Christy Essien – Igbokwe eventually branched into pop music and attained the iconic status as Nigeria's lady of songs with her throbbing melodies, and folk traditional rhythm rendered in a fashionable modernist style.

As a form of entertainment, "The Masquerade" and its sequel, "The New Masquerade" defined and mirrored its age and milieu, and became a benchmark to measure future TV drama creations. *The Renaissance* newspaper, appropriately titled, the South-Eastern newspaper flagship and the home to such bristling journalistic geniuses as the late Jerry Okoro, Xryx Eyutchae, C.de Agomba and a host of other peerless exponents of the truest, finest and purest spirit of newspapering.

13. Fourth Dimension Publishing Co. Ltd, one of the finest examples of indigenous business resourcefulness and creative entrepreneurship, was a product of a double heritage. It began as an

entrepreneurial creation of a brilliant Igbo son, Dr Arthur Agwuncha Nwankwo, called Nwamife Publishers, before its higher incarnation into Fourth Dimension Publishers. The creation of Fourth Dimension Publishers fulfilled Arthur Nwankwo's hopes, expectations, vision and dream of geopolitically balancing academic publishing in Nigeria, and of harnessing global best practices in the production, marketing and distribution of serious academic, intellectual and professional literature. Ultimately, the bulk of indigenously resident Igbo scholars attained their highest academic, scholarly and intellectual peak via local and international exposure through the outlet in the 1970s, 1980s and 1990s, myself inclusive, as well as delivering to the Nigerian public the seminal political writings of Ebenezer Babatope (Ebino Topsy), and the works of the late poet-soldier, Mamman vatsa, among numerous others.

14. See, "General Introduction" to my six-volume *Collected Boyhood Works,* for a brief account of my elementary school days.

15. The **Collected Boyhood Works** which appeared in six volumes have the following titles: Volumes One– *The Wrath of the Gods;* Volume Two–*Book of Knowledge and Great Understanding, and Reflections on School Life*; Volume Three–*Before They Came;* Volume Four–*Poetic Reminiscence, Book of Dislocation and Snapshots of Ancient Ways*; Volume Five–*The Re-discovery of the Arlistoga and Retrospective Vision: Cultural Interactions*; Volume Six–*Ribbings in Youth-Hood and Youth-Hood Scribbling.*

16. SCOBA is the acronym for St Charles Old Boys Association; that is, the alumni who attended the famous and illustrious St Charles College, Onitsha.

My father was an alumnus of the college which he attended in the early to mid-1950s and was very proud of this fact. His academic and intellectual foundation was laid there as a very concrete source of the later day flowering of his scholarship. The group meets, in turns, in the home of one of their members, probably every month. I recall that he hosted the group a number of times in his country home, and usually in attendance was the principal of my secondary school, Chief Ume Ukeje.

The website "Government of Anambra State of Nigeria PPSSC. Onitsha Zone" describes the college thus:

> St Charles College, Onitsha, popularly known as the "Varsity on the Niger", was founded in 1928, by his Grace Most Rev. Dr Charles Heery, Archbishop of blessed memory and was dedicated to St Charles Borrormeo. The college began as a teacher training college for men, and has produced seasoned and renowned teachers, many of whom later branched out and became professors of the science and arts, government administrators and statesman, bishops of the church, business magnates, traditional rulers, barristers-at-law and Judges of the High Court ...

My journey to the University of Benin, Nigeria for graduate studies had a St Charles College touch to it, believe it or not. Uncomfortable with pursuing my graduate studies at my alma mater, University of Nigeria Nsukka, Nigeria, because of my unfounded fears about prolonged studentship as a consequence of my undergraduate Marxist revolutionary agitations, I sought for an alternative environment where my past will not come to haunt me. My father suggested the University of Benin where his junior at St Charles College, Romanus N. Egudu, was already a distinguished professor of literature. He drafted a letter to Professor Egudu who not only admitted me, but took me under his wing as an academic mentor and father-figure.

17. I led a student revolt in my class five in High School. I recall that it must have been either in the second or third term because we had registered for the West African School Certificate (WASC) Examinations conducted by the West African Examinations Council (WAEC) by then. Trouble started when those of us who returned to school on time after the term break were made to eat beans three times in a day for two days. A number of us class five students, including my elder brother, Ben Jr., organized ourselves and ensured that the next round of beans was poured away. Before then the school's Dean of Studies, Mr Obi Okafor, had come to address the students to eat the beans. I spoke on behalf of the students and gave reasons why they should not do so. Tension ran high in the school, almost to an explosive point.

The school authorities issued a strong query to eleven of us who led the revolt, but I was specially singled out in the Assembly Ground by the principal who likened my rebellion to the role of Ndaba I played in Tunji Fatilewa's *Torrents of Soweto*. Rather than do the punishment meted out to me, I wrote an 18-page petition against the authorities and threatened to submit it to the then Anambra State Secondary School Board. A compromise was reached. I did not submit the petition and the punishment was whittled down to fetching a single pail of water. The revolt had a number of positive outcomes. Within days, the school's kitchen store was filled with different varieties of foodstuff. The principal thereafter recruited me as the recorder of the school's major activities, like the inter-house sports event, the Founder's Day's celebration, etc. Indeed, at the next SCOBA meeting in our house, he enquired about how my Law degree programme was working out. He was visibly stunned and disappointed when I told him that I was studying Literature and not Law! This must have been on account of the 18-page petition I wrote against him, a copy of which I submitted to him.

18.   Wikipedia Encyclopedia describes the history and development of the University of Nigeria, Nsukka, thus:

> The University of Nigeria, commonly referred to as UNN, is a federal university located in Nsukka, Enugu State, Nigeria. Founded in 1955 and formally opened on October 7, 1960, the University of Nigeria has four campuses – Nsukka, Enugu and Ituku-Ozalla – located in Enugu State and one in Abia State, Nigeria. The University was the first full-fledged indigenous and first autonomous university in Nigeria, modeled upon the American educational system. The university has 15 faculties and 102 academic departments. The university offers 83 undergraduate programmes and 211 postgraduate programmes."

A law to establish the university was enacted in 1955 by the Eastern Regional Government under the inspirational leadership of its premier, Rt. Hon Dr Nnamdi Azikiwe. This led to the invitation of American and British Educational experts, including Professor J. W. Cook and Dr John A

Hannah and Dr Glen L. Taggart, both of Michigan State University. The team visited Nigeria in 1958 and consequently selected Nsukka as the sight of the new university. A November 30, 1958 government white paper paved the way for the accelerated establishment and development of the university; a process that led to the setting up of an internationalist provisional council in April 1959 made up of Dr Nnamdi Azikiwe, chairman; Dr T Olawale Elias, Dr Okechukwu Ikejiani, J. S. Fulton, from the United Kingdom, and Dr Eldon Lee Johnson from the United States of America. While the university was formally opened on 7th October, 1960, formal classes began on 17th October, 1960 with an enrolment of 220 students and 13 members of the academic staff. This formal opening was followed by the university's first convocation ceremony during which addresses were delivered by Dr Nnamdi Azikiwe and Dr John A. Hannah, the president of Michigan State University.

According to Wikipedia, "the university was fully autonomous, with the power to grant its own degrees. Technically speaking, therefore, it became the first full-fledged university in Nigeria, since Ibadan was still at that time a University College granting London degrees. It also became the first university established by a Nigerian regional government. The University College Ibadan, the old university institution, cut its umbilical cord with London in October 1962, becoming the University of Ibadan. In July, 1965, it turned out the first graduates holding Ibadan (rather than London) degrees, by which time Nsukka had produced two crops of graduates and taken all the publicity for turning out the first graduates of an autonomous Nigerian university."

Interested readers should also see *Portrait of a Nation-Builder: Biography of Chief (Dr) G. E. Okeke,* co-authored by Profs. A. I. Nwabughuogu, G. N. Uzoigwe and myself. Chief Okeke was the first Minister of Education of the Eastern Region and the active driving force behind the establishment of the University of Nigeria, Nsukka. While Dr Azikiwe remained the guiding spirit towards the realization of this worthy dream, it was Chief Okeke who acted as the elemental force that drove the process forward. In countless hours of interview he granted to Professor Nwabughuogu and myself in the course of writing his biography he gave us graphic, phase by phase account about how an almost improbable tall order was translated into material possibility. His account is well captured in the book.

19.   In "In Congruencies in Modern Igbo Politics", a lecture he presented to the Orient Club of Abuja on Dec 1, 2001, at Ibro Hotel, Abuja, Professor Ihechukwu Madubuike stated as follows:

> "By 1897 the Yoruba had produced their first graduate, a lawyer named Sapara Williams. In contrast, the first Igbo graduate could not emerge until about 1934. I believe his name was Dr S. Onwu, a medical doctor. Despite this late start, due to no fault of the Igbo, Ndigbo were able to catch up with the Yoruba by the 1960s. It was the investment in education in the 1930s and 1940s that yielded the dividends of the sixties, which saw the flowering of all aspects of Igbo culture and life."

Prof. Madubuike singled out the late Rt. Hon. Dr Nnamdi Azikiwe, the first indigenous Governor

General and the President of Nigeria during the first Republic and a number of other worthy sons as being the driving force in bridging the enormous educational gap between the Igbo and their southern neighbours. There is even a school of thought which posits that, apart from existing social, political and economic conditions and determinations, Zik waited between 1934 and 1946 to fully launch his political career and anti-colonial nationalist struggle to allow the batch of Igbo students whose overseas educational quest to finish their studies and join him in his agitation he facilitated. Indeed, between 1946 and 1960, Zik could call on the support of his highly educated lieutenants among who were Dr K. O. Mbadiwe, Maazi Mbonu Ojike, Dr Nwafor Orizu, Prof. Godwin Odenigwe and Dr Okechukwu Ikejiani, to mention but a few.

Continuing, Prof. Madubuike asserts that:

"The [Igbo] academic group was led by intellectual giants like Professor Kenneth Dike, first Nigerian principal of the University of London College at Ibadan and its first vice-chancellor for seven years.
There was Professor Eni Njoku, first vice-chancellor and principal officer of the University of Lagos. Writers like Cyprian Ekwensi, Chinua Achebe, and Christopher Okigbo dominated the literary scene. Even though the Igbo were late comers in the field of education – behind the Efik in the Cross Rivers State and the Yoruba of the South-West – by 1960, the year of Nigeria's independence, the Igbo had outstripped the Efik and were about at par with the Yoruba. The Igbo rise was so phenomenal that the Yoruba felt truly threatened and their

leaders wondered aloud why the Igbo should take over the leadership of the University of Ibadan, a university located at the heartland of the Yoruba nation.

20. About April or May, 1984, the military regime of Gen. Muhammad Buhari enacted a policy that would have seen school fees introduced in Nigerian federal universities at the beginning of the 1984/1985 academic session. This unpopular directive was resisted by the National Association of Nigerians Students (NANS) which mobilized Nigerian students to boycott classes and organize demonstrations and sit-ins in all university campuses. I was in my final year, barely one month away from taking my degree exams, yet as the immediate past Secretary-General of the Marxist Youth Movement and one of the architects of the emergence of a new radical Student Union Government, it behooved on me to throw myself once more into the struggle.

Students were quickly rallied to begin boycott of lectures and food until the union executives whom the university authorities had suspended on account of their principled stand and robust opposition to the new directive were recalled. The second day of the protest saw students massed in a strange "lie-in" in front of the Vice-Chancellor's office, at freedom square, and in virtually all the campus major motorways, all lying on the ground, virtually immobile but singing solidarity songs. The nerve of the university authorities cracked and towards evening, after a hastily convened meeting of the university senate, the suspension order was lifted and the eight union leaders were recalled. The story was virtually the same across the country as the students' resistance compelled the federal government to abrogate that obnoxious and anti-people legislation.

Whether there was a precise directive by the university authorities to faculty and departmental heads to fish out and discreetly punish the final year students who either led or participated in the protest, or that some overzealous faculty and departmental heads took it upon themselves to teach the "revolutionaries" in their midst a harsh academic lesson, was only a subject of speculation. What was clear was that we, the final year students who helped organize the protest, ran into all sorts of trouble in our various departments.

In my own case, my somewhat double existence as Lawrence O. Udenta (the official name in my academic record), a dutiful, respectful student librarian in charge of the departmental library, and Udenta O. Udenta, my then political alias, as a troublesome, argumentative radical Marxist, merged into a single entity. My degree lecturers expressed alarm that they never knew that one of Karl Marx's disciples was in their midst. Common sense ultimately prevailed and I was allowed to take my degree examinations which I passed with A scores in virtually all the subjects.

21. During the 1981/1982 academic season, I contested and lost election into the Student Union Parliament principally because I underrated my opponent, believing that being so popular and a good debater, I was virtually unbeatable. I learnt a crucial lesson that electoral politics is far more complex than it ordinarily appears, and may indeed not be the path to the affirmation of my deepest political possibility. I still hold firmly to this stand till date. That experience threw me into a more coherent and strategic study of Marxism and

a direct, practical involvement with the Marxist Youth Movement which I eventually led during the 1982/ 1983 academic session.

22. I met Femi Ahmed in my first year in the university. We instantly connected, I seeing in him the quintessential student revolutionary; fervent, committed to the point of fanaticism, and harbouring an almost professorial understanding of the intellectual content and revolutionary strategies of Marxism, and he seeing in me an eager, articulate pupil willing to learn, and with a more broad social base of relationships that will widen the movement's influence within the community. He instantly became my intellectual guide and ideological mentor, second only to professor Uzodimma Nwala, the movement's Academic Adviser, in shaping my ideological direction.

23. I joined the Marxist Youth Movement when it was sorely rent by factionalism and ideological indirection. The struggle for leadership pitched two groups with diametrically opposed world views about the movement's definition, ideological anchor and revolutionary strategies. The first, led by Femi Ahmed, espoused a near puristic interpretation of the movement's overarching ideological predilection and a classical interpretation of the fundamental Marxist canons. The second group, made up of more liberal members like Nkem Abonta, insisted on the logic of consensus building within wider social publics that will accommodate "radical petty-bourgeois" student elements within the movement's fold.

A panel of enquiry which was set up to examine the crisis bedeviling the movement had me as its Secretary. Femi Ahmed's influence over me was more thorough than his imperious and irrefutable presentation to the panel, a situation that made the outcome of the committee's work fairly predictable. The liberal wing of the movement was thoroughly crushed and Femi Ahmed emerged as the movement's Secretary General and myself, Emma Ezeazu and Mobolade Omonijo emerging as the movement's Secretary for Publicity and publisher of the movement's weekly newsletter, "Revolutionary Path", Secretary for Political Education and Secretary for Ideological Studies respectively. A new era thus dawned in the movement's history, characterized by intense political and ideological education of members, intensification of membership drive and the alignment of the movement to its parent, pan-national platform and outlet, the Patriotic Youth Movement of Nigeria (PYMN), the near invisible power behind the ideological direction of the National Association of Nigerian Students (NANS) for many years.

24. Emma Ezeagu eventually became one of the most resolute, clear-headed and ideologically clear president of NANS, and one of the formidable forces in contemporary Nigerian Civil Society Movement. He is currently the Executive Secretary of one of the most influential and preeminent Nigerian electoral reform and democracy-building platforms, Alliance for Credible Elections (ACE). Mobolade Ononijo is currently the Political Editor of *The Nation*, one of Nigeria's leading daily newspapers. Chris Uyot is the Director of Communications of the Nigerian Labour Congress (NLC) and one of the leading lights of the Nigerian Labour Movement. Dr Sunday Udeze is currently a Senior Lecturer in Mass Communication at the

Enugu State University of Science and Technology (ESUT). Prof. Olu Oguibe is an accomplished artist, curator, poet and scholar. He is currently resident in the USA. Late Ubani Chima died tragically in the struggle to liberate the workers of Nigeria from the stranglehold of oppression. He was and still remains on the A-List of Nigeria's class of pro-democracy and human rights agitators.

25. The term "Petty-bourgeois students" loosely describes those class of students from moneyed and propertied backgrounds, who put on "airs", appear arrogant and superior to the rest of students, wear good clothes, occasionally ride cars, have money to spare and are always successful with the girls. They are usually to be found belonging to such clubs as Victor Sylvester club, Zeta Zee and Beta Sigma.

26. Prof. Charles Chukwuma Soludo is a distinguished professor of Economics. He was between 2000–2008, the Chief Economic Adviser to the President of the federal government of Nigeria and the Governor of Nigeria's Central Bank. Matthew Ojielo (now Ozonnia Ojielo) is an International Peace Scholar and Senior Advisor on Governance to the UN Mission in Kenya. He has held similar high international positions in Nigeria, Ghana and South Africa. Johnny Asuzu (now Chinua Asuzu) is a practicising attorney in Lagos and Abuja, Nigeria, the publisher of the online Legal Journal Assizes at Law and a strong force in Nigerian Civil Society Community. Uche Anioke was a two-time chairman of Awgu Local Government Council, Enugu State (my Local Government Area). He is a distinguished politician who has held numerous high-ranking positions in the government of Enugu State, a publisher, peace advocate and

academic with extensive university teaching experience. Paulinus O. Atta is currently a Senior Officer with the Nigerian Police. C.D Nwosu is a media consultant in Abuja, an author of a number of published books and a regular contributor to newspaper columns in Nigeria's leading newspapers Dr P.C.J. Adibe is an international scholar with expertise in Political Science and Law. The publisher of Africanist and Afrocentric scholarly works, he is concurrently a media consultant and a weekly columnist with a number of leading Nigerian newspapers, including *The Daily Trust.*

27.   Hon. Chijioke Edeoga has held a number of high-ranking positions in the Enugu State Government. A one-time Chairman of the influential Media and Publicity Committee of the House of Representatives, he is currently a Legislative Assistant to Nigeria's President, Dr Goodluck Jonathan.

28.   Apart from the Marxist Youth Movement (MYM), the following radical Marxist groups existed in several Nigerian universities during the 1970s, 1980s and 1990s. Some of them were exclusively student-based, while a number of others had membership drawn from the ranks of students and faculty, and even from the leadership of the workers movements and professional Marxist revolutionaries outside the university: League of Patriotic Students (University of Lagos, University of Benin, Ahmadu Bello University, Obafemi Awolowo University and University of Calabar); Movement of Progressive Nigeria, Calabar Group of Communist and Socialist Workers, Democratic Socialist Movement and Farmers Party all existed in the following universities: University of Calabar, University of Ibadan, University of Lagos, Obafemi

Awolowo University; League of Democratic Students and Socialist Congress of Nigeria existed at Bayero University, Kano; Socialist Forum – Obafemi Awolowo University; Iron Grounders – University of Ilorin; and Marxist Movement of Africa – Bayero University, Kano, and Akanu Ibiam Federal Polytechnic, Afikpo.

Chapter

3

WAKING DREAMS: A VIBRANT LITERARY TRADITION

The development of modern African literature is a field which has been substantially charted by scholars and literary theorists. From the earliest survey method to a deeper explication of the ideo-aesthetic forces that shape the literature and inspire creative writers; from an investigation into the complexity of contemporary literary-theoretical and cultural expressions and the debt it owes to traditional aesthetic forms and elements – forms which have crystallized into a coherent literary category understood as orature; and from the debate over the language issue in African literature, to the examination of its interdependence with history, sociology, psychology, cultural studies and social practice, the modern literature of Africa has consistently shown an awareness of being and becoming in a creative and critical canvas that is as broad as it is baffling in its sheer perspicacity.[1]

There is no doubt that the emergence and development of modern African literature; and the sustenance of that tradition is underpinned by the creative productions of African writers and the critical responses to these. Historically, therefore, the growth of that literature has always depended, at various historical and social moments, on the originality, craftsmanship, skill, commitment and passion of geniuses who have mastered both the matter and manner of artistic cognition through the apprehension and mediation of objective reality. This capacity to transform, expand, reduce or mutate reality is accommodated by the near limitless resources of the artistic image – the most potent creative weapon in the hands of African writers.

An investigation of the modern literature of Africa from the colonial period when creative intervention centred around cultural nationalism and resistance to the early post-colonial period when the critical realist spirit of disillusionment, angst and ennui defined African writers' encounter with society; and from the early 70s to the early 1990s that witnessed the flowering and maturation of the revolutionary aesthetic spirit in both creative authorship and critical practice to the literature of the moment with its persistent search for new idioms of meaning, message and delivery, and which is witnessing the interplay of such forces as postmodernism, reader-response, new renditions of poststructuralist and post deconstructionist ethos and concerns about the human condition, in a universe that is becoming embarrassingly difficult to apprehend and master, African writers have always been the product of the university system, and spend substantial part of their productive life and careers either as university teachers, researchers or writers-in-residence

Of course, while there are exceptions to this rule,[2] the bulk of the literary artists whose imaginative creations have enriched the tradition of modern writing in the continent have all been closely associated with the university environment. This trail was essentially blazed by the likes of Chinua Achebe, Wole Soyinka, Ngugi wa Thiong'o and Nuruddin Farah to mention but a few, and has faithfully been substantiated by the second generation of writers that include the likes of Kole Omotosho, Tess Onwueme, Bode Sowande, Femi Osofisan, Niyi Osundare and the late Ezenwa-Ohaeto.[3]

If the university system is the dwelling place of writers, then it is the secure home base and self-contained, self-sustaining, self-perpetuating and self-reinforcing community of scholars, theorists and critics. The close contact, interaction, occasional distrust, group solidarity and mutual respect between two sets of individuals with different callings, passions, persuasions and instinctual responses to social stimuli have tended to create a sometimes well-structured and sometimes, occasional, accidental, and fairly incoherent tendencies that have come to be associated with such universities as their "Schools of Thought".

It is perfectly rational to speak of the Ibadan, Ife, Nsukka and Makerere schools of African Literature not only because of the presence of Wole Soyinka, Chinua Achebe and Ngugi wa Thiong'o respectively, but also because of the depth and range of representative scholars and theoreticians who sustained the critical craft, some of whom are Emmanuel Obiechina, D. I. Nwoga, Romanus Egudu, Kalu Uka, Ernest Emenyonu, Charles Nnolim, Omafume Onoge, M.J.C. Echeruo, Ime Ikiddeh, Ben Obumselu, Dan Izevbaye, Abiola Irele, and Biodun Jeyifo.[4]

In terms of the theory of literature, however, the identity of these "Schools" does not stem from fidelity to and sponsorship of any coherent ideological or aesthetic theory or movement. If anything, in each school are to be found writers and scholars whose world-views, aesthetic ideologies and temperament are mutually opposed, and some of who are closely allied to other writers and scholars that inhabit the other schools. For example, in spite of the acclaimed revolutionary aesthetic and leftist inclination of key members of the Ibadan-Ife schools, like Biodun Jeyifo, Kole Omotosho and later Femi Osofisan and Niyi Osundare, the key figure of that school, Wole Soyinka, remains an enigma in terms of the complicated nature of his ideo-aesthetics and the high degree of his individual mediation of commonly held traditional heritage and forces. Add to that too is a scholar like Abiola Irele who could be described as being left of centre, and the right-leaning, in terms of scholarship and understanding of the place and role of literature in social processes, Dan Izevbaye.

The Nsukka situation is no less complicated. Chinua Achebe who contributed much in ensuring the international recognition of the English Department at UNN from the early 70s to the early 80s, and who was subsequently celebrated as a cultural hero in 1990 during his sixtieth birthday with a fitting caption "Eagle on Iroko",[5] defies categorization. A humanist to the core, he exemplifies the true spirit of art– calm, turbulent, serene, disturbed, with a dash of revolutionary common sense and conventional and orthodox wisdom. Emmanuel Obiechina, with specialization in the sociology of literature, was closely associated with leftist, socialist academic and scholarly causes. Not so, D. I. Nwoga, a cerebral scholar that was faithful only to his calling as a literary theorist and scholar and nothing more. Worthy of note too in the Nsukka school is Romanus Egudu who left about 1976 to pursue his scholarly career at the University of Benin, Kalu Uka who eventually relocated to the University of Calabar, Obi Maduakor who combines a modernist consciousness with a deep immersion in the sympathetic relationship of literature with radical and populist social causes, Juliet Okonkwo with her profound grasp of the whole range of the African novel, and a commitment to scrupulous research and an inspiring teaching technique, and younger and newer members of the school like Emeka Nwabueze, Chimalum Nwankwo and Nelson Chidi Okonkwo.

The Department of English at the University of Nigeria,

Nsukka was well established. For decades, the department had fostered the role of turning out well rounded students with specialization in Literature, Language, and Dramatic and Theatre Arts. Indeed, for years, while it was merely called "Department of English", there existed also, as part of the department, but operating as a semi-autonomous entity with an administrative head, the Sub-Department of Dramatic Arts. Until the late 1980s the department was located at the Ansah Building which it shared with the Department of Economics while the Sub-Department of Dramatic Arts operated out of the Paul Robeson building complex[6].

While the Ansah building had a complement of lecture halls, a language laboratory, staff offices and a fairly well-stocked library, the Sub-Department of Dramatic Arts was even more well equipped with full complement of lecture rooms, staff offices, a mini proscenium theatre, sound and lighting effects room, costume and make-up rooms, dress rehearsal rooms and a section for speech and voice production. The Sub-Department had also available to it for play productions and other dramatic and theatre arts activities, the Lecture Arts Theatre, the Princess Alexandria Auditorium and the student refectories that could be converted into mini-theatres with minor adjustments. Currently, the Department of English is housed in the imposing Faculty of Arts building complex while the Dramatic and Theatre Arts unit still operates out of Paul Robeson building complex.

When I entered UNN to study English in 1980, I was instantly confronted by a literary event of epical proportions which was either debated openly in lecture rooms or whispered about in low tones along departmental corridors and passageways. This event was the publication of Chinweizu et al's Toward the Decolonization of African Literature, a whole-scale expansion of an ideo-aesthetic thesis which the authors put out in a widely read essay about 1975 as "Prodigals Come Home".[7] Till date, I believe that apart from the critical writings of Ngugi wa Thiong'o on African literature,[8] the two texts that influenced me the most were *Toward the Decolonization of African Literature* and Omafume Onoge's *The Crisis of Consciousness in Modern African Literature: A Survey*. *Toward the Decolonization of African Literature* was an idea whose time had come. It helped in shaking up a continental literature that had fallen into somnambulance, secure in its canons and certain about its heroes. It shaped debate, exploded myths, deconstructed literary theory, history, texts and personalities and expanded the apprehensible frontiers under which that literature had to operate from. It constructed new ideo-aesthetic categories and extended the thematic and stylistic range of Black Aesthetics. It impacted positively on the development of orature as an authentic voice of African aesthetic heritage and inspired a whole generation of writers through its songs of panegyrics to those writers the authors held in high esteem – Achebe, Ngugi, Okot P' Biket and the later Okigbo, to mention but a few.

However, as a young, enterprising student of African literature, the greatest benefit of the work remains its overly polemical and combative style, its passionate and committed statements on the future direction of African literature, its consistent trajectory that nothing should be taken for granted or held sacrosanct or sacred in the continent's literature, and that no writer, no matter the degree and extent of universal recognition, should be spared in this scrutiny unless and until a proper, thorough, and comprehensive investigation of his or her creative productions meet the benchmarks set by the authors.

Today, one can look at that work as being overly prescriptivist in nature, tendentious and paternalistic, and its sometimes harsh and hysterical tones somewhat out of place in dealing with the vitality of an animated life force called literature. Yet, in 1980, such critical thoughts were far removed from my young imagination. My classmates and I were in possession of a masterpiece, an oracular guide to the wisdom reposed in the sacred words of Africa, and as young acolytes who wanted to guard these sacred words, we asked our teachers and the older students pointed questions about their stand on the book, and whether their understanding and appreciation of African literature will remain the same after reading it. Luckily for us and our lecturers, and the older students with maturing vision and fledging creative temper like Esiaba Irobi and Chuma Ezenyirioha[9], most of them, at least ideo-aesthetically, were not far away from the crucial stand taken by Chinweizu *et al* in the work. While some of the lecturers, particularly Professor Kalu Uka, had a few bones to pick with the work given its constricted aesthetic world-view and imperatives, it was generally well received as a commendable addition to the growing corpus of scholarship on African literature.

When I entered Nsukka, Chinua Achebe was set to depart for his sabbatical leave overseas, and though we regularly peeped into his office to catch a glimpse of the literary master, legend and giant and hid in departmental corners to await his comings and goings, I was never taught by him, though we, the first year students, would hang at the window to listen to him teach third or maybe final year students. Also when I entered the UNN, Ngugi wa Thiong'o was completing his sabbatical leave in the Department of English and like Achebe we gave so much just to be admitted into the presence of the writer of such immortal works as *The River Between, Weep Not Child, A Grain of Wheat, Petals of Blood,* and *The Trial of Dedan Kimathi.*[10] Again, one of my regrets was that he too never taught me, but the very fact of their presence, occupying the same atmosphere that we inhabited, provided no less stimulation for inspired studentship, a kind of epiphany that may descend on one by merely encountering such divine or transcendental presence!

Even with Achebe's absence, the "engine-room" as we called the departmental faculty, was well-oiled, managed and maintained by a galaxy of scholars whom I owe a great debt of gratitude to. The department had already developed a vibrant tradition in literary discourses, and had already emerged as one of the renowned centres of instruction on literature and the dramatic arts in Africa. The Nsukka School was recognized and respected globally, not just because of Achebe's presence throughout the 1970s, though his influential standing was a decisive factor, but also because of the presence of other notable scholars whom I have already mentioned.

In our time this vibrant tradition was pursued in various directions: in class instructions; in national and international seminars and conferences hosted by the department; in scholarly publications and book length studies by faculty members; in the creative output of staff and students alike; and in the popularity of the plays produced by the Sub-Department of Dramatic Arts. Of course, the department was closely associated with the publication of *Okike: A Journal of New African Writing* which Achebe edited, and which received high critical acclaim as did his editorship of the African Writers' Series – the single most important factor in the growth, development, and the international standing of African literature.

Prof. Ossie Enekwe was to edit *Okike* much later. There was the *Nsukka Scope,* a magazine that also popularized the creative and critical output of staff and students. Furthermore, Prof. Emmanuel Obiechina served on the editorial board of *The Comrade,* the mouthpiece of the Socialist Movement on campus and which featured articles and essays written by Marxist and other left-leaning members of the university community. Equally at the individual level, faculty members were involved in the growth of the publishing industry as could be seen by the close collaboration between Achebe and Arthur Nwankwo in setting up Nwamife Publishers, a forerunner to Fourth Dimension Publishers which, as I have noted in chapter two, provided the decisive push that drove scholarship in Eastern Nigeria. Fourth Dimension eventually published Achebe's *How the Leopard Got His Claws,* as well as the *Rhythm of*

Creativity and *African Creations* edited by Emmanuel Obiechina and D. I. Nwoga respectively, in addition to many other works in the field of literature, including the poetic works of the late Mamman Vatsa who was a member of the governing council of the university in the mid-1970s.[11]

My first year in the Department of English was partly uneventful because I was still trying to come to grips with the basic rudiments of scholarship and learning in a university setting, and because I was completely distracted by being made to take courses in French, Natural Sciences, Use of English and the Library, as well as Spoken English and other courses in Language and Linguistics. This was so because my conception of the department was a place where I would study nothing but literature from my first year to my final year. I recall that the literature courses I took in my first year were introductions to Fiction, Drama and Poetry. Later will come the Survey of English Literature and an in-depth study of American literature and very great thanks to Fr. Landy, an American priest-lecturer who made this particular course very popular with students.

The high point of my first year was being taught by Prof. Emmanuel Obiechina and Prof. Kalu Uka. Obiechina's use of language, skill of delivery, range of vocabulary and passion for teaching and scholarship was awe-inspiring, and though it was impossible to grasp all his thoughts (he taught us Introduction to Fiction), I made up my mind to speak the way he did, and to have a mastery of literature comparable to his knowledge of the subject. Kalu Uka's own Introduction to Drama was even more baffling. Everything he said sounded strange, esoteric, inscrutable and cultic. With his piercing eyesight and self-possessed mien, he held us spell bound with his sheer oratorical skill, command of English and in-depth of knowledge of drama and theatre. At a point, I started to wonder if these two professors were fully conscious of the fact that they were instructing first year students and not seminar presentations for graduate class students. In retrospect, I have everything to thank them for, as they succeeded in laying a secure and solid foundation that made the appreciation of literature an essentially easy, rewarding and profitable venture in years to come.

At that stage I was yet to confront the late Prof. D. I. Nwoga. This occurred in my final year during which he captured, in a comprehensive manner, the essential ingredients of Studies in Poetry in nine hours, in a breathtaking exercise of the intellect and imagination that was virtually peerless, and which till date still leaves me with goose pimples. To fully appreciate the import of what he did, one had to remember that in the 1980s UNN was still running a three-term system with the almighty June sessional and combined sessional examinations being the test of what had been learned for nine uninterrupted months. To therefore capture in nine hours, the course outline that should take nine months, and to impart in us in those weird, not to be forgotten hours, a knowledge of poetry that far surpassed all that we had learned about the subject in three years, was to say the least extraordinary. Only a genius could have produced that magic. The only other comparable instance of such deep and profound poetic illumination was Prof. Romanus Egudu's handling of Studies in Poetry during my graduate days at the University of Benin.

I have already stated the reasons why I was a poor student in my first year. At the end of the sessional examinations I came out with a 2.79 CGPA that placed me within the second class lower division bracket. While I did well in the three or so literature courses, my French, Natural Science and Spoken English scores dragged the grades down. This trend was to continue in my second year when at the end of the sessional examinations I ended up with a 2.6 something CGPA, failing a 9-credit unit French course. Another reason why my grade at this stage was poor has already been explained in chapter two – my immersion into Marxism and my all-consuming work as a student revolutionary in the Marxist Youth Movement.

However, by the third year, during which time a student

had to "stress an area" in English Studies, I elected to stress literature effortlessly and without any great thought about what I was embarking upon. Having now dispended with in-house departmental Language/Linguistics courses, I began to find my feet, to enjoy my stay in the department and to improve my grades. I was also selected as the departmental librarian under the staff advice of Dr Nzebunachi Oji, a cerebral and enigmatic lecturer who was difficult to understand.

I encountered Prof. Obiechina for the second time, now fairly well equipped to understand him adequately and to fully grasp the essential thrust of his declarations. Prof. Juliet Okonkwo also provided a source of inspiration given her commanding and comprehensive knowledge of African Fiction and the wide variety of texts she prescribed for the course, with the charge that we must provide a detailed summary of all of them. My third year was thus a very exciting one, with a maturing vision of what was expected of us as possible literary scholars and the deepening of our knowledge and grasp of the main trends, currents and forces that shape African and world literatures. My enthusiasm for literature at this stage was such that in spite of my leadership of the Marxist Youth Movement as its Secretary General, my numerous absences and nocturnal journeys to attend PYMN meetings, and my involvement with Student Union Politics I was able to "drag", as it were, my CGPA to 2.83 into the final year, but still short of the 3.0 grade point that would guarantee a 2.1 final grade and a sure step to a possible fulfilling and rewarding career as a literary scholar and potential university teacher.

My final year in the university was fully a defining moment in my life. I had to reconnect fully to the demands of learning and establish my credentials as a leading student and not merely an adequate, uninspiring, unambitious and not too brilliant student, despite my being the Departmental Librarian. The first step towards the realization of this urge was to relinquish the Secretary Generalship of the Marxist

Youth Movement to Chris Uyot, now of the Nigerian Labour Congress headquarters, who guided it competently before handing over to Sunday Udeze, my distant cousin and currently a Senior Lecturer of Mass Communication at the Enugu State University of Science and Technology. Once freed from the day to day administration of the movement and the writing and mass dissemination of the "Revolutionary Path", as well as leading the tutorials in both the ideological and political education classes, I immersed myself completely into my degree examinations preparation. By the end of the first term of my final year, I was easily recognized by my classmates as one of the most advanced students in their midst.

A number of other departmental situations equally contributed to the flowering of my potentials as a student of literature. Nelson Chidi Okonkwo, a former student of the department joined the faculty. His brilliance as a teacher and scholar was acute, absorbing, and because he was closer to us in age than the senior members of the faculty, we gravitated towards him, and pestered him with questions in lecture rooms, along the corridors and in his office where we constantly laid siege. He became both my "Long Essay" supervisor and academic and intellectual guide and was unstinting in the knowledge he freely imparted to us.

About the same time, Emeka Nwabueze, another former student of the department, also joined the faculty as a specialist in Dramatic and Theatre Arts. His charisma, ebullience, oratorical skills and sheer presence awakened our literary and dramatic imagination and helped in laying a secure foundation for my future academic and intellectual pursuits. His range of dramatic knowledge is awesome, particularly given the intimidating array of dramatic texts and critical source books he made available to us. His office became a mecca of a sort for students desirous of deeper knowledge, and his large stock of books and journals, a mini-library of sorts for us.

Not to be forgotten was the introduction of a new course

called "Modern Authors" which was designed for "students aiming for higher pursuit in scholarship". The course was taught by Obi Maduakor, a seasoned lecturer and a deeply knowledgeable and brilliant scholar. For the first time, modernist movement became instantly illuminated and the acclaimed obscurantism of Ezra Pound and T.S. Elliot, as well as the difficulty in apprehending Virgina Woolf's "stream of consciousness" method, became a thing of the past. In retrospect, I can safely assert that my exposure to the modern authors and the modernist movement through the course, even though I rebelled against that ideo-aesthetic tendency and philosophical vision of reality through my encounter with Antonio Gramsci, Walter Benjamin, Christopher Caudwell, Louis Allthusser, Lucien Goldmann, Raymond Williams and Terry Eagleton,[12] contributed significantly in my electing to pursue a higher degree in Literature and become a university teacher.

My final year also witnessed a maturing creative spirit and vision which found expression in a disquieting, vulgar and pejorative poeticization of the female genitalia. A number of my classmates and myself who started experimenting in this less than noble poetic form came to regard ourselves as belonging to the "Marsh-land" School of Poetry; marshland being our Elliotian objective correlative[13] because while retaining its essence as a material force, elliptically alludes to, impersonates, explains and refers to either sets of material reality, emotion and feeling. We wrote our poetic sketches on the lecture hall blackboard, and regaled our bemused and increasingly embarrassed classmates with readings and performances of our poetic creation and heritage! We even contemplated putting out an anthology of "Marshland" poetry but soon put such foolish thoughts out of our minds. The leading lights of this "School of Poetry", that I still remember are C. B. Asomugha, Emeka Onuorah, S. B. C. Nwankwo, Emeka Gregory Okeke, Azubike and Chinedu Okonkwo.[14]

However, an event occurred in my final year which almost

derailed my academic plans and carefully re-constructed career as an outstanding student of literature. It was the envisaged introduction of tuition fees in federal universities by the Buhari/Idiagbon regime beginning from the 1984-1985 academic year by which time I would have graduated. The Student Union Government, with the inspiring leadership of Olu Oguibe, who was its Secretary General, rallied the students to a long-drawn resistance to what was considered an anti-people imposition. Those of us in our final year who had been battle tested over years of student mobilization, donned our revolutionary togas once more and provided the leadership and moral strength the students needed. We ensured that there was a comprehensive boycott of food in the night and the following morning, and as early as 6.00 am, we had begun massing in large numbers in front of the Vice-Chancellor's office, not in a stand up protest fashion, but with every student lying on the ground and singing revolutionary songs. Our demand was both the abrogation of the new fees and the recalling of our nine student leaders expelled or suspended, including the charismatic and hugely popular Olu Oguibe.

I played a leading role in mobilizing the students, in solidarity rallies called before the "Lie-in" and was among the first students to lie in front of the Vice-Chancellor's office. Eventually, the stalemate was broken and the expelled or suspended students recalled. Ultimately, the Federal Military Government reversed itself and abrogated the new fees. Yet, a huge prize was to be paid by some of the final year students who participated in the protest. Matters became worse at the departmental level when it was revealed that some lecturers indeed taught students during the struggle. I led the charge in condemning the students and lecturers who sought to break the strike. Inevitably, matters got out of control when I was reported to the senior members of the faculty as a student "anarchist" and revolutionary. I became instantly popular or notorious depending on people's stand on the issue.

In essence, my carefully concealed identity as a student revolutionary was revealed and I had a thin time convincing Dr Emeka Nwabueze, Obi Maduakor and Nzebunachi Orji that we meant well in our protest and that I had the highest regard and respect for them.

This season of disquiet, anxiety and uncertainty endured into the degree examinations but the fact that I had A scores in virtually all the degree courses meant that my lecturers considered my activities as a case of youthful exuberance. Indeed, it was Dr Nwabueze who first broke the news to me that I was among the three students who made a second class upper division, and that I scored A in his paper. However, the Masters and PhD programmes I had taken for granted would be done at UNN was not to be, since I was still apprehensive that my lecturers would take out their resentment on me at that stage of my career. In retrospect, I now feel that my fears were unfounded and childish, and that I would have been welcomed with open arms, as indeed a number of my lecturers encouraged me to come back for the M.A. programme after the compulsory national youth service.

My period of study at the Department of English of UNN laid the foundation for my future academic and intellectual pursuits. By the time I left the university, I had discovered myself and had awoken fully from the slumber of my early years. I encountered a vibrant literary tradition and was taught by the best scholars and lecturers in the discipline. I was profoundly influenced by their industry, hard work, discipline and commitment to learning, teaching and scholarship. And though a number of gaps in the departmental curriculum was eventually detected by me as an advanced and mature student, particularly in the area of Russian and continental European literature (we only studied Dostoyevsky's *Crime and Punishment* in our final year), particularly European Classical Novels of the 19th century (I do not think that Tolstoy and Dostoyevsky have any peer in the full range of English and American fiction),[15] and the absence of scholarship on Marxist aesthetics, the programme fully and more than competently prepared me for higher studies in literature, so much so that when I started the M.A. programme at the Department of English and Literary Studies of the University of Benin, I was very much at home with the issues raised by my lecturers.

Let me confess that I am not familiar with the faculty strength of the department today, and though it is easy to gather this kind of information by obtaining the faculty list and examining the credential of the present-day lecturers, this exercise falls outside the main focus of this work. What I do know is that, like all great traditions, the department has the capacity for self-renewal, self-sustenance and self-perpetuation. A product of a great heritage and a well established "School" of African Literature, there is no doubt that it has been and will continue to enrich this noble inheritance, inspire students and extend the goals of research, scholarship and great learning for many more decades to come.

CHAPTER THREE
NOTES AND REFERENCES

1. From its relatively modest beginning, African literature in English has attracted and continued to attract the attention of literary and cultural theorists, literary critics, scholars and academics in such broadly related inter-disciplinary fields as philosophy, history, linguistics, sociology, ethnology and psychology. Mention must be made, in this regard, of the research efforts and critical enterprise of the following scholars whose critical and ideological approaches and world view are as wide and diverse as ever could be. Apart from the traditional approaches to literature, these critics' and scholars' ideo-aesthetic canons also encompass Eurocentricism and Euro-modernism, Marxist revolutionary aesthetics, semiotics, structuralism, post-structuralism, deconstructionism, feminism and reader response. Scholars and critics worth mentioning in this regard include Claude Wauthier, Adrian Roscoe, James Olney, John Povey, David Cook, Eldred Jones, Eustace Palmer, Charles Larson, Bernth Lindfors, O.R. Darthorne, Joseph Okpaku, Chinweizu, Omafume Onoge, Ngugi wa Thiong'o, Chidi Amuta, Biodun Jeyifo, Emmanuel Ngara, Emmanual Obechina, Romanus Egudu, Donatus I. Nwoga, Ben Obumselu, M. J. C. Echeruo, Funso Aiyejina, Adebayo Williams, Niyi Osundare and Kole Omotoso.

2. Examples of non-university based or located African writers include: Sembene Ousmane, Alex La Guma, Cyprian Ekwensi, Gabriel Okara, Onuora Nzekwu, Elechi Amadi, T. M. Aluko, Ferdinand Oyono, and to an extent Chukwuemeka Ike, though he was associated with the university

system for a number of years in a non-teaching and research capacity.

3. African writers who are associated with university teaching and research work are legion and they include the following: Chinua Achebe, Wole Soyinka, Ngugi wa Thiong'o, Femi Osofisan, Niyi Osundare, Tess Onwueme, Kole Omotoso, Esiaba Irobi, Obi Nwakamma, Okey Ndibe, Ezenwa Ohaeto, Ayi Kwei Armah, Kofi Awoonor, Jared Angira, Mongo Beti, Okot P. Bitek, Dennis Brutus, Nuruddin Farah and Mazisi Kunene.

4. While it is true that hundreds and possibly thousands of critics and scholars have continued to shed light on the theoretical and ideo-aesthetic direction of African Literature, there are perhaps only a handful of them who have made what amounted to the construction of the theoretical-critical, aesthetic and ideological canons of the literature. These include Bernth Lindfors, not on an account of any coherent ideo-aesthetic world-view, concrete and materially manifest, but on the length of his staying power, the literary and other resources at his disposal, the pervasive influence of *Research in African Literatures* and the whole generation of scholars he either molded or influenced and who now belong to what could loosely be called the "Lindfors Tradition or School of African Literature"; Ngugi wa Thiong'o, Omafume Onoge; Sunday Anozie; Emmanual Obiechina; Abiola Irele; Dan Izevbaye; G. G. Darah, Olu Obafemi and perhaps Chidi Amuta and Emmanuel Ngara.

5. The "Eagle on Iroko" celebration was mounted for the renowned novelist and humanist, Chinua Achebe, in 1990 to commemorate his 60th birthday. Appropriately conceived as a metaphor of sublimity,

material transcendence, superlative and quintessential exultation of glory and honour, it celebrated the eagle–the most golden of all birds, dwelling on the Iroko–the tallest and most majestic of all trees.

6. Before the construction of a composite Faculty of Arts building in the University of Nigeria, Nsukka, the Department of English was located at the "Ansah Building" which it shared with the Department of Economics while the Sub-Department of Dramatic Arts was housed at the "Paul Robeson building", named in honour of the African-American concert singer, recording artist, athlete and actor who was also noted for his political radicalism and activism in the civil rights movement.

7. *Toward the Decolonization of African Literature* was like a critical thunderbolt out of heaven. It shattered illusions about the direction of African Literature, deconstructed canons, demystified aesthetic principles and demythologized literary icons. It virtually threw African Literature into tumult, ferment and soul-searching, energized its practitioners and extended the space, range, scope and breadth of its legitimacy and authenticity. *Toward the Decolonization of African Literature* remains one of the most influential works on African literary theory and literary scholarship, its combustible language, combative and disquieting tone and prescriptivist paradigm notwithstanding.

8. Before the publication of Omafume Onoge's "The Crisis of Consciousness in African Literature: A Survey", and with the exception of the theoretical and critical writings of Ngugi Wa Thiong'o and a few others, the African literary-critical-theoretical dialectic was cluttered with a plethora of

Eurocentric and Euro-modernist cant. "The Crisis of Consciousness" was the first rigorous materialist reading of African literature, a major statement on its ideological content, direction and obligations and an organic attempt to locate and domesticate the operation of Marxist aesthetic principles and philosophy in the historical development of African literature. It influenced, and continues to influence generations of African scholars and literary theoreticians, myself inclusive.

9.   Esiaba Irobi and Chuma Ezenyirioha, who both graduated from the English Department of the University of Nigeria, Nsukka in 1983, were prolific student literary practitioners. While Esiaba's craft was drama-based (he wrote and performed a number of his student plays at both the Sub-Department of Dramatic Arts auditorium and in various other campuses across Nigeria), Chuma's craft was in the field of short story. He wrote and self-published a number of his stories which motivated a number of other students to discover and realize their own latent potentials.

10. Ngugi wa Thiong'o never set out to construct a postcolonial literary and cultural theory, yet in the depth of his intellect, the profundity of his creative genius and the practical impact of his monumental cultural, literary and dramatic creations, he has had far more meaningful impact and influence in the materialist conceptualization and ideological reinforcements of the dialectic of a liberationist postcolonial cultural struggle than all the university constructors and systematizers of postcolonial literary and cultural theory put together. Between *Home Coming* and *Penpoints, Gunpoints and Dreams: Towards a Critical Theory of the Arts and the State in Africa,* Ngugi has put

out such resounding canonical revolutionary literary and cultural works as *Writers in Politics, Barrel of a Pen, Detained: A Writer's Prison Diary, Writing Against Neo-Colonialism, Decolonizing the Mind, Moving the Centre: Struggle for Cultural Freedom*, and *Dreams in a Time of War,* all of which are the constitutive ingredients of a continent-wide cultural ideology of protest, resistance, emancipation and re-humanization.

11.   The Nsukka literary environment of the 1980s was a lively and vibrant one inspired, as students and staff were, by the presence of high quality literary magazines, periodicals, journals and anthologies that contained the best of Nigerian and African creative and critical writings. Worthy of mention, in this regard, are *Okike: A Journal of African Writing,* which Chinua Achebe edited, *Nsukkascope, The Comrade* (which contained literary, political and ideological materials) and the two fiction and poetry anthologies: *Rhythm of Creativity* edited by Emmanuel Obiechima and *African Creations* edited by Donatus I. Nwoga. Both were published by the Fourth Dimension Publishing Company Limited.

12.   In retrospect, I can readily concede that one of the glaring, fundamental limitations of my scholarly research of the mid-1980s was my lack of full exposure to the critical thinking and philosophical, ideological and theoretical writings of "Western Marxists", beginning with the groundbreaking works of the Frankfurt School of Critical Theory (Max Horkheimer, Theodor Adorno, Herbert Marcuse, etc), and up to and including Jurgen Habermas, Donald Kellner, Axel Honnth and N. Kompridis, not to talk of a close reading of the works of Antonio Gramsci, Walter Benjamin, Louis Althusser, Raymond Williams, and even Terry

Eagleton. Though I did manage to glean some of their thoughts in fragmentary pieces I could lay hands on, as could be attested to from a reading of *Revolutionary Aesthetics and the African Literary Process,* I have taken the opportunity of its second edition, as well as the second editions of *Art, Ideology and Social Commitment in African Poetry, Heroism and Critical Consciousness in African Literature* (previously titled *Ideological Sanction and Social Action in African Literature)* and the unpublished *Art and Identity: Essays on African Literature* to redress this theoretical and philosophical imbalance.

13. Objective Correlative is one of T. S. Eliot's eternal literary coinages. The term pertains to a metaphoric composition that operates at the level of materiality and ideal consciousness (feelings, emotions passions, and other sensuous responses). Eliot conceived it as sets of images that, while retaining their materiality, adequately express thoughts and emotions.

14. Chibuzo Asomugha is currently a Senior Lecturer at the Federal Polytechnic, Oko, Nigeria. Before then, he was a lecturer in the Department of English at Nnamdi Azikiwe University, Awka, Nigeria. Emeka Onuokah is currently the Head of the Corporate Affairs Division of the Pension Commission Abuja, Nigeria. He was for years a top staff of the Business Division of the Nigerian Television Authority. Emeka Okeke is a management consultant in Lagos, Nigeria. SBC Nwankwo subsequently read Law and is practicing in Anambra State, Nigeria. Chinedu Okonkwo is a senior staff of the Anambra State Secondary Education Board as a secondary school principal.

15. The literature syllabus of the Department of English

at the University of Nigeria, Nsukka, was weighed heavily in favour of English and American literature. Exposure to Continental European and World Literature was grossly limited. Dostoyevsky was the only Russian writer ever studied (*Crime and Punishment*); Stendhal, Balzac, Emile Zola, Flaubert, Goethe and the other masters of European literature had no mention. It was during my compulsory one year National Youth Service, and at graduate school that I began to appreciate the power of Russian literature and its superiority to English literature. Only then, too, did I begin to appreciate the fact that the best novels were not written by Charles Dickens, George Elliot and the Bronte Sisters but by Leo Tolstoy *(War and Peace)*; Dostoyevsky *(The Brothers Karamazov);* Alexei Tolstoy *(Peter the First)*; Maxim Gorky *(Mother);* Mikhail Sholokhov *(And Quiet Flows the Don)*, and Boris Pasternak *(Doctor Zhivago)*.

Chapter

4

SEARCHING FOR POSSIBILITY

When I left UNN in June-July 1984, it was very clear what my principal intention in life was going to be: to acquire a second and maybe a third degree in literature and make my mark as a university teacher, scholar and researcher. I was also convinced that I had some writing talents as exemplified in my boyhood stories, and I knew that I would devote quite a significant portion of my productive years to writing. Yet, while I wrote essentially creative works in my high school days, I was convinced that my destiny lay elsewhere; in literary scholarship, in critical studies of literature, and in intellectual works with a philosophic bias.

This desire recorded two huge boosts shortly after my graduation, for though I was apprehensive about applying for the M.A. and PhD programmes in UNN, in spite of my lecturers' assurances, I was determined to acquire one elsewhere.

The M.A. programme of the Department of English and Literary Studies of the University of Benin, Benin City, was thus the only course that I applied for, in part because of the presence of Prof. Romanus Egwu who was my father's junior colleague at St. Charles Teacher's Training College in the 1950s, and again because I was deployed to the old Bendel State for the one year compulsory National Youth Service programme. This choice (I never had any doubt that I would be admitted given my estimation of my scholarly and intellectual abilities) was a very deliberate and practical one: I would be "safe" in the hands of a profoundly brilliant professor who had a connection with my family, and Benin City was the capital of old Bendel State, my location for the National Service.

The first was thus the awareness that I had available to me a Department of English with a strong literature stress or component at the head of which was somebody I would trust to protect, guide and encourage the flowering of my intellectual and scholarly abilities and disposition. The second boost was my being posted to the headquarters of the then Aniocha Local Government Area of the state as a Corps Liaison Officer for the Local Government Area – the highest posting in any Local Government Area of the Federation made to those corps members with leadership potentials and organizational skills. As a Corps Liaison Officer, I oversaw the welfare of Corps Members, ensured that they received their monthly allowance in good time (I always went to the NYSC headquarters in Benin City every month with the Local Government Accountant for this purpose), visited them at their various stations, and generally listened to their problems and complaints, and tried my best to address them. I also doubled as an Under Secretary in the local government with a schedule of duties and support staff. For the execution of my duties, I was assigned an official Peugeot 504 from the local government pool of vehicles.

It may be worth recounting here how I became a Corps Liaison Officer. I got into the Auchi Polytechnic Camp very late in the day because I mistakenly boarded a car going to Ibadan from Onitsha rather than boarding the one that would take me directly to Auchi in a very short time. I was thus forced to board yet another car from Ibadan to Auchi, and by the time I arrived it was pretty late in the night. This meant that I could not start the registration processes and the collection of NYSC kits as many other corps members did on that first day. I resolved to be at the registration/collection centre early the following morning.

However, when I got there, I discovered that hundreds of corps members were already queuing up for the same purpose. I looked with dismay at the long, snaky line and wondered when I would be attended to. To make matters worse, a lot of "shunting" (breaking the queue) was going on and the line was hardly moving. I made an arresting appearance in my jeans trousers, jeans jacket and a Che Guevara-type cap, and with the jacket pockets bulging with *ABC of Dialectical and Historical Materialism*[1] and other pocket-sized classic works of Marx and Lenin. And when I self-imposed on myself the task of keeping the line moving by sternly rebuking "the shunters", the whole line erupted with uproarious laughter and cat calls. I persisted, and in a short time it was my turn to be attended to.

Little did I know that the NYSC Chief Store Executive, Mr Idakwo, was observing all my valiant efforts and stoic acceptance of the cat calls. Rather than permit me to be attended to he asked if I would like to continue with my endeavour. My positive answer was greeted with more cat calls to the effect that I had now been "promoted". I continued with the work till late evening before he now assigned one of his officers to provide for me everything I needed. On the following day, he asked me to work with his team in the store, sorting out kits and distributing them, and to recruit two or three willing Corps Members that would keep watch over the line. The volunteers were many, principally because the story of my dramatic transformation from a late arriver to a leader with privileges had made the round.

From that stage I never looked back. I was virtually a semi-official of the NYSC, eating with the staff and advising them on the best approach in handling Corps Members. I worked closely with "Spill-over"[2] Corps Members who studied overseas and different categories of other staff. I became quite influential and popular in the camp; at weekend parties, on parade grounds and during the endurance trek. When the time for posting for the primary assignment came, I was among the few privileged Corps Members who were not only asked to make a choice about where they wanted to serve, but who also were virtually commanded to accept postings as Liaison Officers on account of all that we did at the orientation Camp. That was how I was posted to Ogwashiuku, the Headquarters of the then Aniocha Local Government Area as a Corps Liaison Officer, courtesy of a consensus probably reached by the NYSC camp officials, but in part facilitated by Mr Idakwo who had taken me under his wing.

Ogwashiuku proved to be a turning point in my intellectual and academic advancement. This was surprising in that though bursting with a dynamic social and cultural life, it was a semi-urban enclave bounded by other such notable towns as Ibuzo and Ubulu-Ukwu. I discovered that the town had a public library and my investigation of this was an eye opener. I saw displayed on the shelves and in the reference rooms, the classics of philosophy, history and national literatures, from England to Germany, and from America to Russia and France. The library was particularly strong on the 19th century Russian literature and for the first time I had before me the novels I had always wanted and desired to read since the first intimation of the richness of this literary tradition was fired by my exposure to Dostoyevsky's *Crime and Punishment.* There were also some 20th century Russian works, including Maxim Gorky's *Mother,* the three autobiographical trilogy[3] and *Forma Gordeyev;* Lev Tolstoy's

Peter the First (one of the most brilliant and compelling historical narratives ever written given its social and historical fidelity, and the transformational nature of its realism); Mikhail Sholokhov's *And Quiet Flows The Don* (a classic of modern Russian literature and a landmark Socialist Realist work); and Boris Pasternak's *Dr Zhivago* (which together with *And Quiet Flows The Don, War and Peace,* and *The Brothers Karamazov* I consider the greatest novels ever written).[4]

I virtually read without restraint, making copious notes as I did, and comparatively examining the literary achievements of England, Germany, France and Russia. I came to the stark and disturbing conclusion, which was a substantial denial or refutation of the curriculum content of my B.A. programme at UNN that with the exception of the Shakespearian works written by Edward de Vere, the 17th Earl of Oxford,[5] nothing in English literature, particularly the 19th and early 20th centuries, could match the literary productions of France, Germany, and especially Russia of the same period. I became instantly immersed in these works and succeeded in achieving a balance in my literary and intellectual progression by acquiring a more rounded view and perspective on literature, life and culture. I read Zola's *La Assommoir* and *The Earth* and Balzac's *The Thirteen* and *Cousin Bettle;* Lermontov's *The Hero of Our Time;* Turgenev's *Fathers and Sons;* Gogol's *Dead Souls,* Leo Tolstoy's *War and Peace, Anna Karenina* and *Resurrection* (which I found highly illuminating and morally edifying); and Dostoyevsky's *The Brothers Karamazov, The Devils, Note from the Underground* and *The Idiot.*[6] Till date, Dostoyevsky remains my favourite world novelist, as Achebe *(Arrow of God)*[7] and Ngugi wa Thiong'o remain my favourite African novelists.

Apart from these classics of world literature, I was also exposed to the philosophical works of Plato, particularly *The Republic,* and Aristotle (I read *The Poetics* for the first time, though aspects of it, including extracts, have consistently formed an integral part of my dramatic studies from first year to final year). The library also had a rich stock of historical discourses, including Herodotus' *The Histories,* Caesar's *The Civil Wars* and Thucydides' *The History of the Peloponnesian Wars*. All these and more I read, though I cannot remember all their titles or authorship now.

Thus, while I enjoyed my service year as a Corp Liaison Officer and Local Government Area Under Secretary, I more than adequately prepared myself for higher pursuit in literary scholarship. I had read literally hundreds of books, and filled up exercise books and file-sized paper clippings with jottings, extracts, personal interpretations and commentaries, inter-textual references and comparative analysis of the works I encountered. There was no doubt whatsoever in my mind that I was more than ready for an M.A. and a PhD literature programme in any university, in the middle of my service year, and this period of heavy reading and intense study made available by the Ogwashiuku Library was to stand me in good stead as a graduate student and a university teacher.

In my quest for academic excellence and intellectual development I owe a debt of gratitude to Prof. Romanus Egudu who became my intellectual guide and mentor between 1985-1987, and whose passion for and commitment to literature helped in sustaining my deep love for and interest in the discipline over the intervening years. Before I even applied for the M.A. programme in the University of Benin, I sought his advice on my anticipated undertaking. He not only encouraged me to seek for admission without delay but went out of his way to brief me about the structure and content of the programme. He ended by making available to me the course title and description of the six prescribed courses and generally behaved as if I was already one of his students even before I purchased the admission form.

Armed with this information, and fully convinced that I would be admitted into the M.A. programme, I really went to work. I created files for each of the courses and filled them with critical notes, summaries, lengthy analysis on different aspects of literature and bibliographic listing and annotations of critical and scholarly works that I could find. I re-read virtually all the African novels, stories, drama and poetry works that I had ever come across and made lengthy notes on them, placing these notes in the appropriate files. Together with the notes I had already made from my wide readings from the Ogwashiuku Library, the files became a formidable academic weapon that would guarantee for me a smooth, stress free and successful career as a graduate student.

I next turned my attention to the likely areas where I would conduct my research for the M.A. thesis. This exercise was absurdly easy, for I was convinced that of all African novelists (prose fiction has always been my strongest point and first love of all literary genres), the only two novelists that would yield the kind of ideo-aesthetic insight I was committed to were Ngugi wa Thiong'o and Alex La Guma.[8] Ngugi, particularly, held an attraction for me as one writer who had successfully combined fidelity to art and commitment to progressive social, cultural and political causes to the degree that his life and work had already become the sum total of the general and specific encounter with a traumatic historical evolution for all Africans. Growing out of the liberal humanist/critical realist ideo-aesthetic[9] affirmations of the sixties with such works as *The River Between, Weep Not Child, A Grain of Wheat* and *The Black Hermit,* he had, by the late 70s and 80s, completely abandoned, in form, language and content, all Eurocentric aesthetic criteria and prerogatives, and with such works as *The Trial of Dedan Kimathi, Petals of Blood, Devil on the Cross, I Will Marry When I Want, Mother, Sing for Me, Matigari, and The Wizard of The Crow* had established his reputation as a disciplined literary creator, a passionate Africanist and a Marxist revolutionary.

Ngugi is one of very few African writers who has broken down and successfully deconstructed the conventional notions of aesthetics, craftsmanship and historical vision in Africa; has deployed the rich resources of orature and other traditional verbal art forms not for literary embellishment but for the construction of a new continental aesthetic idiom; and has merged two contending cognitive and perceptual currents: a concrete and proactive response to imperialism, neo-colonialism and national oppression via material action, struggle and labour, and a profound, multi-layered exploration of the various dimensions of literary mediation, with near peerless aesthetic and authorial ideologies.[10] In making this statement, Ngugi has reached out and mastered the cogent cultural and social nuances of a transformational milieu, and handled, with remarkable dexterity, the key issues in history, culture and language of creative delivery.

Illuminating too are his numerous books, lectures and essays on African literature, history, politics and cultural and social processes starting with the seminal essays in *Homecoming* to the universal thesis on the multiplicity of authentic cultural centres in *Moving The Centre*.[11]

In between these two works are such other works that challenge the imagination and extend the frontier of cultural apprehension as *The Barrel of a Pen, Writers in Politics, Decolonizing the Mind,* and *Detained: A Writer's Prison Diary.* All taken together, Ngugi's works–creative and critical–demonstrate the capacity of the human mind and imagination to assimilate, digest and codify reality in a coherent manner and form; and the force of balance that comes out of a lifelong pursuit of fusing intellect with procreative social action, creative vision with popular causes.

One of my regrets so far in my intellectual development has been not writing a definitive study of Ngugi's ideo-aesthetics, because by the time I completed my M.A. degree programme in 1986-1987, I was already priding myself that I would turn out to be the definitive authority on Ngugi's art. Maybe that project will still be executed. I was thus clear on the author whose works I would base my M.A. thesis on:

Ngugi wa Thiong'o, either as an individual author study, or in comparison with Alex La Guma, Maxim Gorky, and Mikhail Sholokhov. I stated as much in the thesis statement that accompanied my admission form. Having made this resolve, I set about formulating various titles for a potential M.A. thesis and building up a body of scholarly knowledge around them. This process continued unabated throughout my service year so much so that by the commencement of the M.A. programme I had about two or three fully developed notes on the works of Ngugi.

I thus entered University of Benin bursting with enthusiasm and fortified with the notes I made on the classics I read at Ogwashiuku Library, the six files bulging with notes on all the courses I would be offering throughout the duration of the programme, and of course, my two or three fully written notes on Ngugi's works. It was not every easy for me at the start, the story having spread among faculty members, that a Marxist ideologue had virtually smuggled himself to study literature, a field that was being jealously protected by the guardians of the sacred word, with canons ad criteria that should not be distorted or corrupted. Professor Egudu fired the first salvo when I visited him to enquire about the status of my admission. He admonished me to remain faithful to the canons of literature and not let myself be engulfed in the ideological pyrotechnics (abstracted from philosophy, sociology and political economy) which are masquerading as critical scholarship. He drew attention to my admission form's thesis statement which was laden with Marxist "cant", a matter he discussed with the respected Professor Dan Izevbaye when he visited him and he showed him that thesis statement. On enquiring whether my ideological stand would affect my admission, he was emphatic that I was already admitted as a student, that the thesis statement, shorn of those ideological encrustations, was very sound academically and intellectually and that I should not expect any backlash.

He and the other faculty members were true to their

words, even though Dr Emeka Okeke-Ezigbo cracked a joke when I went to see him when I commenced the programme. He wanted to know "whether our Ngugi friend (meaning me) has already completed his thesis". I was taken aback but took it in my stride. He was to become one of my strongest sources of inspiration in the department and, with the exception of my supervisor, Dr V. U. Ola, and Prof. Egudu, became my most respected and trusted intellectual mentor and guide. I still treasure the reference letter he wrote on my behalf when I graduated, and still remember that he was one lecturer who advised me to complete the M.A. programme rather than move straight to the PhD programme without writing the M.A. thesis and earning the degree, on account of my outstanding scores in the course work.

The only suggestion that some sort of bias lingered in the minds of faculty members regarding my immersion into Marxism was the rejection of all M.A. thesis topics I submitted which had the remotest relationship to Ngugi's art, and this was in spite of the robust defence and tenacious insistence of my supervisor, Dr V.U. Ola, who was not just my lecturer, but a mother, auntie and guardian.

After submitting various topics, sometimes craftily drafted, yet seeing them rejected at the departmental graduate seminar/thesis defence meetings, I told her that I would make another try, and that I would settle for the examination of the novels of Mega Mwangi from the standpoint of critical realism.[12] She was quite sympathetic and understanding, and helped in guiding me to a successful defence of my proposal and the submission of the finished thesis in record time.[13] In retrospect, I have everything to thank Prof. Egudu and the entire faculty for insisting that I broaden my literary and critical perspective, and in examining literary texts from a more rounded perspective and standpoint. This is so because, in all honesty, if I had been allowed to write my thesis on Ngugi wa Thiong'o, I would have learnt very little from the M.A. programme and the thesis defence processes, given the wealth of information and data at my command.

The M.A. degree programme was indeed a tough one. The course content covered all of African and world literature (prose fiction, drama, poetry, short stories, etc) with two special courses on Afro-American Literature and the Theory of Oral Literature taught by Professor S.E. Ogude and Dr Okpure O. Obuke respectively. The M.A. student was also expected to defend his thesis proposal in an intellectually challenging graduate seminar as well as participate in and present papers during other graduate seminar activities. Added to this was the fact that even if the proposal succeeded he was expected to defend all the chapters of his thesis at the various graduate seminars.

When I was admitted, no one had as yet graduated with an M.A. in English degree and this situation was a constant source of worry to members of the faculty, particularly, Prof. Egudu who could be described as the doyen of the department. In fact, he told me that it would give him immeasurable joy to get a student who would complete the programme in one year. I gave him my word that I would achieve that feat. The academic condition in the department was ideal for sustained intellectual growth and development. Graduate students had a well-appointed office all to themselves. There were also classrooms exclusively designated for graduate teaching and seminar. The departmental library was well stocked, and so also was the literature section in the main university library. Though we commuted daily from Ekenwan campus to Ugbouho campus for our lectures, our Ekenwan campus residence was very comfortable. A graduate student either had a room to himself or shared a room with another student.

However, the greatest asset I had as a graduate student was the quality and commitment of members of the department. Led by Professor Romanus Egudu, the faculty was made up of such distinguished, brilliant and committed scholars as Prof. S. E. Ogude, Dr Okeke-Ezigbo, Dr V. U. Ola, Dr Odun Balogun, Dr Okpure Obuke and Dr Tony Afejiku. I can justly say that on the basis of my subsequent readings and advanced study of literature over the years, my lecturers can more than hold their own, globally speaking, with their colleagues in any university in terms of the quality of intellectual output, passionate commitment to teaching and scholarship and unalloyed love for literature. I owe a lot to them individually and collectively for helping to ignite the fire I had into becoming a roaring flame, and for their guidance, mentorship and wise counsel.

However, I have to single out Prof. Egudu, whose lecture on the poetry of Chris Okigbo could only be matched in intensity, brilliant execution and sheer mastery of the ideo-aesthetic craftmanship and poetics of that somewhat difficult writer, by the late Prof. D. I. Nwoga's nine-hour lecture on Studies in Poetry, which I alluded to in chapter three; Dr (Mrs) V. U. Ola, an Igbo woman married to a Yoruba man, a mother figure, teacher par excellence, passionate, and intellectually stubborn when necessary, as exemplified when she rose to a stout defence of my thesis proposal which somehow became controversial.[14] Dr Okeke-Ezigbo, a deeply, thoughtful, profoundly brilliant teacher and scholar, whose command and use of English baffled me, and reminded me very much of my experience with Prof. Obiechina's lecture, during my first year at UNN; Dr Okpure Obuke with his original ideas about orature and folkloristic scholarship as demonstrated in his constructing a universally acclaimed theoretical and aesthetic method of studying oral literature called "aesthetic-multi dimensional approach"[15]; and of course, Dr Odun Balogun, who ennobled and edified my imagination with his sheer, comprehensive knowledge of prose fiction. Dr Balogun came to represent in my consciousness the authentic picture of what academic discipline should be, and what efforts the younger generation of teachers and scholars are putting into advancing the reaches and frontiers of literary discourses in Africa beyond their received inheritance.

Apart from my colleagues, Segun Agbaje and Elo Lesso

who became my close personal friends, I was lucky to have such distinguished writers as Tess Onwueme and the late Ezenwa Ohaeto as fellow graduate students in the department though they were pursuing their PhD programmes. There was also another PhD student who inspired and influenced me. He is U. B. Uwatt, who is currently a Professor of Dramatic Literature at the University of Abuja. Mention will also be made of Mike Dibia who was completing his M.A. programme when I was admitted to the university. He too influenced me tremendously, especially in the sense of providing practical tips that would make my stay in the department as short as possible.

Tess Onwueme, who has been a distinguished Professor of Literary and Multicultural Studies in various universities in the USA since 1989, and who is one of Africa's leading contemporary playwrights,[16] exercised perhaps the most profound influence on my intellectual development. She was not only a soulmate, a kindred spirit, an older sister, a guide and a mentor, but was also very generous with the knowledge she impacted. A radical left-leaning dramatist who is profoundly influenced by Bertolt Brecht – whose exposition of the aesthetic of distantiation in the "epic theater"[17] construct she domesticated for her PhD dissertation at the University of Benin. She came to Benin with the same baggage as I did: belief in the revolutionary and transformational possibilities of art; passion for the interface between literary craft and progressive social causes; and the bridging of the distances created by the individuality of a mediating agent and the social, cultural and political context under which he or she creates or produces.

Our connection was instantaneous and therein began a friendship and close collaboration that time has but tried its teeth in vain.[18] By the time we met in about 1985-1986, she had already authored and produced several dramatic works and had already won the prestigious Association of Nigerian Authors (ANA) drama prize with *The Desert Encroaches*, an explosive creative dramatization of the contest between the dark forces of oppression and negation and the committed struggle of the champions of a just social order, rendered with the dramaturgical resources of the Brechtian Epic Theatre tradition.

Throughout our stay in Benin we debated several literary, dramatic, philosophical and political issues, sometimes late in the night, and would continue from where we left off on the following morning, I journeying to Ugbowo from Ekenwan Campus, and she from Prof. Sagay's residence in the university staff quarters, where she usually stayed while on campus. As far back as 1986, she had an intimidating library and lent me books on aesthetics, dramaturgy and literary scholarship unstintingly. It was therefore no surprise that she literally fished me out from Federal Polytechnic Oko where I was teaching Use of English and together with Prof. G. N. Ugoigwe, brought me to the Centre for Igbo Studies/ School of Humanities of Abia State University, Uturu, as a researcher and lecturer.

The late Prof. Ezenwa-Ohaeto was yet another distinguished PhD student who exercised an enormous influence on me. By the time we met in Benin he had already published highly acclaimed collections of poetry, including the *Songs of a Traveller, I Wan Be President* and *Bullet for Bunting*[19] all crafted in the modern, revolutionary style of the 1960s song school tradition popularized by Okot P. Bitek.[20] The new conception of the song school was a poetic movement that probably began with Chris Okigbo's "Path of Thunder", and which was the dominant feature of the poetic creations of the 1980s and 1990s, especially in the works of Ohaeto, Niyi Osundare, Odia Ofeimun and Tanure Ojaide.[21] The periods he spent in Benin were as exciting as they were invigorating because we – himself, Tess Onwueme, E. B. Uwatt and myself – would literally transform the graduate students' office into a mini-literary convention. It was not surprising that I explicated some of his works and those of Tess Onwueme in *Revolutionary Aesthetics and the African Literary Process,* and *Art, Ideology and Social Commitment in*

African Poetry,[22] two studies of modern African literature that I completed while a student at the University of Benin.[23]

I was a very good student and must have impressed my lecturers on several scores. But oftentimes, I was given to excessive exuberance and impetuosity that may be explained as a trait in someone eager to master all he could in as short as possible a time, and who was occasionally impatient with established rules and procedures. My course work result was outstanding, judging by the comments made by my course work external examiner, Professor Charles Nnolim and by Prof. Egudu. My thesis defence was very smooth and my external examiner, Prof. Ime Ikiddeh (a specialist in Ngugi's art) may have been very impressed too. I completed my thesis nine months into the M.A. programme and spent close to one year waiting for its defence, occasioned in great part by the long-drawn strike action embarked upon by the Academic Staff Union of Nigerian Universities (ASUU). I recollect that about three postponements were made before I finally defended my thesis.

This must have been about July, 1987 (I had completed the thesis, to all intents and purposes, about September, 1986), by which time I was already a lecturer at the Federal Polytechnic, Oko in Anambra State.

I was not involved in any serious revolutionary agitation while at University of Benin. The main reason was the absence of a national Marxist revolutionary platform that student members of the various moments would embrace on leaving school. The labour movement was ideologically weak and rent by crass opportunism and intellectual laziness. It, therefore, did not provide the necessary anchor on which ex-student comrades could rally around. However, I became part of a Marxist study group in Benin, led by the distinguished novelist, Professor Festus Iyayi, and the notable Pidgin English playwright, Professor Tunde Fatunde.[24] We usually met once a week in either Iyayi's or Fatunde's office with other comrades on campus whose identities I cannot now recollect. Yet probably I was influenced more by their literary works than by any practical involvement in revolutionary activism, and the debt of gratitude I owed them could be seen in some chapters dealing with their works in *Revolutionary Aesthetics and the African Literary Process.*[25] Till date, Iyayi's *Violence* (a classic example of a proletarian novel), *The Contract* and *Heroes,* and Fatunde's *No Food No Country* (a play that made Pidgin English instantly transmissible and accessible and created a new linguistic-aesthetic paradigm of literary craft), *Blood and Sweat, Water No Get Enemy,* and *Oga Na Tief Man* remain some of my favourite African novels and plays.

My University of Benin years laid a secure foundation for my intellectual development and provided a platform for my growing confidence as an emerging critical voice in African literature. After my intellectual and academic orientation and maturation during those years I came to the inescapable conclusion that the subsequent years to come would be nothing more than deepening, strengthening and consolidating the strides I had recorded. And I have not been disappointed in this assessment till date.

The Oko years, when I was a lecturer at the Federal Polytechnic,[26] was a historical juncture between the completion of my graduate studies at the University of Benin and my transition to a tenured position as a researcher and a lecturer at Abia State University, Uturu. Yet in a strict chronological rendering of my intellectual development, an account of my stay at Oko, no matter how brief, necessarily dispenses with a full explication of my first serious scholarly productions while still a student at the University of Benin. The reason for this structural device subsists on the fact that by the end of my studies at Benin, I had finished the first draft of four scholarly works on African literature, as well as most of the poems that later appeared in the collection *37 Seasons Before the Tornado.*[27] The significance of these studies and intellectual output is such that I am devoting an entire chapter to it. The implication of this is that while I had already "made my intellectual statement as a scholar", as it were, before I joined the academic faculty of the polytechnic, the account of the Oko years still precedes an explication of that statement in this work.

The Oko years were significant in several other respects. When I joined the polytechnic as a lecturer in Use of English (I was eventually to become the Coordinator of English in the polytechnic with over thirteen lecturers, some senior to me, who were in the department and over 4000 students who offered the course), in May 1987, I was 23 years old. I was not yet fully aware of the challenges that lay ahead of me, and the possibility that I could still exploit the opportunities that existed in that environment and setting in advancing my intellectual career. My only regret was that while my primary desire was a university appointment which would have meant teaching African and comparative literature and nothing else, I had to make do with nearly thirty credit hours of teaching every week of essentially Use of English study, with the occasional exploration of literary issues in a number of prescribed literature texts.

However, I found my heavy teaching load an exciting pursuit, particularly when I discussed a literature text with students. I found their eagerness to learn, enthusiasm for my teaching method and their sheer adoration a source of constant joy. Though I still yearned for a university appointment I was very comfortable and relaxed at Oko both as a very much beloved lecturer and an energetic Secretary General of the Academic Staff Union of Polytechnics, Oko branch.[28] I also gained a tremendous insight into the workings of an academic environment, and the promises, challenges, setbacks and successes that condition the life expectations of the average lecturer. The significance of the Oko years could thus be seen in my easy adaptation, at a relatively young age, of the nuances of faith and belief that characterize an academic community, the necessary maturity to head the largest department in the school at age 24, and the rich social and cultural experiences that enriched my life and molded me into a fully formed adult.

Yet, a few other bigger significances still awaited me at Oko. I kept up with my serious intellectual studies and wide readings, and would spend very many hours in my office, after the regular school time, polishing the drafts of the four scholarly works I had completed at Benin. I presently recall that the chapter of *Revolutionary Aesthetics and the African Literary process* on J.U. Obuefi's novel, *The Time Between*, was written about 1987 at Oko. It was one of the literary texts I recommended for the ND (National Diploma) I and ND II programmes. The reason for its inclusion in the book, and somewhat different mode of its presentation in relation to the other chapters, was because of the time-gap between the composition of the original draft and my time at Oko, but most particularly because I wanted to use the novel to test out some of my findings in my study of the Eagletonian Schema; a critical-theoretical construct developed by Terry Eagleton.[29]

One other remarkable highlight of my stay at Oko was the completion and subsequent publication by Meks–Unique Publishers, of a work on the Use of English which I co-authored with Dr Osita Nwosu, a senior colleague of mine at the polytechnic, and the Director of School of Technical Teacher Education between 1987 and 1988. The book emerged out of his gentle prodding and insistence that we translate our copious lecture notes, study exercises and general reading of the subject into a usable text for students of higher institutions who were offering the Use of English course. The result was the book, *Use of English Studies for Higher Education,* which was completed by mid-1988 when I was 24 years,[30] and which went on to become a very popular English Studies text for students of polytechnics, colleges of education and universities in South-Eastern Nigeria. Its second, revised edition has been issued in 2014.

Though I was very reluctant to engage that subject and really dragged my feet in writing great portions of it, in spite of Dr Nwosu's insistence that the work must see the light of day, I felt immensely proud when it was completed and deeply satisfied upon its being published, principally because it created a balance in my academic and intellectual pursuit, together with the feeling that I have left a modest mark in the field of English as a language – the branch of English Studies that I am least comfortable with and in which I am most insecure. The book thus proved a point that I, indeed, absorbed a great deal on language as an undergraduate student, as well as justifying my skill, experience and standing as a lecturer and Coordinator of English in a polytechnic.

It was also while I was at Oko that I met Ego Alowes Jimanze, an accountant–turned publisher, who created Oko Heritage both as a veritable publishing house as well as an institution for the development of human intellectual resources. We were to go on to create a unique partnership that endures till date, even though it has been hard for us to see as often as I would have desired. Ego Jimanze exercised a measure of influence on my intellectual growth, both as a publisher who published a remarkable volume on *Functional English* in which I contributed a chapter[31] (the book was to become a very popular text for students offering the Use of English in tertiary institutions, in essence all students), and as a friend who would engage me in wide-ranging discussions on philosophy, politics, the state of the humanities in general, the dilemma of Igbo civilization, and on many other sublime subjects.

I met him when he came to the polytechnic to market *Letters to Sarah*, a journal and diary-type of narration that had been previously published. I decided to prescribe the text for my students' use because of its thematic and stylistic utility, but more because of the remarkable personality that was marketing it. My first visit to his house was an eye-opener. I had previously believed that I had amassed a near unsurpassable collection of the classics of history, philosophy and literature. This myth was embarrassingly exposed when he let me into his intimidating collection of the classics. I was baffled that someone who read accountancy, and who had had no previous training in the humanities could possess so rich a library as I saw. And most importantly that he demonstrated a complete grasp and mastery of the academic and intellectual discourses in the humanities, as well as a poignant insight into the state and condition of contemporary Nigeria.

Ego Jimanze is an intellectual through and through and lives the constancy of illumination and mental exaltation that only few people are capable of possessing. The Nietszcherian notion of mountain-top dwelling, over and above the mundane and banal din of the valley of ordinary life is his forte, in his disdain for material things, pompous self-importance, vulgar exhibitionism, and the vain-glorious but pertinently vacuous, empty and cultureless lifestyle and philistine existence of the rich and famous. Till date he remains one of the few Nigerians who have truly influenced the course of my life, and who have made a worthy contribution to my intellectual development.

But, perhaps, the most significant development during the Oko years was my encounter with Comrade Viktor Kalu, one of the leading Marxist theoreticians in Nigeria, and whose ebullient and forceful use of language influenced my style of writing for a considerable length of time. By then, he was a lecturer at the now defunct Anambra College of Education, Awka, where he developed and systematized a young and dynamic Marxist cell, made up of students, lecturers and workers who engaged ceaselessly in a robust debate about the Nigerian condition and the possibility of a socialist revolution in the country. I eventually became a leading member of that group, and would journey from Uturu (when I became a researcher and lecturer in the university there) and spend days with the group in one of the most productive dialogical exchanges of my entire life.

Viktor Kalu had come to the polytechnic to deliver a lecture on behalf of Dr Arthur Nwankwo, the chairman of

Fourth Dimension Publishers and one of the radical elites in contemporary Nigerian politics (Viktor Kalu also doubled as an Editorial Consultant to Fourth Dimension) on a topic I have now forgotten but which had to do with the possibility of social revolution in Nigeria. I respected him as a fellow comrade by not asking him embarrassing questions about the contradictions inherent in his promoting the cause of somebody I classified as a "petty bourgeois element" whose lip service to the cause of socialism and popular revolution may be more harmful than the antics of the conservative reactionary ruling national elite during the course of the lecture but demanded an explanation when the lecture ended. This was in front of the lecture theatre, amid my students who cheered me on as I fired salvo after salvo at him on his "betrayal of the cause of Marxism and the prospect of a socialist revolution in Nigeria" by presenting a paper written by an "enemy of the revolution". He took my diatribes in his stride, smiled away my self-righteous indignation and only uttered: "Comrade, I will create the opportunity for you to meet the man, Arthur Nwankwo, in person, after which you will form your own opinion and render your judgment."

He kept his promise by taking me to Enugu to meet Dr Arthur Nwankwo; a journey that changed my life, altered my destiny and led to both quantitative and qualitative transformation of my identity, personality, being and total essence. I was to meet Arthur Nwankwo one more time while I was still at Oko. This was at the Chalk Valley Hotel which was built by Dr Alex Ekweme, former Nigerian Vice-President and a native of Oko, when he came to personally deliver another lecture on the Nigerian condition.

As well adjusted as I was at Oko, and as popular as I was with both staff and students, by mid-1988 I was already planning my exit to higher pursuits and challenges. By then Tess Onwueme had completed her PhD at Benin and had gone back fully to her teaching and theatrical production job at the Federal University of Technology, Owerri. We kept a close contact, mostly by mail. I learnt from her about the decision of the authorities of the then Imo State University, Okigwe, to establish a Centre for Igbo Studies - a research centre that would be exclusively devoted to the study of Igbo civilization, history, culture, language, literature, sociology and politics from a multi-disciplinary perspective. She told me that she had joined the centre and was about to open a Performing Arts Unit within it, and encouraged me to apply as a research fellow, stressing that the centre would be directed by Prof. Godwin N. Uzoigwe, a renowned Professor of African history.

Without hesitation, I sent in my application, as well as an application to the University of Calabar for my PhD, the admission of which I got in late 1988. About the same time I was invited for an interview for the job of a Research Fellow (as well as a lecturer in English and Literature in the School of Humanities, the idea being that all the researchers in the centre would be made to teach their core subjects at the various university schools and colleges), and had my first meeting with Prof. G. N. Uzoigwe. Apparently because of the steady push that Dr Tess Onwueme was exerting on my behalf, Prof. Uzoigwe reminded me that it was only the result of the interview that would determine my suitability for the job. To this I replied that, among all the categories of academic staff to be interviewed, not just those at the same level with me, if I came second in the whole interview, that I should not be employed. He looked at me sharply, and we continued discussing other matters. A few weeks later I was informed that I had been offered the job in the centre, and between December, 1988 and January, 1989, I resigned from the polytechnic and relocated to Uturu to start life as a researcher and lecturer in the university, and as a doctoral student in the Department of English at the University of Calabar.

CHAPTER FOUR
NOTES AND REFERENCES

1. *ABC of Dialectical and Historical Materialism* is a Marxist Bible of sorts, if I should so express it, a sacred, holy work that must be read every day, from dawn till dusk by all true believers. I did read the work virtually every day for over five years, imbibing its tenets and developing my intellectual consciousness along its charted paths and courses. It is to be eventually joined among the list of "Sacred" writings I would never be parted from, by Alexander Ovcharenko's *Socialist Realism and the World Literary Process;* Dmitry Markov's *Socialist Literatures: Problems of Development*; I. Frolov's *Marxist Philosophy and the Arts, Marxist Leninist Aesthetics and the Arts;* and Vassily Novikov's, *Dialectic of Creative Work.* The height they and countless other soviet Marxist philosophical, ideological and aesthetic writings took my scholarship, and the limits they set to my all-round materialist reading and appreciation of the totality of leftist intellectual thoughts, will remain an eternal debate in my mind and consciousness. Operating out of a social, political and ideological space in the 1980s in a Third World country in which the only path to true Marxism was unarguably the Soviet path; meaning that the only true path to Marxist intellectual scholarship was the Soviet Marxist paradigm, the collapse of the Soviet Union and the retreat of Sovietized Euro-Marxism was a liberating experience that freed my intellectual consciousness and has led me to where I am today.

2. Spillover National Youth Service Corps members in the 1980s (when there was a single batch of

Corps Members) were graduates from foreign universities who were deployed to serve no matter the time of their graduation. They would eventually join the new batch of Corps Members at the orientation camp, when some of them may have spent four, five or even six months doing their primary assignment. They were "senior" Corps Members and the new batch members had a lot to learn from them. My camp friends, Ben C. Okonta and Eddy Ibinabo, were spillover corps members who helped out in the camp store, distributing kits to new Corps Members. I eventually joined them in this work, learnt a lot from them, and rapidly became a "senior" Corps Member just days after I reported to camp.

3.   Maxim Gorky was a towering figure in Soviet and world socialist literature and cultural studies, and the intellectual force behind the emergence of the association of Soviet writers and the formulation of Socialist Realism as the guiding philosophical, aesthetic and ideological paradigm of Soviet literature. A self-educated writer with a piercing intellect he wrote, among other works, such influential books as *Mother, Forma Gordayev, My Childhood, My Universities,* and *My Apprenticeship.*

4.   Alexei Tolstoy's *Peter the First* was a socialist oriented work that incorporated substantial elements of "Classical Realism" in its mediation of long historical processes in the evolution of Russian society. In sheer scope, subject matter, aesthetic devices and fidelity to historical truth, it has been compared to Leo Tolstoy's *War and Peace* and considered one of the success stories of Soviet literature. Mikhail Sholokhov's *And quiet Flows the Don* won worldwide recognition and respect for Soviet literature, and for the author, a Nobel Prize

for Literature. Readers and critics alike applauded its piercing, almost brutal honesty, its unsparing portrayal of life's tragic moments, its historical sincerity and unpretentiousness, and even-handed treatment of characters, red and white. Boris Pasternak's *Doctor Zhivago* is a thinly concealed poetic and philosophical work that brought romanticism to the fictive form, transformed reality and mediated history as very few writers ever did. Its sense of trenchant poignancy, a pervasive and inscrutable aura and sheer deconstruction of the revolutionary process and the spirit that infused it, place it as an artistic entity onto itself.

Together, these three works and Aleksandar Solzhenitsyn's *The Gulag Archipelaga, Cancer Ward, The First Circle,* and *One Day in the Life of Ivan Denisovich* exemplify the highest achievement of 20th century Russian literature, official and dissident, and together with *War and Peace, Anna Karenina,* and *The Brothers Karamazov,* are considered mankind's greatest achievement in the fictional craft.

5.   Long before I read Charlton Ogborn's *The Mystery of William Shakespeare;* and long before I became aware of and read widely on the raging debate over the authorship of Shakespeare's works, I had come to the conclusion that the Stratford–Upon-Avon character whose biography I read in high school could not have written the works ascribed to him. All the arguments– historical, educational, artistic and aesthetic– considered, (and there cannot be absolute certainty in this matter, either way), I have comfortably settled for Edward de Vere, the 17th Earl of Oxford as the author of the Shakespeare works and I am sticking to him. I will

continue to reflect this standpoint in all my works where Shakespeare and his works are mentioned or discussed, until an overwhelming, irrefutable evidence turns up to state otherwise.

6.   Gogol (*Dead Souls*), Ivan Turgenev (*Fathers and Sons*); Leo Tolstoy (*War and Peace, Anna Karenina,* and *Resurrection*); Emile Zola (*Earth* and *L'Assomoir), Dostoyevsky (Crime and Punishment, The Brothers Karamazov, Notes From the Underground/The Double, The Idiots);* and Honore' Balzac's (*Cousin Bette* and *The Thirteen*), over and above the hundreds of European novels I read between 1984 and 1986, influenced my artistic consciousness, cultural understanding and illumination and intellectual development, in a profound way.

7.   Yes, readers and critics point to *Things Fall Apart* as Achebe's most significant work whose half-centennial was celebrated with pomp and aplomb globally in 2008. It defined Achebe's place in the context of global literature and culture and gave modern African literature its authentic and legitimate independent claim, status and stature. However, apart from the fact that *Arrow of God* is one novel by Achebe that I would be caught sitting down to read again, (preface to the second edition of *AOG*), there are abundant textual evidence that it is by far a much more mature artistic-aesthetic, structural-thematic, ideological, cultural and mythic composition than *TFA*. On the basis of this evidence, I have no doubt that *AOG* is Achebe's most mature work and his masterpiece.

8.   Ngugi wa Thiong'o and Alex La Guma are unpretentiously revolutionary in their approach to art and life, combining the aesthetic principles of realism, symbolism, transmogrification and even

magical realism and the politics and ideology of Marxism in mediating reality in its process of social, political and cultural transformation. This viewpoint addresses such works as *A Grain of Wheat, Petals of Blood, The Trial of Dedan Kimathi, Ndeenda Ngaahikaa, Mother Sing for Me, Devil on the Cross, Matigari,* and *The Wizard of Crow* (Ngugi) and *A Walk in the Night, In The Fog of the Season's End, The Stone Country,* and *Time of the Butcher Bird* (La Guma).

9. The critical realist/liberal spirit emerged in Africa in the 1960s (coinciding with the attainment of flag independence by many African States) and is defined by the use of bristling and caustic criticism, satire, lampoon and irony, through the meditational resources of the artistic image, by literary artists, against the political and economic management of the state by the newly installed postcolonial leaders. This ideo-aesthetic tendency is to be found in Achebe's *No Longer at Ease* and *A Man of the People;* Wole Soyinka's *The Interpreters;* Ayi Kwei Armah's *The Beautyful Ones Are Not Yet Born, Fragments,* and *Why are we so Blest?;* Nkem Nwankwo's *My Mercedes is Bigger Than Yours;* Mongo Beti, *Perpetua and the Habit of Unhappiness;* Amu Djoleto's *The Strange Man;* Nuruddin Farah's *A Naked Needle;* Okot P' Bitek's *Song of Lawino;* and Chris Okigbo's "Path of Thunder" sequences in *Labyrinths.*

10. The Eagletonian Schema is the ideo-aesthetic principle codified by Terry Eagleton in *Criticism and Ideology.* Operating under the term "Categories of Materialist Criticism", it is a qualitatively higher form of the structuralist approaches to Marxist aesthetics associated with Louis Althusser and Lucien Goldmann. Academicist in orientation and

poignantly intellectualized, Eagleton sought to fuse two broad categories; the materially existing Marxist political economic thought (Base, Superstructure, Forces of Production, Social Relations of Production, Ideology, etc), and their rendition, via aesthetic mediation, into artistic form and content.

Regarding this method of aesthetic enquiry, Eagleton has this to say in the "Preface" to *Walter Benjamin or Towards a Revolutionary Criticism* (WB/TRC, verso, 1981, 2009): "I wrote it (the book) because I thought I could see ways in which Benjamin's work might be used to illuminate some key problems now confronting revolutionary criticism: in the manner of Benjamin himself. The book is deliberately not an *'Organic Unity'* (emphasis mine): the logic of its second part in particular is as much to be constructed by the text.

In these ways, then, the book marks a development from my *Criticism and Ideology* (NLC, 1976), which was less overly political in timbre and ***more conventionally academic in style and form*** (emphasis mine) … I would still defend the principle of that project, but it is perhaps no longer the focal concern of Marxist cultural studies. Partly under the pressure of global capitalist crisis, partly under the influence of new socialism, ***the centre of such studies is shifting from narrowly textual or conceptual analysis to problems of cultural production and the political uses of artifacts"***. (Emphasis mine.)

Eagleton explains that part of his personal evolution since writing *Criticism and Ideology* stems from his engagement in a creative project (*Brecht and Company,* 1979) in which he "raised questions of the relationship between socialist cultural theory and cultural practice, the relevance of both to revolutionary politics, the techniques of intellectual production of theatre and comedy". He has more than justified himself and realized this possibility if we examine closely such seminal works of his as the *Illusions of Postmodernism, After Theory, The Task of the Critic:* (Terry Eagleton in Dialogue, with Matthew Beaumont), *The Idea of Culture, Sweet Violence: The Idea of the Tragic, Why Marx Was Right,* and *Trouble with Strangers: A Study of Ethics.*

11. Ngugi's wa Thiong'o is not just a great writer of revolutionary literature he is also a passionate cultural worker and activist who has fused the potentials of the creative craft and the possibilities of cultural struggle. His active involvement in the historic and revolutionary postcolonial struggle of the Kenyan people for true liberty, democracy and popular participation in governance, has led him to detention without trial, seen his cultural project razed to the ground, forced him and his book, *Matigari,* into exile and much more recently witnessed a direct personal assault on his wife when he came back from exile after almost two decades.

From *Devil on the Cross* onwards, Ngugi ceased to write his creative works in English, writing them originally in his native Gikuyu, before subsequently translating them into English, as an affirmation of the thesis he enunciated in *Decolonizing the Mind.* The mobilizational capacity of native language literature and the fear it inspires in the neo-colonial managers of the postcolonial state is best appreciated through an examination of the publication and subsequent exiling of the Gikuyu edition of *Matigari.* Ngugi's involvement with the Kamirithu Educational and Cultural Centre, one of the first genuine communally owned theatre platforms, and out of which *Ndeenda Ngaahika* evolved, and a project which a panicky and repressive neo-colonial regime burnt to the ground, made an eloquent statement about Ngugi's grounding as a political and cultural activist.

12. I initially wanted to do my M.A. thesis on a comparative study of the works of Ngugi, La Guma and Gorky, but later switched to a study of the novels of Meja Mwangi from the perspective of critical realism.

13. I virtually completed the M.A. programme (course work and thesis) in about 9 months, but waited a further fourteen or so months before I could defend my thesis, occasioned in part by a spate of strikes embarked upon by Nigerian university teachers.

14. There was a mix-up regarding the defence of my M.A. thesis proposal when it was presumed to have failed in my absence. However, at a new thesis proposal defence which I attended, this view was corrected, and my proposal was passed after very minor amendments.

15. The "Aesthetic multi-dimensional" approach to the study of oral literature was constructed by Okpure Obuke in 1976. This aesthetics is eclectic in nature, harnessing and fusing the best ingredients of the evolutionary, diffussionist, structuralist and poststructuralist approaches into a new aesthetic category.

16. Tess Onwueme is an accomplished multi-award winning Nigerian dramatist whose play, *The Desert Encroaches,* won the 1986 Drama prize of the Association of Nigerian Authors (ANA). She has published major dramatic works such as *A Hen Too Soon, The Reign of Wazobia, The Broken Calabash, Ban Empty Barn and other Plays, Mirror for Campus,*

Legacies, The Missing Face, Tell It To Women, Why the Elephant has No Butt, Shakara: Dance Hall Queen, Then She Said It, What Mama Said, No Vacancy and Riot in Heaven.

17. Tess Onwueme's PhD thesis was a highly successful attempt to domesticate the Brechtian epic theatre aesthetic method to the examination of revolutionary Nigerian drama.

18. My relationship with Tess Onwueme has endured over time, and is a reality that, as Nietzsche would say, "time but tries its teeth in vain". This relationship started from when we first met at the University of Benin in 1985 to the present day.

19. The late Ezenwa-Ohaeto was a star of African literature whose life was cut too short. From *Bullet for Buntings* and *Songs of the Traveller,* to *I wan Bi President,* he was a powerful creative and critical voice whose passion for literature and commitment to cultural education have been hailed by his contemporaries.

20. Okot P'Bitek "launched" the "Song School" with the English Language publication of *Song of Lawino.* He followed it up with *Song of Ocol, Song of Malaya,* and *Song of a Prisoner.* It created an aesthetic movement in East Africa and influenced such other writers as David Rubadiri and Okello Oculi. The Song School became a continental aesthetic method, signposts of which could be seen in Chris Okigbo's *Path of Thunder* (critical realism on the threshold of revolutionary poetry), and at a qualitatively higher Ideo-aesthetic formulation in the poetic constructions of Ezenwa-Ohaeto, Niyi Osundare, and to an extent Odia Ofeimun and Tanure Ojaide.

21. Niyi Osundare's published collections of poems

include *Songs of the Market Place, Moon songs, Eye of the Earth, The Word is an Egg,* and *Pages from the Book of the Sun: New and Selected Poems.* Tanure Ojaide's collected poems include *Labyrinth of the Delta, When it No Longer Matters Where You Live, Invoking the Warrior Spirit: New and Selected Poems, In the Kingdom of Songs, I want to Dance, In the House of Words,* and *Waiting for the Hatching of a Cockerel.* Ofia Ofeimun's collected poems include, *The Poet Lied, London Letter and Other Poems,* and *I Will Ask Questions With Stone If They Take My Voice.* He is the editor of the compendium, *Lagos of the Poets.*

22. The first drafts of *Revolutionary Aesthetics and the African Literary Process* and *Art, Ideology and Social Commitment in African Poetry* were finished between 1986 and 1987, though editorial work on them continued and some new ideas were added till the books were published in 1993 and 1996 respectively.

23. *Revolutionary Aesthetics* has two chapters devoted to the plays of Tess Onwueme, and both *Art, Ideology and Social Commitment in African Poetry* and the then unpublished *Art, Society and Identity: Essays On African Literature* contains a study of Ezenwa-Ohaeto's early poetry collections both as a recognition of their stature as accomplished dramatist and poet, and as a mark of my fidelity to our friendship which started in 1985.

24. Both Festus Iyayi and Tunde Fatunde are radical Nigerian novelists and dramatists who adopted revolutionary aesthetic method in their creative enterprise. Iyayi is the author of the highly engaged and socially committed *Violence, The Contract,* and *Heroes,* while Fatunde popularized the Nigerian Pidgin English in his drama works such as *No Food*

No Country, Blood and Sweat, Water No Get Enemy,
and *Oga Na Tief Man.*

25.   I treated, in some detail, some novels of Iyayi and
some plays of Fatunde in *Revolutionary Aesthetics.*

26.   I was first engaged to teach English at the Federal
Polytechnic, Oko, Nigeria, in 1987. I subsequently
relocated to Abia State University, Uturu, Nigeria,
(originally Imo State University, Okigwe, Nigeria)
in late 1988/early 1989 at the prompting of Tess
Onwueme who was then a Senior Lecturer in
English and Senior Research Fellow at the Centre
for Igbo Studies because of the need to further my
intellectual and research pursuits, and because of
the doctoral programme I commenced at the
University of Calabar, Nigeria, during the 1988 -
1989 academic session.

27.   Between 1986 and 1989, I wrote *Revolutionary
Aesthetics and the African Literary Process;
Ideological Sanction and Social Action in African
Literature* (now re-issued as *Heroism and Critical
Consciousness in African Literature*); *Art, Ideology
and Social Commitment in African Poetry; Art,
Society and Identity: Essays on African Literature*
(then in manuscript form), and *37 seasons Before
the Tornado* (collection of poems). *RA* was published
in 1993; *ISSA* in 1994; *AISC* in 1996 and *37 SBT* in
1997.

28.   When I joined the teaching staff of Federal
Polytechnic, Oko, in 1987, The Academic Staff
Union of Polytechnics (ASUP) was in a state of
moribundcy and inertia. Together with Innocent
Okoye (now a Professor of Mass Communication
at the University of Ilorin, Nigeria), Ikem Nwosu,
O.U. Emele, Engr E. Nwankwo (who are still
academic staff of the polytechnic), and a few others
I cannot recall, we set in motion the process of

reviving the inert platform. We brushed aside the opposition from our conservative colleagues who questioned our motive, as the Polytechnics Senior Staff Association (POSSAN) (for both academic and non-academic staff) was alive and well, and went ahead to proclaim the rebirth of the body. I emerged as its Secretary General and with O.U. Emele subsequently elected as the Secretary General of POSSAN, my caucus was in firm control of the two strongest platforms in the institution.

29.   See note 10.

30.   I was engaged to teach the "Use of English" at the Federal Polytechnic, Oko, Nigeria, a course that blended grammatical application of English, comprehension and summary, writing techniques, public communication methods, introduction to literature and the use of the library, among other core ingredients. Dr Osita Nwosu (now a professor at the Abia State University, Uturu, Nigeria), was the Director of Technical Teacher Education at the polytechnic. He convinced me about the need to publish a Use of English Studies textbook to be used by polytechnic, college of education and university students. Our joint effort yielded the *Use of English Studies for Higher Education* which was published by Meks-Unique Publishers, Awka, Nigeria, in 1990 by which time I had already relocated to Abia State University, Uturu, Nigeria (then Imo State University, Okigwe, Nigeria) as a lecturer in literature and a researcher at the Centre for Igbo Studies. A second revised and expanded edition of the book has just been recently published.

31.   I contributed a chapter on "Summary Writing" to *Functional English: A Developmental Approach* published by Ofo Heritage Press, Onitsha, Nigeria, in 1990.

Chapter

5

INCARNATION OF THE INTELLECT

By December 1988 when I relocated to Abia State University, Uturu, from the Federal Polytechnic, Oko, as a researcher and lecturer, I had completed the draft of the following works: *Revolutionary Aesthetics and the African Literary Process; Ideological Sanction and Social Action in African Literature; Art, Ideology and Social Commitment in African Poetry; Art, Society and Identity: Essays on African Literature; English Studies for Higher Education* (with Osita Nwosu); and most of the poems that make-up the collection, *37 Seasons Before the Tornado.* I had also contributed a chapter to *Functional English: A Developmental Approach* as well as a scholarly article in the journal, *Sechaba.*

Interestingly though, as many young and inexperienced writers can reveal, a very wide spatio-temporal gulf indeed exists between the writing of a book and its eventual publication. Most of the above manuscripts suffered this fate. While *English Studies for Higher Education* found a ready and willing publisher in a matter of months after the revision of the final draft, ostensibly because it was structured to meet the curricular needs of the Use of English course in tertiary institutions and could thus be commercially marked, it took the intervention of Dr Arthur Nwankwo and the Fourth Dimension Publishers to cause the publication of some of them years later.[1] This was after they had been either rejected outrightly by some publishers who saw them, or could not be published by publishers who liked them but had no means of putting them out. Most disappointingly, *Art, Society and Identity* had never been published till just a few months ago in 2014, a clear 26 or so years after it was originally written.

When I began my graduate studies at the University of Benin, I began to formulate in my mind a plan for a series of scholarly works on African literature. It was my ambition to complete these critical studies when I completed my graduate work. Thus, as I read to pass my course work and gathered materials for my thesis, I was also researching for the books I knew I would eventually write. By the time I wrote the final examination for the course work I had virtually completed the draft of my thesis as well as having amassed sufficient materials that would support the book project I had in mind. This process was facilitated by the enormous time I had at hand, in that while I completed both the course work and the first draft of my thesis about July 1986, I never got to defend that thesis till about July 1987. I therefore had the remaining part of 1986 and the first six or so months of 1987 to complete the writing of the work that I began at the beginning of 1986.

It was quite clear in my mind the kind of books I wanted to write and the ideological and aesthetic perspective that would condition, and even overdetermine them. These two issues had been settled long before I entered the University of Benin. My commitment to Marxism, at the political and ideological plane must, of necessity, become translated into a commitment to its aesthetics. Those works would therefore be substantially influenced by my understanding of dialectical and historical materialism, as well as some of the existing theories of Marxist art, in relation to history, culture and the social processes that define any given social formation.

Equally, since my high school days, I had developed a tremendous enthusiasm for African literature, particularly African fiction and dramatic literature. This was reinforced by the strength of that literature in the course content of the UNN Department of English programme. During my National Youth Service, I deepened my appreciation of African literature, both as a creative process and its critical practice, as well as my exposure to and enchantment with Russian and French literature. The books I had in mind would thus reflect my modest readings in these areas, especially the theoretical sections of the books I intended to write.

I therefore had a plan of action to write three or four scholarly works that would demonstrate my commitment to Marxist aesthetics and the Marxist epistemological and cognitive world views; that would show the depth of my investigation of the main historical and aesthetic lines in the development of African literature, as well as a close examination of a number of literary texts; and that would also reflect my understanding and appreciation of world literature. I intended to devote the first two books to a theoretical analysis of the aesthetic and ideological properties of African prose-fiction and dramatic literature, as well as the main currents and tendencies that shape artistic responses and mediational strategies in select literary works. The third book would be devoted to the study of African poetry – the subject that I am least comfortable with in African literature but had continued to fascinate and challenge me. The fourth, a collection of essays on African literature, was inspired by my reading of J. M. Gugelberger's edited work on *Marxism and African literature*.[2] I hoped to provide an adequate meta-critical rebuttal of his insights, postulations and theoretical constructs in the leading article in the collection.

How did I go about the task of realizing this potentially ambitious vision and scheme? I was just a few months old in an M.A. Literature class, and about 22 years old when the desire to attain this scholarly objective occurred. I knew that my reading was grossly limited to withstand and propel this undertaking and that I needed to cover substantial ground in my study of literary works and critical text if I was to make any headway. But I had a few things going for me; my boundless love and enthusiasm for literature, an irrepressible spirit, a stout and determined mind, and an ambition to make an eloquent statement on literature long before I turned 30 years. These strengths, as it went, overwhelmed my gross limitations and inadequacies and provided a secure platform on which to push ahead. Probably because failure never crossed my mind, I was able to complete this set objective before I turned 24 years.

My first strategy was to read in a very structured manner and not just for pleasure, edification and basic enlightenment. I read with the purpose of discovering and unearthing every bit of information that would aid the scholarly quest. I read with this essential objective in mind, absorbing those facts that would support its realization and discarding materials that appeared tangential and peripheral to the central thesis around which the entire project was organized. I made use of my personal collection, the departmental library, the university's main library and books, and journals and articles borrowed from colleagues and teachers. Tess Onwueme, for example, provided me with all the materials I needed on Bertolt Brecht's Epic theatre – the subject of her PhD dissertation as well as theoretical works on popular and revolutionary theatre.

Two or three events occurred about this time that not only strengthened my desire to embark on the book project but provided the rich insight and deep knowledge that would make such a precarious venture to have any hope of succeeding. The first was my discovery of Georg Lukacs, easily one of the most influential philosophers and theoreticians of history, culture and literature of the 20th century. I became instantly his fan, especially with the reading of *The Historical Novel, The Theory of the Novel,* and *Studies in Contemporary Realism.*[3] Its impact on my intellectual development and influence on my critical scholarship could easily be seen through a close study of *Revolutionary Aesthetics and the African Literary Process.* I also discovered S. S. Prawer's outstanding work on Marxist aesthetics, *Karl Marx and World Literature,*[4] which provided the much needed historical structuring and developmental stages in the evolution of Marxist aesthetics and the relationship between ontological, cognitive and ideological systematizations and social practice.

The significance of this development was that while previously I was fully exposed to Marxist literature as an artistic expression, I lacked the theoretical knowledge and equipment necessary for the interpretation of all literary expressions from a Marxist aesthetic perspective. Lukacs and S. S. Prawer provided this theoretical-philosophical anchor and helped in streamlining and coherently systematizing my wide but disconnected readings in the field. At this stage, the other missing link in my study of Marxist aesthetics was bridged when I stumbled on three or four books displayed by an itinerant bookseller on the floor in front of one of the University of Benin's buildings. These works which emphasize the place of socialist realism in the overall development of Marxist aesthetics and as the official ideo-aesthetic and socio-aesthetic method of the then Soviet art are: Alexander Ovcharenko's *Socialist Realism and the World Literary Process* (it provided inspiration for the title of *Revolutionary Aesthetics and the African Literary Process); Dmitry Markov's *Socialist Literatures: Problems of Development;* and the collection *Marxist Aesthetics and the Arts.*[5] A close study of *Revolutionary Aesthetics and Ideological Sanction* will reveal the extent of my indebtedness to these scholars. But more on this later.

Armed with a towering intellectual and scholarly ambition, driven by an intrepid will, and fortified by a profound immersion into the philosophical and aesthetic thinking of Lukacs, Prawer, Ovcharenko and Markov, I was ready to plunge into the book project that may herald the dawning of a new era in African literary scholarship. Yet, I encountered a rude awakening from an unexpected source. Periodically, I would travel home to my hometown of Mgbowo from Benin during my course of study. This would be for the semester break, and particularly when I completed my course work about July 1986. During one of those visits I was introduced to a Youth Corps member serving in one of the secondary schools in the community, by my close friend, Arobath Eze. The Corps Member, (whose name I have forgotten, most unfortunately) I learnt taught English and Literature and was highly regarded by the students, staff and other social acquaintances. He was indeed somewhat of a local celebrity, a peerless honour I naively reserved for myself.

How wrong I was, for the Corps Member who had read English and Literature at Bayero University, Kano, was a rare breed.

In the course of our first meeting over bottles of Stout beer and pepper soup in a popular joint in the town, surrounded by friends and admirers, a spark occurred that would ignite an intellectual explosion of indescribable magnitude. Inevitably, our discussion turned to literature, its philosophy and aesthetic method, ideological movements, shifts and historical progression, and its relationship to and interface with social practice. I was raring to go because I wanted to put him in his place, having been sufficiently informed by accounts of how good he was. From an analysis of African, English and American literature, and even in the context of the explication of Continental European literature–Russian, German and French – I more than held my ground and was scoring points after points.

Then, I made the mistake of launching into literary ideo-aesthetics and held up Lukacs and the socialist realist theoreticians I had read as the supreme ideological and aesthetic constructionists in the field. It was then that he really sparked into life. He must have been overwhelmed by my sheer grasp of the subject and the perspicacity and breadth of my literary and intellectual vision and depth, but now he felt that I had trodden on a path I had scarce information about. From him poured out a torrent of data about the neo-Marxist aestheticians, mostly Western, who had elevated the discourse on Marxism, art and literature to a new, academicized height. He took me to task on my knowledge of the work of Terry Eagleton, Raymond Williams, and Lucien Goldmann, and my familiarity with genetic structuralism and all its other theoretical-ideological constructions and variants. From him too I heard for the first time about Pierre Marcherary and the theory of literary production, Theodor Adorno, Antonio Gramsci, Walter Benjamin and Christopher Caudwell.[6]

Though I left the discussion with my dignity and social and intellectual standing fairly intact, great thanks to my erudition, articulation and robust use of language, far more than the depth and range of information at my command, I considered that debate one of the most stimulating, challenging and difficult dialogical exchanges I have ever been part of till date. I made up my mind to deepen my knowledge about the aesthetic issues he discussed, and the purveyors of the main ideo-aesthetic philosophies he was so familiar with, so much so that a few months later when I came home again, I easily withstood and even surpassed his knowledge of the subject to his amazement. The secret of this profound knowledge was that as soon as I got back to Benin, I began a ceaseless study of this difficult branch of aesthetics – especially the writings of Eagleton, Williams and Goldmann – to the extent that I became an expert of a sort of their aesthetic categories and literary-philosophical systems. This is reflected in the theoretical piece in *Art,*

Society and Identity and the chapters on "Revolutionary Aesthetics" and "Materialist Criticism" and "The Eagletonian Schema: "A Materialist" reading of Festus Iyayi's *The Contract*" in *Revolutionary Aesthetics and the African Literary Process.*[7]

Thus, when I began to seriously contemplate such an ambitious book project as I resolved to do, I had a road map about where to start, what to read, what to select and what to discard. I was already sufficiently exposed to the creative productions of African and world literary artists. I had over the years assimilated the main traditional canons and "universal critical criteria" of interpreting literature, and I was also fortified with an adequate understanding of revolutionary aesthetics, socialist realism and materialist criticism through a close reading of the works of their chief exponents. I was therefore intellectually equipped to embark on such an undertaking; what was essentially required was to organize and systematize my reading and writing with a clearly developed and well enunciated strategy.

It may be necessary to elucidate the full range of literary works I would be analyzing in the books I had planned to write, as well as the intellectual tradition on which my analysis will be predicated. But one thing was clear at this stage in my mind. I would be studying those works which would yield sufficient and significant insight into the problems of art, politics, ideology, society and social action. Yet in this choice, and in the eventual works that emerged, only one of Ngugi wa Thiongo's novels, *Matigari,* was studied even when I had read virtually all his literary and critical works and could easily hold my own with the well established authorities, specialists and experts on his works.[8] The reason for this is not far-fetched. I had intended to write a definitive work on Ngugi's art and had collected, as I stated elsewhere, hefty materials for the project. I held him in so much regard that I had no intention of studying him alongside any other writer. I do hope that I would accomplish that task someday.

For textual analysis in the book project, I began to re-

read Chinua Achebe's *Things Fall Apart* with a dialectical insight into its historical, cultural and sociological determinations. I was keen to apply Marxist aesthetic methods and considerations to the study of the novel and develop new insights into the class structure, social relations and the dialectics of social change in Igboland as reflected in the novel. The inspiration for this approach to the reading of the novel derived from Ngugi wa Thiong'o's profound dialectical insight into Achebe's novels in which he charted the development of modern dependent, neo-colonial capitalism in Nigeria as reflected in Achebe's novels from *Things Fall Apart* to *A Man of the People*.[9] Till date I consider that materialist perspective the most instructive of all critical assessments of Achebe's novels, the possible exception being a mythopoeic illumination of transcendental consciousness and supra-natural reality that engages the ritual sequences in *Arrow of God*, unarguably Achebe's greatest novel and his masterpiece.[10]

I next turned attention to Meja Mwangi's novels, particularly *Kill Me Quick* and *Going Down River Road*, the two texts that formed the primary basis for my M.A. thesis. Because of my involvement with Meja Mwangi, I studied in-depth the socio-aesthetic and ideo-aesthetic properties of critical realism,[11] and for an effective inter-textual commentary and analysis, I literally read hundreds of African and non-African novels and short stories written by critical realist-liberal humanist writers. I knew that the study of critical realism, a qualitatively lower artistic and social category than revolutionary art, but which nevertheless constitutes a marked progressive tradition in the exploration of social reality and social change using the instrumentality of the artistic image, will occupy a strong space in one or two of the books I was to write.

My close ideological collaboration with Festus Iyayi and Tunde Fatunde, both lecturers at the University of Benin, and both established writers,[12] would mean an analysis of their works. I studied all their published works very closely and eventually made extensive use of them in at least two of the books that eventually emerged. My decision was, however, not merely an ideological one. Tunde Fatunde revolutionized the language of dramatic literature in Nigeria by his innovative and creative reliance on pidgin English as a means of "popularizing the dramatic craft" and making it accessible to a wider audience, and also by the eclectic dramaturgical resources he employed which include elements of the Brechtian epic theatre, communal-participatory popular theatre, authorial commentary and audience participation. On his part, Festus Iyayi was, already in the mid-1980s, a major creative voice in African prose-fiction and *Violence, The Contract,* and *Heroes* would hold their own among the rank of Africa's best novels. That he went on to win the Commonwealth Fiction Prize attests to the artistic maturity of his works.

Equally, too, my close collaboration with Tess Onwueme meant an examination of her dramatic works from *A Hen Too Soon* to *Reign of Wazobia,* with *The Broken Calabash* in between them. Later, I was to direct the premier production of *Legacies* (originally titled *Legacy* in manuscript form), and wrote on it in *Art, Society and Identity.*[13] I consider her the most fascinating of the younger generation of African playwrights, and given the poetic range of her language, her use of traditional, oratorical verbal art forms, the application of the epic theatre dramaturgical method and the progressive nature of her social and cultural imagination which forms a nexus around authentic African feminism and revolutionary social possibilities, she has grown in stature over the years, to become today, arguably, the leading, dominant voice in African drama. I made a promise to write a definitive work on her art and craft, and still hope to accomplish that set goal. These are some of the primary prose and drama texts I interrogated and scrutinized closely, but a reading of the books would reveal a wider range of textual reading which came in handy in inter-textual cross references and analysis.

In the field of modern African poetry, I structured my reading around the discernible historical-thematic phases in the development of that aesthetic tradition and imagination. In this connection, I went to a great length in studying the social, cultural and political setting of what has later become known as "Nationalist Poetry" – a poetic phenomenon that thrived in Anglophone West Africa in the 1940s and 1950s. Juxtaposed to this poetic effort is the more internationally known, recognized and respected "Negritude Poetry" – a Francophone West African phenomenon, that could again be sub-categorized into two tendencies; the progressive, ideologically driven aesthetic of African renascence and resistance to oppression and racial bigotry, humiliation and negation represented by Aime Cesaire and David Diop, and the romantic-transcendental notion of African history and its pseudo-humanist symbiotic relationship with European cultural exposition and nuances represented by Leopold Sedar Senghor.

Close attention was also paid to the second historical – thematic phase in the development of modern African poetry, a period which coincided with political independence in the 1960s and 1970s and was defined by a poetic imagination characterized by disillusionment, despair, angst and ennui. I studied in some considerable detail the spirit of liberal humanism and critical realism that undergirded the poetry of Wole Soyinka, Kwesi Brew, Lenri Peters, Gabriel Okara, J. P. Clark-Bekederemo and such younger poets as Jared Angira who started writing from the late 1960s and early 1970s. Not to be left out are Chris Okigbo and Okot P'bitek, two poets who straddle the ideo-aesthetic world of critical realism and that of revolutionary art which they clothed with an oracular vision given the enormous use they made of such traditional verbal art forms like song, incantation, music and sound accompaniment, repetitions and allegorical references in some of their poems.

The third historical-thematic phase that I concentrated effort on was the poetic experimentations of the late 1970s and the 1980s which were characterized by a revolution in poetic language, diction, ideo-aesthetic direction and commitment to progressive revolutionary social change. Some of the poets who exemplify this tradition took the "song tradition"[14] to a new and higher ideological height, while others boldly and courageously threw their lot with the popular masses in an innovative and refreshing poetic mode that communicated shared experiences. In examining this revolutionary aesthetic tradition in modern African poetry, I studied closely the poetry of Niyi Osundare, Ezenwa-Ohaeto, Tanure Ojaide, Esiaba Irobi, Afam Eke and a host of other poets that share similar vision.[15] I have pushed forward this poetic discourse to the post-2000 era in the second edition of *Art, Ideology and Social Commitment in African Poetry* by examining, in some detail, contemporary Nigerian poetry of the past one and half decades.

Finally, because of the special position the then apartheid system occupied, as a structure of oppression, racial alienation and dehumanization of peoples and entities, I studied South African poetry as a separate poetic movement in Africa. I considered that political and social experience unique in relation to the burning issues raised by a more conventional form of colonialism and postcolonial dependency, and was able to find a coherent and objective manifestation of this formation in the poetry of Dennis Brutus, Arthur Norfje and Oswald Mbuyesini Mtshali[16]. I have equally expanded this section in *Art Ideology and Social Commitment* by studying poetic craft of the post-apartheid South African poetry.

All put together, as in the case of prose fiction and dramatic literature, I never limited my reading to the poets whose works I would primarily study. I read extensively about other African and non-African poets whose writings would yield the kind of insight I was investigating and this would be seen in the richness of the inter-textual and cross reference analysis and interpretation in the books dealing with modern African poetry.

Because of my profound interest in philosophy, it was apparent that theoretical issues would predominate in whatever books I would eventually write. As I pointed out earlier I was adequately prepared for this undertaking given my familiarity with the works of African, American and European critics of African literature. I had read the works of Eustace Palmer, Adrian Roscoe, Bernth Lindfors, Gerald Moore, O. R. Darthorne, E. D. Jones, Emmanuel Obiechina, D. I. Nwoga, R. N. Egudu, Abiola Irele, Dan Izevbaye, Charles Nnolim, Ime Ikiddeh, Sunday Anozie, Ben Obumselu Chinweizu, M. J. C. Echeruo, and Chukwuma Azuonye,[17] to name but a few of the critics with tested credentials whose writings I studied not just for classroom and examination purposes, but most importantly for my future intellectual and scholarly pursuits.

In addition to this, I had already pointed out that my encounter with Georg Lukacs and the philosophers and theoreticians of socialist realism had equipped me with a philosophical and theoretical understanding of the relationship between literature, history, class structure and class consciousness, social change and revolutionary social practice.[18] Added to this was my exposure to the works of such theoretical constructionists of literary aesthetics like Raymond Williams (cultural materialism); Lucien Goldmann (genetic Structuralism); Terry Eagleton (categories of Materialist criticism) Pierre Marcharey (theory of literary production); Louis Althusser, Walter Benjamin, Christopher Caudwell, Ernest Fischer, Roger Gaurady, Antonio Gramsci and Theodor Adorno.[19] My major regret was in not being exposed to the writings of Edward Said at this stage, an omission that is much regretted given the fact that an assimilation and utilization of his views on literature, postcolonial theory, cultural processes, imperialism, dependency, human identity and multiplicities of authentic universal cultural centres would have deeply enriched my works.[20] Happily, I am now very conversant with his works and have demonstrated that knowledge in my current writings.[21]

Philosophical and theoretical issues abound in the books I wrote at this stage, and the reason for this is not far-fetched. I have always held up philosophy as the foundation of all human knowledge, and always believed that in the search of meaning (epistemology); in the apprehension and cognition of reality; in the utilization of mediational strategies and artistic devices, utilities and resources by literary artists; and in the determination of the balance between objective phenomena and their various forms and layers of significations (hermeneutic or heuristic), the literary mode owes a great debt to philosophy. From philosophy are thus abstracted those theoretical structures and systems that reinforce the place of literature as a significant part of humanity's cultural inheritance, and establishes its connectedness and mutual affinity with other manifestations of material and transcendental reality.

Four major works eventually came out of this period of intense preparation, with the exception of the *English Studies for Higher Education,* a number of chapters in book collections and a few published articles and reviews. I cannot remember if I set out to write four books, but as the materials kept growing, and new structures kept emerging out of the original scheme I had developed, the result was the four books, three of which were published between 1993 and 1996, and the last just issued out some months back after an extensive editorial revision.

The book project that I got really caught up with, and which was written with passion, thundering heart and scorching intensity was *Revolutionary Aesthetics and the African Literary Process.*[22] The intention was not merely to make my own statement on the development and direction of African literature, but also to join issues with my literary adversaries, real or imagined, and to deconstruct certain canonical constructions about African literary scholarship. In the end, the book emerged as a two-part effort, with a polemical introduction, and a near hysterical appendix on the literary situation in Nigeria.

Part one attempted to resolve and settle the main philosophical, theoretical and ideological issues pertaining to African literature which I have become obsessed with. It dealt with such issues as revolutionary aesthetics and the African literary process (the main paper from where the book title was gotten), the democratization of dramaturgy or an exploration of the democratic potentials and possibilities of African dramatic literature, the popular spirit in African literature, where I tried to situate the modern African literary tradition in the context of progressive literary forces of other societies, peoples and cultures, and a comparative assessment of the ideo-aesthetic standing of revolutionary aesthetics in relation with the materialist criticism purveyed by Goldmann, Williams, Eagleton and others. Part two is textual analysis of the novels of Achebe, Iyayi, Mwangi, Ogbuefi, and the plays of Futunde and Onwueme from the perspectives of ideology, politics, class structure and social relations, revolutionary feminism and radical consciousness.

Ideological Sanction and Social Action in African Literature[23] is closely related to part one of *Revolutionary Aesthetics and the African literary process*. It is completely philosophical and theoretical, in that while textual analysis abounds in it, the essential argument is pursued along broad, generalized lines. Probably, in developing the material on revolutionary aesthetics, I had also wanted to do a detailed analysis of critical realism with the hope that these two ideo-aesthetic subjects will make-up a book. However, as I gathered more material, I wrote a lengthy piece on the "Positive Hero in African literature", and subsequently decided to restructure the entire research process. The result was that *Revolutionary Aesthetics* eventually stood on its own as a separate book with its part two being textual discourse, while the second book in the project became equally composed of two parts: "The Positive Hero in African Literature" and "Critical Realism and the African Literary Process".

The part of *Ideological Sanction and Social Action in African*

Literature dealing with positive heroes and positive heroism covered such issues as the genesis of the positive hero in world literature; the qualities, characteristics and identity of the positive hero; the socio-historical antecedents of the emergence of the positive hero in African literature; the positive heroic types in African fiction; and the characterization of the positive hero in African drama. The part that dealt with critical realism covered such grounds as the ideological and aesthetic properties of critical realism, particularly the question of the transformation of objective reality; an analysis of the characteristics of critical realism – a comprehensive depiction of reality, a negation of reality, a revolutionary historical perspective; the ideo-aesthetic of apology and the transformational and transitional nature of critical realism; critical realism in the period following political in- dependence; critical realism in the later postcolonial period in Africa (1970s, 1980s); and the future of critical realism in African literature.

The work on modern African poetry which came out as *Art, Ideology and Social Commitment in African poetry*[24] is equally theoretical to the degree that it is structured not as a systematic examination of various poetic texts (though there is sufficient textual analysis in the work) but essentially as a sustained, and sometimes, passionate analysis of the historical sources, shaping socio-cultural ideas and ideals, and the ideo-aesthetic impetuses, nuances and stimuli that collectively overdetermined this poetic tradition and provided the poets with the ready materials cogent to their poetic signification of objective and transcendental reality. The work that emerged was thus a blend of close examination of the matter and manner of poetic experimentation, and a generalized, theoretical account of the forces that were worked into these experiments.

In pursuing this line of argument, I structured the work as follows: while part one was cast as a socio-historical overview of revolutionary poetry with materials drawn from Africa, Europe and Latin America, part two contained materials on the genesis of art and ideology in African poetry, with examples drawn from the "Negritude" and "Nationalist" poetry that flourished in Francophone and Anglophone West Africa respectively in the 1940s and 1950s. Part three examined the place of art and ideology in the immediate postcolonial period in Africa (early mid - 1960s), from the perspective of critical realism and the radical variant of liberal humanism. Part four covered the later historical period in modern African historical development; the 1970s and 1980s, and a period that witnessed the flourishing of the revolutionary aesthetic phenomenon in African poetry, created by the poets whom I have already mentioned earlier. And as I stated elsewhere, because of the special nature of the then apartheid system in South Africa and the poetic responses it elicited, part five was devoted to the study of poetry and politics in South Africa.

The fourth book which emerged out of this research is being published for the first time since the research was completed 22 years ago. Titled *Art, Society and Identity: Essays on African Literature,*[25] it has both a theoretical part and chapters that deal with detailed textual analysis. The theoretical piece is, as I stated elsewhere, a meta-critical response to J. M. Gugelberger's article in the book *Marxism and African Literature.*[26]

The chapters dealing with textual analysis – again exploring the issues of identity, social relations, social change, politics and ideology – examined Achebe's *Anthills of the Savannah, Tess Onwueme's* Legacies, Ezenwa-Ohaeto's *Songs of a Traveler* and *I Want to be President,* Ngugi wa Thiong'o's *Matigari,* and Meja Mwangi's *Kill Me Quick* and *Going Down River Road* in some detail.

I had wanted for some time to bring out the second edition of these works but was never able to do so till now, essentially because of my disconnection from the university system and heavy involvement with human rights and pro-democracy causes as an activist.[27] Happily, that task has been accomplished with a thorough editorial revision of the works, new prefaces, additions to their introduction and expansion of the texts with new materials as part of the bargain. These second, revised editions were all published in 2014.

It is only fitting that I end this account by emphasizing that these works must be looked at from their historical conditioning, circumstance and context. They were all written when I was between 22 and 24 years, and when I was just beginning to master the philosophy and theories of literature and aesthetics. They embody the pitfalls of all youthful, apprentice scholarship, and probably its strengths too. They are essentially combative, polemical and adversarial. They constitute a statement made by a highly impassioned and ideologically driven young man who probably was eager, if not in a hurry, to make his mark in the field of scholarship and learning. Where I stand on some of the issues that engaged me between 1986 and 1988 has changed somewhat, leading to a crisis of consciousness and identity that nearly affected the issuing of the second edition of the works. I am happy to have weathered that crisis, and summoned all the necessary courage to bring them out again, together with their imperfections, pitfalls and deficiencies, for failure in this regard would have inflicted an enormous damage to my sense of being today, and meant a loss of a vital phase in my intellectual development.

CHAPTER FIVE
NOTES AND REFERENCES

1. See note no. 27 of chapter three.

2. I bought a copy of J. M. Gugelberger's edited work, *Marxism and African Literature* after I had completed the draft of *Revolutionary Aesthetics*. My reading of Gugelberger's elucidating but controversial and problematic leading essay, "Marxist Literary Debates", inspired me to write the theoretical essay in my book *Art, Society and Identity: Essays on African Literature,* titled "Revolutionary Aesthetics and the Development of Radical Criticism in African Literature. Issues in Meta–Criticism" I have radically re-worked the chapter, added substantial new material and extended the historical range of the debates in a book which had remained in MS form since 1988 when the first draft was finished.

3. Unfortunately, and most frustratingly, I never read Lukacs' *History and Class Consciousness* before I completed *Revolutionary Aesthetics*, though I did read a number of critical commentaries on it. I did read over and over again, his *The Meaning of Contemporary Realism, The Historical Novel,* and *The Problem of Contemporary Realism.* The impact of Lukacs' philosophical and ideo-aesthetic system on me was profound, leading to a charge by some critics that I over relied on his epistemological world view in the preparation of some of my published scholarly works.

4. The strength of S. S. Prawer's *Karl Marx and World Literature* derives less from its canonical theoretical insights and more from its comprehensive command and presentation of the relationship between Marxism, creative practice and aesthetic judgment. A ground breaking work, it helped lay

the foundation for Marxist aesthetic methodology.

5. I have already stressed elsewhere that Alexander Ovcharenko's *Socialist Realism and the World Literary Process* and Dmitry Markov's *Socialist Literature: Problems of Development* influenced my intellectual development in a profound way. Indeed, *Revolutionary Aesthetics* was initially titled "Socialist Realism and the African Literary Process" in frank imitation of Ovcharenko's book.

6. See note 10 of chapter three.

7. My fascination with Terry Eagleton is abiding. I started by being a measured critic of his philosophical and ideo-aesthetic system as demonstrated in the chapter dealing with his works in *Revolutionary Aesthetics* and *Art, Society and Identity* to the present stage in which I not only consider him as one of the most profound literary theoreticians and cultural thinkers of all time, but is also now an unabashed Eagletonian.

8. The chapter on Ngugi's *Matigari,* which I conceived as a journey of search for revolutionary possibility, was probably the last part of *Art, Society and Identity* to be written. This was in 1989 when I got a copy of the book from Tess Onwueme.

9. Revolutionary aestheticians in Africa have tried to underscore the historical materialist content of Chinua Achebe's novels, from *Things Fall Apart* to *A man of the People*. Ngugi is one such commentator who has undertaken an analysis of the historical, political, economic and cultural forces at work in this regard.

10. Achebe's *Arrow of God* could be read at several levels. One of such readings underscores the archetypal oedipal quest that progresses from the "brink of knowing", to use Chukwuma Azuonye's

term, to a full confrontation with the psychic trauma and ritualistic victimhood that prefigure an encounter with divine knowledge. The possibilities for mythopoeic excursions and excavations are inexhaustible; limitless also are the tragic nuances of the nature of power, its comprehension, use and abuse that bestride the thresholds of materiality and culture-in-transcendence.

11. Critical realism, as many scholars in the field of literary theory have pointed out, Georg Lukacs and Damian Grant inclusive, is the sheer, merciless, pitiless and comprehensive depiction, interrogation and mediation of reality, which allows for a historical perspective and sometimes, ideological awareness and movement, but which sometimes is restricted by the limit-situations set by social stasis and an undialectical apprehension of objective reality.

12. See note 24 of chapter three.

13. See note 16 of chapter three.

14. See note 20 of chapter three.

15. See note 21 of chapter three.

The late Esiaba Irobi, Uche Nduka, Emman Usman Shehu and Afam Eke belong to what Funso Aiyejina describes as members of the "alter-native tradition" in Nigerian poetry, younger, more vibrant, iconoclastic and very revolutionary in content and form, and in the ideo-aesthetic imperatives of their poetry.

16. Denis Brutus, Arthur Nortje and Oswald M. Mtshali are representative South African poets who wrote the bulk of their works during the apartheid period. Using different poetic devices, and adopting varied ideological postures, they imaginatively

reconstructed experience of ordinary people during the apartheid era and the soulless, ruthless and reprehensible logic that defined that inhuman and atavistic system.

17. While very many critics have commented on African Literature, the scholars enumerated in note 1 of chapter two are representative of the highest critical scholarship African Literature has attained.

18. See note no. 1 of chapter three and note 3 of the present chapter.

19. See note no. 7 above, note no. 10 of chapter three.

20. Edward Said is credited with the formulation, elaboration and canonization of a liberal, cooptative/syncretic postcolonial theoretical literary and cultural framework. From *Orientalism* to *Representation of the Intellectual,* with *Literature and Society* and *Culture and Imperialism in between,* he has pursued a cultural and intellectual crusade aimed at the freeing of universal cultural centres and the recognition of varied cultural units as carriers of distinct forms of human knowledge from the perspective of liberal humanism. Together with Homi Bhabha and Gayatri Chakravorty Spivak (the triumvial postcolonial theoretical force), he has more than accorded the structuralist variant of postcolonial scholarship a pride of place in global cultural centres of learning and research.

21. Edward Said's writing exercised a measure of influence over me in the composition of *Autonomy of Values*, especially in the context in which I borrowed his notion of legitimate and authentic universal cultural centres (another way of expressing Ngugi's notion of moving the centre through the struggle for cultural freedoms) in mediating "amorally" existing reality and life-forces with determining, affirming and reinventing

properties and capacities.

22. *Revolutionary Aesthetics* makes a case through theoretical discourse and close textual analysis of an enduring revolutionary Marxist aesthetic tradition in African literary process, and as an ideo-aesthetic method that best approximates African peoples' struggle for cultural, political, economic and economic liberty in the postcolonial era.

23. *Ideological Sanction and Social Action in African Literature* (now republished as *Heroism and Critical Consciousness in African Literature*) is an investigation into the twin issues of the heroic tradition in African fiction and drama, and the place of critical realism in the African literary process.

24. *Art, Ideology and Social Commitment in African Poetry* is an examination of the historical, political, ideological, cultural and social forces at work in African poetry through a materialist reading of representative poets and poetry collections using the epistemological tools of Marxist dialectics and aesthetics.

25. *Art, Society and Identity: Essays on African Literature* has two parts: a theoretical part which is a direct meta-critical response to J. M. Gugelberger's *Marxism and African Literature*, and a textual analysis part which examines some African novels and plays essentially from the search motif.

26. See note no. 2 above.

27. In 1997, I took my sabbatical leave as Editorial Consultant to Fourth Dimension Publishing Company Ltd/*New Outlook* newspapers, based in Enugu, Nigeria. Indeed, even before then, from about 1990, I had become heavily involved in Nigerian politics and democratic struggle, as a

leading member of the Eastern Mandate Union (EMU) and the National Democratic Coalition (NADECO). I suffered political detention on several occasions between 1994 and 1998, and was selected as the National Secretary of Alliance for Democracy (AD), one of Nigeria's three legal political parties, in 1998. In 2001, I was appointed, by former President Olusegun Obasanjo, as the Director of Internal Conflict Prevention, Management and Resolution in the Institute for Peace and Conflict Resolution (IPCR), The Presidency, Abuja, Nigeria.

Chapter

6

A JOURNEY OF ILLUMINATION

Abia State University, Uturu, previously known as Imo State University, Okigwe, was established by the government of late Chief Sam Mbakwe in 1981 during Nigeria's Second Republic. As the first elected Executive Governor of old Imo State, Chief Mbakwe responded to the growing educational needs of such a front line education state as Imo by establishing a state university, in the liberal tradition of university education, with a take-off campus at Etiti.[1] This was a period of extraordinary explosion in the quest for university education in Nigeria that led eventually to the emergence of such other third generation universities as the Anambra State University of Science and Technology (now Enugu State University of Science and Technology) and a number of federal universities of Science and Technology, including the one sited in Owerri, the Imo State Capital, at about the same time as the state university was taking off.[2]

The university continued to be wholly owned and funded by the Imo State government from 1981 to 1991 when it was ceded to Abia State with the state creation exercise of that year. Thus, a university which had hitherto been known as Imo State University, Okigwe, became, till date, Abia State University, Uturu. To confer legitimacy on the young university, ensure its national standing, and create an institutional mechanism and basis for its ultimate pursuit of excellence, the Sam Mbakwe government adopted two strategic approaches: the erection of a befitting campus at Okigwe-Uturu Valley, and the appointment of an internationally renowned literary scholar and cultural theorist, Prof. M. J. C. Echeruo, as its pioneer Vice-Chancellor. Prof. M. J. C. Echerou's outstanding stature as an intellectual, directly or indirectly led to the migration of other respected scholars and academics such as Professors Osita Eze, Chukwurah, Umezulike, Fabian Osuji, M. A. Mkpa, Afam Ebeogu, A. I. Nwabughuogu, S. O. Igwe and Ogwo O. Ogwo, among so many others to the university. Later, such universally acclaimed historians as G. N. Uzoigwe and Afigbo were to join the teaching and research staff of the university, as well as leading contemporary African playwright, Tess Onwueme.

The evolving or emerging vibrant intellectual and academic tradition and culture in the university was reinforced and stimulated by its physical location and infrastructural endowments. Situated on the valleys, and lowlands created by the undulating Okigwe hill range, the university is an architectural marvel in its total structural harmony with nature and the rich, though erosion-prone vegetation, forests, cashew plantations, groves and hills that surround it. It is precisely because of the topography of the soil and in order to achieve environmental balance through the preservation of the ecosystem that a modern-day architectural marvel emerged. Mid-Eastern in outlook, with a total absence of long beams, and roofing sheets (undetectable by the eye) the buildings were literally imperceptibly imposed on the natural environment without disputing its rhythm, ebb and flow. Spaces were simply created for administrative buildings, lecture theatres, university student hotels, parking spaces, etc, in such a way and manner that nature remained intact, with the impression created that this is a very old university community with a rich history, tradition and culture dating probably decades, if not centuries. Indeed, the impression one gets on first entering the university is one of a young-old study centre, with modern, beautiful buildings and very ancient trees, forests, streams, brooks, caves, deep gorges and crevices, and a well-laid out cashew plantation stretching as far as the eye could see, to crest the towering and undulating hill ranges that skirted the university in three directions.

The combination of eye-catching structural design and beautiful landscape with a systematically developed and aggressively pursued drive for intellectual excellence made the university an instant hit just a few years after its establishment. It soon developed a tradition of robust academic exchanges, passionate teaching programmes, and a near stingy culture of academic excellence going by its sheer unwillingness to turn out first class students for over a decade[3]. It was thus to this exciting academic setting that I relocated in late December, 1988-early January, 1989, as a researcher in the Centre for Igbo Studies and a lecturer of English and Literature in the School of Humanities.

After my introduction to the research and teaching staff of the centre and the School of Humanities by Prof. G. N. Uzoigwe, who also doubled as the Dean of the College of Humanities and Social Sciences, that included Professors Afam Ebego and Tess Onwueme, Dr J. O. J. Nwachukwu, Dr A. Chukwu, Dr P. A. Ezike Ezeojiaku, Okechukwu Okeke, Chief Ogbonnaya Onuoha, Dr U. D. Anyanwu, Rev. Fr (Dr) Jude Aguwa, Dr Emma Inyama, Okechukwu Okoro, Uzoma Nwokocha, and Isidore Diala among others, I quickly settled down to work. Because of the initial slow start in the take-off of the Performing Arts Unit headed by Tess Onwueme, to which I was attached, I had to begin my academic life as a lecturer.

When Tess Onwueme introduced me to the third and final year students of English and Literature as their new lecturer in Drama and Prose Fiction they were clearly baffled and highly agitated. They thought I was too young and casual to be a lecturer (indeed the age difference between most of the students and myself was not much), and set out from the onset to give me a run for my learning, preparation and adequacy as a lecturer. They were initially hostile and unruly in class and bombarded me with ceaseless questions. However, I was fully prepared for this challenge, and would once in a while summon my Marxist-trained debating, argumentative and polemical skills, in sustaining their interest and thus guaranteeing my very high standing amongst them.

I won them over easily, and we developed such a strong partnership that broke down the traditional and conventional boundaries of student-lecturer relationship. Led by such students as the late Nnamdi Abara, Emeka Obiakonwa and Vivien Jonathan, they had a free run of my house and office, where we would spend countless hours debating issues in literature, drama, theatre and other forms of performing arts. This relationship was to be further strengthened and deepened when we made the choice of producing the premiere edition of Tess Onwueme's play script, initially titled *Legacy* but subsequently published as *Legacies* by Heinemann Publishers. We would spend hours in the university auditorium, my office or house discussing the play, mapping out acting and stage roles, and allocating functions, amidst the flow of brandy and whisky and the unending spiraling of cigarette smoke. Yet, they accorded me full respect and regard as their lecturer, a sense of adoration that sometimes bordered on hero-worship.

The command performance of *Legacies* was my first serious exposure to a near professional play production. My qualification to assist Tess Onwueme in developing the institutional and creative potentials of the Performing Arts Unit in the Centre for Igbo Studies stemmed from my modest exposure to dramatic literature and theatre arts studies while at UNN. While it is true that I took courses that ranged from introduction to drama and theatre, speech and voice production, stage management, costuming, make-up and lighting and sound effects to play production, and while the production of a class group play was a requirement for passing the play production course (I played the lead role in *Laughter and Hubub in the House* which we re-titled *The Birds are Singing* in my group work), I cannot reasonably claim to have a sufficient mastery of the mechanics and techniques of directing or producing a play. Thus, even though I was the director of *Legacies'* premiere production, Tess Onwueme wisely engaged the services of such a tested and renowned director and theatre scholar, as Prof. Chris Nwamuo, and an experienced lighting and soundman as Elendu from the University of Calabar, where I was then pursuing my PhD programme, as consultants.

The premier command performance of *Legacies* was organized as part of activities celebrating the intellectual standing of the university and the height of excellence it attained under Professor Umezulike's watch as Vice-Chancellor. The second command performance of the play was organized as part of activities mapped out for the celebration of Bishop Ilonu's 25-year priestly ordination anniversary. The contact with and sponsorship by the Bishop of these two command performances was undertaken by a truly remarkable Reverend Father, Pan-Africanist and Scholar, Rev. Fr (Prof.) J. I. Okonkwo (Okosisi), a colleague in the university and now a professor of Linguistics at Imo State University, Owerri.

The two command performances were a tremendous success and a major theatre achievement. Everything was done on a grandiose, professional scale, from costume to make-up, and from stage construction to very realistic lighting and sound effects. On their opening nights, virtually all the lecturers in the university, including the Vice Chancellor and Senate members, members of the Governing Council, over 25 Bishops, Reverend Fathers and church workers, dignitaries from Owerri and Okigwe, as well as students filled the university auditorium to capacity to watch the play. My parents also came with their friends from my village of Mgbowo, which was a mere 20 minutes' car drive from Okigwe-Uturu to witness their son's triumph.

Producing *Legacies* was a tasking experience, and exposed me to the tensions, psychological and emotional stresses, triumphs and impediments in drama production. It brought out key issues in human and resource management, and the bonding, deep fraternal fellowship and interdependence among human agents driving such a process. It also showcased an exhilarating feeling of fulfilment on any success recorded along its numerous stages and the depth of despair, collapse of relationships, alienation and isolation, on encountering setbacks and disappointments. The theatre is truly a vital, living organism, with an inherent capacity for self-reinforcement, self-regeneration, self-sufficiency and self-renewal. It is a self-contained entity that rejects intrusive outside social reality, while harnessing and caressing those social idioms and leverages that further its interests. It thus excludes, via keeping at arm's length, the stimuli and phenomena that resist its temperament and sense of being. I experienced all this and more and particularly with *Legacies,* my health suffered after the first command performance, for there were stretches of months that I lived virtually exclusively on cigarettes, whisky and brandy. It took me weeks to recover from the sense of disorientation and physical loss of balance I got afflicted with.

However, with the garnering of experience in play production through repeated practices, I was able to reduce this scale of intensity in myself, and among my students. Between 1989 and 1994, I had succeeded in institutionalizing the Performing Arts Unit as a fully functioning organ, and ensured that at least three plays were produced a semester both for classroom, examination purposes and for the entertainment of students. I set up an association for theatre practitioners that drew its membership from as far afield as Architecture, Biochemistry, History, Government and Public Administration and Law. The plays my students directed and produced under my supervision included Esiaba Irobi's *Hangmen Also Die, Gold, Frankenstein and Myrrh, Nwokedi* and *The Colour of Rusting Gold;* Bode Sowande's *Flamingo;* Wole Soyinka's *The Lion and The Jewel* and *The Jero Plays;* and Femi Osofisan's *Morountodum* and *Red is the Freedom Road.* Play scripts written by students were also produced. The one that readily comes to my mind is *The Claws of the Vulture* written by Azubuike Erinugha, now a successful film director and producer.

There comes once in a while in the career of a university lecturer when he or she achieves a sublime feeling of epiphany, spiritual exultation and sublime fulfillment, not on the basis of his deep penetrating researches and intellectual and scientific discoveries and revelations, but essentially by the quality, imaginativeness, dynamism and creativity of his or her students. It is during such a period that he or she achieves the most profound degree of affirmation based on a coherent articulation of the essential substances of his discipline, and begins to truly enjoy his calling or vocation as an illuminator, an enlightener, and a proselytizer. The lecturers who achieve this state of affirmation on constant basis as a consequence of the special potentials of different classes and generations of students over an evenly spread period of time are most often those who come to worship knowledge, who see the university community as a self-contained, self-replenishing, inviolate system that must resist the intrusiveness and contamination of the outside world.

My class of 1991; that is, those students who I started teaching from their second year in 1989, and who graduated in 1991, best exemplifies the tendencies I have tried to describe above. It was a class made up of students who were not merely content or satisfied with classroom work; but were substantially driven and propelled with the desire to excel in knowledge and intellect. Led by Chris Abani, who had already published a novel, *Masters of the Board,* before he entered the university, and who is now a professor of literature and cultural studies and an award-wining writer in the USA, some other members of the group whose names I can still remember were the late Emma Opara a.k.a Echeruo; Lenin Chigbunadu; Obinna, Uruakpa, Gabriel Okorie who is one of the leading figures in the Nigerian Film/Home Video Industry called Nollywood; Nkiru Okere, Christy Otuka, Chinyere Nwagbara, and Uchenna Abadom (I guess the surnames of the girls would long have changed with marriage). Added to them were three male students who did not offer English but were an integral part of the team, and the informal, intellectual study tradition that evolved out of their interaction with me: Tony Anyadike who read History but played the lead male role of Uli in Tess Onwueme's *Legacies* during its premiere production, and now a management consultant in Abuja; Dr Kelechi Akubueze who read Government and Public Administration but was very deeply committed to the group, and a one-time Special Assistant to the Special Adviser to President Obasanjo on Inter-Party Relations, and Chris Ekeagwu who read Biochemistry, was an understudy to Anyadike as Uli, and played leading roles in other subsequent plays I produced.

We made an instant hit during my first ever lecture with them, and the deep bond that eventually developed was to, almost totally, breakdown the conventional barriers in academic and social interaction between students and their lecturers. Yet, this occurred after they played a sophisticated academic prank on me. After a 2-hour lecture, usually attended by students from other Humanities and Social Sciences disciplines, they demanded its continuation at the university auditorium as the classroom we were using in "Lecture Theater West" was now to be used by another lecturer. So to the auditorium we proceeded, for another two-hour of the most intense academic performance of my career as a lecturer. Hardly had I settled down to commence the teaching than well rehearsed, intellectually challenging questions began to fly about from all directions. It became clear to me that there was a deliberate, well planned attempt to test the depth of my knowledge and grasp of the issue at hand. I accepted the challenge, elevated the discourse beyond their understanding and unleashed a well crafted, virtuoso linguistic delivery that ended with a resounding applause, a standing ovation, a collective bow and a choreographed chant of "warhead, warhead".

From that day onward, I became their undisputed intellectual leader and hero, academic adviser and counselor, moral guide, social mentor and soulmate. While Prof. Afam Ebegu enjoyed the status of a father-figure, it was to me they turned to for the clarification of their deepest impulses and yearnings, doubts and uncertainties. The key members of this unique group had access to me virtually 24 hours a day, sharing ideas, asking questions and disputing my standpoints on several literary, ideological, cultural and social issues. The lecture hall became an incidental contact point; discussions about class-work went on in corridors and hallways, in the auditorium, along the road, in my office and in my house. They had the keys to my office and house, and it was a normal occurrence for me to enter my office to see four or five of them already seated drinking, smoking and debating some issues in literature and performing arts. The same was true of my house, and on a number of occasions the ones closest to me will spend their weekend there – reading, watching films on video, discussing, arguing, debating and occasionally quarrelling.

The theatre also brought us very close, and they would sometimes rehearse plays up until the early hours of the morning. I really pushed them hard in all academic and intellectual directions, and expected and got great academic returns from them. For the African Drama Course, they would study at least 15 plays; produce at least three per semester for an outside audience, and over five for internal class work. For the history of the novel course, I would prescribe over 20 novels for them to read, drawn from the works of African, South American, Caribbean, English, American and European writers. I expected them to present at least one individual, well-researched term paper and two group term papers that would be presented by team leaders, in class, with questions asked the members of the group by the rest of the students. The result was that my students hardly failed my papers, because by the time examinations drew near, the least intellectually endowed amongst them would have put in such an amount of work that would guarantee them an average pass.

Within the context of such great fraternal fellowship and bond, I enjoyed their support, encouragement, respect, and even veneration. They became fiercely partisan and partial towards me, and would go to a great extent in promoting and popularizing my academic and intellectual credentials. My strategy was essentially the strategy adopted by my parents in bringing us up: social, intellectual and cultural liberalism that was counter-balanced by strict parental discipline and control on the domestic sphere. I was a very strict and exacting lecturer and very free with a biting and insulting tongue. But I was also a radical intellectual who saw them as near social equals and related with and to them on this basis. This phenomenon baffled my colleagues and other students who were not so close to me: how inexplicable it was for a group of students to drink and smoke in their lecturer's office, sleep in his house and at the same time speak about him with awe, hold him in near absolute high esteem and were ready to pay any sacrifice he demanded of them.

In retrospect, I can say that one of the drawbacks, or negative consequences, of this situation was that it led to the creation of an informal caste and social cult system, between the chosen few, who flaunted their closeness to me and the many others who only had a limited access to me. Though I tried very hard to break this barrier down, and draw as many of the students as close as possible to myself, the feeling of insecurity, rejection and jealousy persisted in the minds of some. This situation became very serious when a number of students reported me anonymously to the Faculty Board about being partial with my award of marks. In the presence of such distinguished scholars as Profs. G. N. Uzoigwe, Aja Akpuru Aja, Afam Ebeogu, A. F. Nwabughuogu and J. O. J. Nwachukwu-Agbada, Dr Chukwu and Chief Ogbonnaya Onuoha, I made an eloquent defence that went beyond the issue at hand, to incorporate such ideas as the necessity of vigorously and systematically nurturing students' potentials as a spiritual calling, the tragedy that no student as of 1991 had earned a first class in the university which may be a reflection, not of student's academic deficiency, but a consequence of intellectual deficiency at the faculty level, and the notion that examination is, has always been and should always be a test of knowledge and not ignorance. When some of the scripts were remarked by a select committee, I was accused of being stingy with my marks. Additional marks were awarded to all the students concerned without exception.

This experience never affected my relationship with any of my students; rather, it reinforced in my mind, the correctness of my academic and social strategy, and to even deepen my relationship with them. I hasten to add here that while the class of 1991 was very special in every sense of the word, the class of 1992 was equally very special to me. Indeed, from 1989 to 1997 when I was fully involved with teaching, researching and heading the Performing Arts Unit, (I took my sabbatical in 1997 to spend a year at Fourth Dimension Publishers as an Editorial Consultant), I have always had very special students who were eager to learn, to advance themselves academically and intellectually, and who would always occupy a space in my mind and consciousness.

I led an active social, academic and intellectual life while at the Abia State University, Uturu. My circle of friends and colleagues was quite large and we drew strength from one another. High on the list of these colleagues are Prof. G. N. Uzoigwe whose work on the Bunyuro-Kitoro Kingdom of Eastern Africa is virtually peerless; Professor Tess Onwueme who instrumented my relocation to the university but who left in late 1989 for the Montclair State University in the USA as a Distinguished Professor of Multicultural Studies; Professor Afam Ebeogu, intellectually intense and passionate and a committed academic with deep knowledge of African literature; Professor Aja Akprou Aja, who was then beginning to establish himself as one of the most reputable scholars of political science, government and strategic studies; Professor A. I. Nwabughuogu, a distinguished Professor of History; Dr U. D. Anyanwu, who succeeded Prof. Uzougwe as the Director of the Centre for Igbo studies, warm, friendly and a father-figure; Prof. P. A. Ezike Ojiaku, a thorough and well published scholar of Igbo language, literature and culture, and a committed Igbo nationalist and cultural exemplar; Chief Ogbonnaya Onuoha, who combined academic erudition with a passionate commitment to the welfare of academic staff (he was for several years the Chairman of the ASUU, ABSU chapter); Rev. Fr (Prof.) Jude Aguwa who exposed me to the world of classical music, and together with Rev. (Fr) Prof. J. I. Okonkwo, was my spiritual adviser and counselor; Dr Okechukwu Okeke, an emerging voice in historical studies and discourses by then, and with a penchant for long sustained intellectual disputation and dialogical exchanges; Barristers Patrick Ugochukwu and Nnamdi Obiareri, two experts in law that became my social companions. Ugochukwu would eventually become my best man during my wedding, and together with Uzoma Nwokocha (Uzo daddy) and Isidore Diala who joined the teaching staff of

English and Literature discipline later, were my closest friends in the university. Other colleagues worth mentioning are Okechukwu Okoro, Dr Emma Inyama, Bob Onuoha and the late Chiemela and Udo Nwokocha.

It was indeed a vibrant academic environment that use created which was defined by vigorous, robust and stimulating intellectual disputations and exchanges, both on campus and in our various homes. Bar Patrick Ugochukwu became my closest intellectual soulmate, essentially because we shared a common passion for politics, cultural processes and reading (he is a compulsive reader who has a sizeable collection of classical and modern popular novels). This period gave me instant joy and deep spiritual fulfilment and satisfaction. I truly felt that, at long last, I was in the midst of those who thought as I did, who had the same social, cultural, academic and intellectual desires and pursuits as myself and who accepted me as a major force in the university's evolving intellectual tradition.

This period of fulfilment was to find its highest expression in a biographical research project I became part of. It was the writing of the biography of the late Chief G. E. Okeke, Igwe Ozuome of Ihiala in Anambra State, the first Minister of Education in Eastern Nigeria in the 1950s and early 1960s, the founder of the Abbot High School in Ihiala and one of the leading figures in the establishment of the University of Nigeria, Nsukka, in 1960.[4] It was a project sourced by Professor G. N. Uzoigwe, with modest funding provided by Dr B. U. Nzeribe, one of the most passionate Igbo political and cultural nationalists of all time, and who had endowed a centre devoted to Igbo Historical and Cultural Studies.[5]

While Professor Uzoigwe oversaw the general direction of the research enquiry, including its structural design and post-research editing of the drafts, the day to day research responsibility fell upon me and Professor Nwabughuogu. We literally lived at Ihiala for long spells of time, intervening Chief Okeke, his contemporaries, associates, friends, staff and students of the two Abbot colleges, and even his political and traditional adversaries at home. We transcribed cartons of tapes made out of the recordings of these interviews. Interviewing and discussing with Chief Okeke was an experience I would never forget. I learnt truth, wisdom, moral principles and high ethical and spiritual standards and authority from him. I learnt about selfless service, the love of the fatherland, philanthropic passion and causes, and a stimulating history of the social, cultural, educational and political transformation of Eastern Nigeria from the 1930s to the 1960s. The research into his biography became a sheer educational odyssey for me, and at the completion of the project I further deepened my knowledge about the course of modern Nigerian history and the labour and sacrifices of the heroes past who drove that process and laid a firm foundation for a secure modern nationhood – efforts which have been substantially negated by the drift, directionless, and unimaginativeness of large portions of successive national political leaderships. The result of that research was the publication of *Portrait of a Nation Builder: The Biography of Chief G. E. Okeke* which I co-authored with Professors Uzoigwe and Nwabughuogu.

However, while I was building my reputation as a lecturer/researcher and head of the Performing Arts Unit in the university, I was inexorably being drawn towards a wider participation and involvement in the political process and pro-democracy agitation and struggle that defined Nigeria of the 1990s. I had already related how I met Dr Arthur Nwankwo twice in the late 1980s while still a lecturer at Federal Polytechnic, Oko. I was to meet him a third time in 1990, shortly after the Okar-led coup attempt,[6] a meeting that was to fundamentally alter the course of my destiny, opened a new vista of challenges and opportunities, and deepened the meeting point between intellectual illumination and positive social practice in my life. It was indeed a journey of illumination, and I will try, as best as I can, in the following pages to narrate the compulsive social and political circumstances that made that journey a reality.

I had an encounter with Dr Arthur Nwankwo in Enugu, sometime after the lecture delivered on his behalf by Viktor Kalu at Federal Polytechnic, Oko. Apart from Dr Okata, then a lecturer at the Institute of Management and Technology, Enugu, I cannot recollect the other people with him when I was introduced to him. It was a meeting of the Editorial Consulting team of the soon to be launched *New Outlook* newspapers[7] which he was floating. But I remember vividly that during my contribution I was harshly critical of the editorial and ideological direction of the newspaper as I saw it, condemned the standpoints of most of those who spoke before me, called for a radical re-evaluation of its editorial thrust in favour of revolutionary Marxist approach and ended by recommending Femi Ahmed as my choice for the paper's editor.

I had not yet finished my passionate submission when a chorus of voices started shouting me down, demanding to know who I was to have the audacity in criticizing "the leader's" vision and insisting that I should be made to shut up. Surprisingly, Arthur Nwankwo took my position, told them to leave me alone, and urged me to continue, with a thinly veiled suggestion that he was hearing for the first time what he intended to hear. Such an encouragement baffled me for I came to the meeting with revolutionary battle in my eyes, intent on rubbishing everything he stood for as I indicated to Viktor Kalu earlier on. I was instantly won over by his unstinting support and encouragement of a very unpopular viewpoint in the meeting, and right there I began to form a totally different and altogether positive impression of the man. I saw instantly a man of courage and great vision and wisdom, who is not unduly swayed by conventional or orthodox sentiment and who is prepared to support any individual with a refreshingly original, creative and imaginative disposition no matter the odds.

I left the meeting knowing that he had made a tremendous impact on me and feeling too that I had not let myself down in my delivery and convinced that I too made a tremendous impression on him. I tried seeing him again in the company of Viktor Kalu in late 1989 but he was on an extended overseas tour. My next encounter with him was shortly after the Okar coup of April 1990. I had ruminated on the national implication of the release of Nelson Mandela in February 1990 and the decisive impetus that this would inject in the world revolutionary process, including the possibility of the revolutionary transformation of Nigerian society. As a student Marxist activist I had made my own financial contribution to the South African nationalist, anti-apartheid cause, apart from leading the Marxist Youth Movement in the periodic celebration of important dates in the South African revolutionary struggle, especially the Sharpeville massacre and the Soweto uprising of 1976. I was also aware that the fundamental social and ideological strength of the South African anti-apartheid struggle was the revolutionary collaboration between the ANC and the South African Communist party, as well as between these two political formations and the South African Trade Union Congress and Youth, Student and Women Revolutionary Vanguards and Cells. I knew the role people like Joe Slovo and Chris Hani played in the struggle and were set to still play in post-apartheid South Africa.[8]

I wanted to share all these thoughts churning in my head with Viktor Kalu at Awka. So about the 17th or 18th of April, 1990, I journeyed from my base in Abia State University, Uturu, to Awka to engage Kalu on some of these matters and more. We did not waste time dwelling on the political implications of the failed coup attempt which occurred while I was at Awka, or even the implications of Mandela's release, for Viktor Kalu told me that Arthur Nwankwo was around, and that it would be most profitable if we shared our thoughts with him and listened to his own perspective and viewpoint.

We thus took off to Enugu, to the headquarters of the Fourth Dimension Publishing firm at Fifth Avenue, off Upper AV Chime New Haven, Enugu, a sprawling complex of several duplexes and machine rooms that also served as Arthur's residential quarters. In actual fact, Fourth Dimension has two headquarters, so to say, an extensive publishing complex that housed the firm two streets off Arthur's residence, and the residential complex itself that housed the Fourth Dimension Institution, a semi-formal Think-Tank, Brain Trust and Research Centre, different from the publishing empire itself. When we entered the upper floor living room in Arthur's own residential building, which is among the mass of buildings in the complex, we met him seated on his favorite sofa reading a book and watching television. When Viktor Kalu made the introduction (it was three long years since we last met back in 1987), he stood up quickly and shouted my name twice. I saw the joy, enthusiasm and unadorned welcome in his eyes, heard it in his voice and knew that I really scored a hit with him during our last meeting. In that instantaneous burst of rapturous greeting, the years peeled away effortlessly and it was as if we had been together over those silent years of broken dialogue. I felt truly at home, and the Fourth Dimension Institution was to become my home, vicariously, between 1990 and 1992, full-time and completely between 1993 and 1999.

The encounter with Fourth Dimension was truly a journey of illumination in the sheer, almost effortless merging of my intellectual conscience and social practice and my deep exposure to the mechanics of dialogue and agitation espoused by the institution. It also facilitated my constructive engagement with the Igbo, nay Nigerian elite, who crossed its path and temporarily dwelled therein. The Fourth Dimension Institution is equally almost peerless in its ceaseless search for curative therapies to Nigerian national maladies in discourses and publications, and in its construction of a coherent and articulate road map for Nigeria's resurgence and self-discovery.

It was there that my four books were eventually published between 1993 and 1997. It was there that the

Eastern Mandate Union (EMU) was born. It also gave birth to the All-Politician's Summit of 1995 and hosted countless meetings of Patriotic National groups such as the Afenifere, the NEPU-PRP, the New Dimension and the National Unity Organization led by Gen. Olusegun Obasanjo and Professor Ben Obumselu. It was there too that the People's Mandate Party (PMP) was born in 1995 (Arthur Nwankwo has re-incarnated it with life in Nigeria's Fourth Republic after a long period of dormancy), and from 1996-1998, the second of the two recognized base of NADECO's operation. And because of the dominance of EMU as a major platform and tendency in the formative days of the old APP and, eventually Alliance for Democracy, (AD), to a considerable extent it was there, too, that these two parties were formed. These issues, tendencies and social and political processes defined my relationship with Fourth Dimension, and the remaining chapters of this volume, as well as substantial portions of the other two volumes of this study, will examine them in great detail.

CHAPTER SIX
NOTES AND REFERENCES

1. Educational statistics over the years have seen Imo State (before 1990, the then old Imo State consisted of the current Imo and Abia States) topping Nigerian educational charts in the areas of school enrolment, pass in the West African School Certificate Examinations (WASCE) and the Joint Admissions Examinations (JME) for entry into Nigerian universities

2. The third generation state universities emerged from about 1981 to complement the efforts of the first and second generation federal universities by absorbing intending students who were graduating from high school at a rapid and exploding rate. The then Imo State University, Okigwe, Nigeria (now Abia State University, Uturu, Nigeria) is one of such third generation Nigerian universities.

3. When I had an issue about my liberal award of marks before the College Board of the College of Humanities and Social Sciences of the then Imo State University, Okigwe, my defence was that one of my principal teaching strategies was to discover students with outstanding academic and intellectual ability and help groom them into first class materials. I had a number of such students in my final year class of 1991. Most rewardingly, the university produced its first batch of first class degree holders in 1991, a feat never achieved since its establishment in 1981.

4. Sometime in 1989, the late Chief Dr G. E. Okeke, Igwe Ozuome of Ihiala and first Minister of Education of the then Eastern Region of Nigeria commissioned the university to write his biography.

The job, coordinated by Prof. G. N. Uzoigwe, fell on Prof. A. I. Nwabughogu and myself to do. Our research took us to Ihiala, Chief Okeke's hometown, and exposed us to the life and time of a truly remarkable man who established the famous Abbot Schools, and was the active driving force behind the establishment of the University of Nigeria, Nsukka. The book eventually came out as *Portrait of a Nation-Builder: The Biography of Chief G. E. Okeke.*

5.   Dr B. U. Nzeribe was passionate about Igbo culture and civilization and set-up a centre in his home town of Awo-Omama dedicated to the study of Igbo life, history, culture, language, civilization and arts. He facilitated the contact between the university and Chief Okeke for the writing of the latter's biography.

6.   The Orkar aborted coup of 1990 was a highly disruptive national phenomenon that exposed Nigeria's ideological, class, political, religious and ethnic fault lines as few other events had ever done. Even though the coup failed it significantly disrupted the Babangida regime's democratic transition programme, heightened ethnic tensions and foregrounded the Niger Delta question – a mere whisper in the national political context before the event occurred.

7.   *New Outlook* newspaper was established by Dr Arthur Nwankwo in the late 1980s as a platform to give voice to the people of Eastern Nigeria in the context of the national question, and in balancing the ownership, management and control of Nigeria's print media across ethnic and geo-strategic lines. The paper's editorial policy was robust, leftist in political orientation and ideological outlook.

8. The fraternal relationship between the African National Congress (ANC) and the South African Communist Party (SACP) was deep-rooted and ideologically anchored through decades of struggle and resistance against the oppressive and inhuman apartheid regime. This fraternal relationship was very manifest in the key role the late Joe Slovo, the leader of the SACP, played in the transition from apartheid to inclusive democracy; a role that saw him occupying a first among equal position in the construction of the post-apartheid South African Constitution. Conspiracy theories abound about the tragic death of Chris Hani, next to Nelson Mandela, the most popular South African of his time, and the heir apparent to South African Presidency after Mandela. One of the persistent theories was that Hani was murdered in a plot hatched and executed by renegade elements in the ANC and groups closely associated with the apartheid regime's security forces to forestall Hani's emergence as President, and the likely anti-big business, far-left leaning ideological direction post apartheid South African State would have taken under him.

Chapter

7

THE FOURTH DIMENSION INSTITUTION

The Fourth Dimension Publishing Company Limited, founded by Dr Arthur Nwankwo in 1976, was an idea whose time had come. It emanated out of the objective intellectual circumstances in Nigeria, particularly the eastern part of the country in the mid-1970s; circumstances that were rooted in a burgeoning academic culture driven by the University of Nigeria, Nsukka, and the newly established ones in Calabar, Benin and Port Harcourt; the presence of well educated elite and university professors, teachers and researchers eager to write for intellectual and academic advancement and for public edification; and the sheer lack of publishing outlet which was stifling academic expression and the availability of much needed reading materials by students at the secondary and tertiary levels.

Indeed, the 1930s, 1940s, 1950s and the early part of the 1960s were characterized by advancement and explosion in learning and enlightenment in Eastern Nigeria which coincided with the intensification of the anti-colonial, nationalist struggle spearheaded by the articulate, well-educated, eloquent and flamboyant Dr Nnamdi Azikiwe, an Easterner, whose oratorical skills and prowess was near matchless. It was a period, as I stated elsewhere, that witnessed the expansion and deepening of educational opportunities and outlets for ambitious students thirsting for higher education, initially at the University College Ibadan, and subsequently at the University of Nigeria, Nsukka, as well as in overseas schools of learning.

The tremendous impetus generated by Dr Azikiwe was further reinforced by the presence of an erudite scholar like Professor Kenneth Dike, the innovativeness of the cultural nationalist like Mbonu Ojike, the timeless labour of educationists like Alvan Ikoku, and the administrative sagacity of the Minister of Education in Eastern Region, Chief G. E. Okeke. When the work of other enlighteners and educational proselytizers like Akanu Ibiam, Okechukwu Ikejiani and the relatively self-educated genius, Mokwugo Okoye, were added to the mix, the picture was one of a formidable educational ferment that propelled a relatively backward region, educationally speaking, to the foreground of national educational attainment in less than three decades (1930-1960).

By the early seventies, even when allowance was made for the massive disruption caused by the civil war of 1967-1970, the generation that gained admission into the university between the mid-1940s and early 1960s, had matured educationally and intellectually. Most were with a second or third degrees and were either teaching in universities around the country or had come back after the war years to take up available research and teaching positions at such universities. A number of them too were to be found in government bureaucracy, special parastatals, research institutes and business corporations during the postwar reconstruction efforts.

While examples abound in virtually all academic disciplines, I can only cite the members of this generation in the Human and Social Sciences; fields of study that I am fairly familiar with. Heading this list would, of course be the celebrated novelist and humanist, Professor Chinua Achebe, who took up a teaching post at the University of Nigeria shortly after the war. Other novelists worth mentioning include Chukwuemeka Ike, an educationist to the core, university registrar and administrator of WAEC for several years; John Munonye, Nkem Nwankwo, Cyprian Ekwensi, Elechi Amadi, Obi B. Egbuna, and the medical doctor-turned writer of fascinating children's stories, Anezi Okoro. Among the literary critics and scholars worthy of mention here are Profs. M. J. C. Echeruo, Ben Obumselu, Emmanuel Obiechina, D. I. Nwoga, Romanus Egudu, Ernest Emenyonu, Charles Nnolim, Ime Ikiddeh, and Chidi Ikonne. From history came Profs. Achufusi, A. E. Afigbo and C. C. Ifemesia. From political science would be mentioned Dr Chuba Okadigbo, Miriam Ikejiani-Clark and Okwudiba Nnoli. From Sociology would be mentioned Ikenna Nzimiro and Inyang Eteng. From Economics, two names readily come to my mind; Ukwu I. Ukwu and Okey Emordi. From Law came Prof. Osita Eze, and from the Sciences such towering figures as Profs Martin Ijere, Gaius Igboeli, Mkparata Ekpete, Anya O. Anya, Frank Ndili, Fabian Osuji, G. Umezulike and ABC Nwosu.

The 1970s were therefore the golden age of intellectual maturity and ceaseless activity. Yet, for the scholar, the high point of any career is the publication of both scholarly articles in learned journals as well as the production of book length studies for general readership. While they encountered literally no serious problem in the first regard because of the existence of peer reviewed journals, both locally and internationally in a number of universities, some of them came unstuck when it came to publishing their book length studies locally. The few reputable publishing houses in Nigeria then were owned by expatriates, and even with the indigenization decree of 1972, Eastern Nigerian entrepreneurs lacked the capacity to invest in such ventures, battling as they did with the painful reality of surviving the peace even at the most rudimentary material level. The publishing houses were thus either wholly or partly owned by expatriates and non-Easterners, and were concentrated in the Lagos-Ibadan publishing axis. Naturally they turned to the local resources that were available and handy, and given the presence of University of Lagos, University of Ibadan and Obafemi Awolowo University (formerly University of Ife), the materials they published were heavily skewered in favour of scholars and writers, mostly non-Easterners, from their immediate catchment areas.

Fourth Dimension was thus born as a child of compelling historical circumstance, as a dialectical end result of an irresistible and inevitable cultural process. It emerged to redress this imbalance, and to present and match, in the public arena, the scrupulous researches and intellectual endeavours of scholars in the private realm. Its vision was to be a pacesetter in the publication of creative, innovative, and even provocative studies in the sciences and the arts, and to consistently represent, affirm and sustain the African viewpoint. To execute this vision, it evolved the mission and strategy of seeking out the best available materials, to subject them to the most rigorous editorial test, and to publish them with the highest level of professional thoroughness and efficiency discernable in all leading publishing houses the world over.

This revolution in publishing was orchestrated by Arthur Nwankwo who had gathered considerable exposure and experience in publishing from his days in the Nwamife publishing experiment. A USA-trained historian and political scientist, he caused a stir with the publication of his *Nigeria: The Challenge of Biafra, Biafra: The Making of a Nation* and *My People Suffer.*[1] A fearless intellectual, historian, social scientist and radical thinker, who eventually embraced a domesticated variant of Marxist historical dialectics as his method of social enquiry, he had developed close social relationship with some of the scholars I have mentioned, and had a deep insight and knowledge into their academic strides and intellectual outlook. He was therefore well placed to blaze this trail and had the intellectual and financial resources he could count on in successfully instrumenting such a hazardous business venture.

While he remained the chairman of the publishing enterprise he relinquished its day to day management to a management team headed by a Managing Director. Ever present were also members of the Editorial Board, as well as Editorial Consultants, assessors and reviewers drawn from several universities. The first Managing Director during its formative years was his younger brother, Hon. Ejike Nwankwo, another USA-trained management consultant who brought a professional approach to publishing, based on his rich international exposure, to bear on the young firm. He was eventually to go on to contest the House of Representatives election for the Aguata Federal Constituency in 1983 under the National Party of Nigeria which he won, when his brother Arthur was the gubernatorial candidate of the Peoples Redemption Party (PRP) in old Anambra State.

However, the golden age of Fourth Dimension Publishing Company Ltd. was defined by the Managing Directorship of the firm by the late Engr Victor Nwankwo, Arthur's immediate younger brother. He broadened the publishing base of the company, expanded its thematic reach, pushed it into the forefront of African and world publishing, and exposed its authors to the international market in a development programme that spanned over a decade. Until his brutal, senseless and politically motivated assassination in 2000, he was for many years one of the leading figures in Nigerian publishing industry, the President of African Publishers Network (AP-NET) and an advisor to the UNESCO Director General on publishing and culture.

He and Fourth Dimension occupied a pride of place at the distinguished Harare and Frankfurt Book Fairs, as well as other world renowned book exhibitions for decades, and as a partner to the African Book Collective (ABC) in London, he used that outlet to achieve a worldwide distribution of the books published by Fourth Dimension, mine included, and a measure of international recognition for both established and younger authors, myself included. An intellectual to the core whose sheer brilliance is dazzling, Victor Nwankwo was a Nigerian and Igbo patriot, a social philanthropist, a humanist and a quiet but effective dialogician.

By the time I came calling again in 1990, Fourth Dimension Publishers had been in existence for fourteen years. During those years, it not only established its relevance as a leading Nigerian and African publishing house but achieved worldwide significance and stature as an intellectual base. Gradually, from the tradition of publishing, there emerged from it the tradition and spirit of intellectual enquiry, the systematization of its institutional base and location and the creation of a semi-informal discussion group that became translated, over the intervening years, into a centre of research, leadership training and public policy. It is this transformation and the tendencies it harboured and symbolized that fascinated all the people who came into contact with it. The institutional design of Fourth Dimension was socially, culturally, intellectually, politically and ideologically capacious.

My first impression of its operation was baffling. On a daily basis, between the hours of 9 am and sometimes up to 2 or even 3 am the next day, streams of visitors poured in, each bearing a different ideological perspective and political viewpoint that ranged from an insular Igbo nationalist ethos to the most liberal position on the necessity of national integration, inter-ethnic co-existence and understanding and the subsumption of different ethnic and national persuasions into a vision of a coherent nation-state with mutual affinities, indissoluble links and interdependent structures. Between these two poles ranged those whose political and ideological loyalty and sympathy predilected towards liberal democracy, radical humanist-welfarist philosophy, a domesticated variant of Marxism-Leninism, and even apologia to the military option to democracy in Nigeria. Yet, beneath this welter of apparent irreconcilable ideological persuasions, ran a dialectical encapsulation of the national question in a logical, coherent, and rational manner. This dialectical premise was always arrived at after a thorough examination of all the issues and the deconstruction of all leading arguments before a reconstruction of a mutually acceptable viewpoint was canvassed and advanced.

Yet, more often than not, perspectives remained unchanged and unchangeable, hardening as the explosion of dialogical exchanges threatened to get out of hand. However, while the members of the institution may end up not yielding any appreciable ground and remained steadfast and resolute in defence of their ideological position, the overall impression which was consistently projected was one of a group of patriots and fervent nationalists who were incurably optimistic about the destiny of their country, and were prepared to deploy their talents, energies and experiences in its service.

The uniqueness of the Fourth Dimension institution is that it abhors the prescriptive and tendentious mindset that restricts, narrows and resists social evolution; that cripples the inherent capacity and predilection of people towards free expression; and that arrogates to itself the status of an all-knowing intellectual base with ready-made answers for all national malaise. Either in the selection of publishable materials by the publishing arm of the institution or in the choice of columnists and selection of articles to be published in the *New Outlook* newspaper, which became the media arm of the institution, careful thought was given to wide social, political and ideological representation. The picture that readily emerges is one of an institution intent in giving voice and providing platform for anybody who has something important to say, no matter what, and who desires to share his thoughts, altitudes and opinions with a wider audience, provided that there was and remains a consistent fidelity to the nobility and depth of thought. A careful reading of the titles issued by the publishing house and a close study of the editorial opinions and the variety of articles published in editions of the *New Outlook* newspaper will make this position abundantly clear.

To ensure that his viewpoints and perspectives on the national question are accorded a central position in the context of the multiplicities of perspectives canvassing for attention, recognition, validity and authenticity; viewpoints which represent the mainstream ideological stand of the institution, of which I was part, Arthur Nwankwo endeavoured to pour out his thoughts and ideas in a torrent of books in a style that was at once personal, yet very representative of the majority of opinions shared in the house. From his early concentration on the fate and place of the Igbo nation in the Nigerian enterprise, in the books I had already mentioned, he began a systematic engagement of the Nigerian condition in a series of researches and book length studies that re-conceptualized and re-defined the conventional approaches to understanding, articulating and projecting Nigerian political transformation and democratization processes.

The first phase in the evolution and systematization of this mainstream tendency is to be found in his *The Power Dynamics of Nigerian Society, The Military Option to Democracy, Before I Die* and *The Retreat of Power: The Military in Nigeria's Third Republic.*[2] The key ideological theses that defined his work at this phase are the theory of cimilicy,[3] a radical-ideological renovation of the theory of "diarchy" which was advanced by Dr Nnamdi Azikiwe in the 1970s, and the defence of multi-party, plural democracy when he successfully deconstructed Olusegun Obasanjo's thesis on the one-party state in the *A Constitution for National Integration and Development,* in *Before I Die: Obasanjo-*

Nwankwo Debate on the One-Party State.

In the first thesis, he ideologized the objective contents of civil-military relations in Nigeria through a careful, scientific analysis of the relevant social forces that have shaped and may continue to shape Nigeria-type social formation, and came to the inescapable conclusion that national integration, social stability, accelerated economic development and sustainable democratic transition would be best served by "civilianizing the soldiers and militarizing the civilians" in a dialectical equation in which the elemental force of democratization will remain the binding and fusing of national element or categories. In the second thesis, he shows his fidelity to the liberal disposition of the Fourth Dimension institution through a trenchant opposition to Obasanjo's politically and ideologically narrow and constricted worldview which would hinder democratic progress, repress contrary views and systematically impose on the nation a one-party monopolistic power structure driven by a culture of silence, fear, intolerance, arrogance of power and impunity.

In dismantling this thesis, he posits a vision of society that would grow and advance through the objective interplay of plural thought; through the heavy reliance on ideological and patriotic education; and through the inculcation on the citizenry the culture of dialogue, tolerance, respect of contrary ideas and recognition and acceptance of national diversities as the symbol of national strength. Viktor Kalu eventually codified Arthur Nwankwo's thoughts and perspectives in a detailed scholarly study titled *The Nigerian Condition: Arthur Nwankwo's Thoughts and Viewpoints.*[4]

The second phase in the evolution of his thought started with his *Nigeria: The Political Transition and the Future of Democracy* and ended with *Nigeria's Stolen Billions.* In between these two works were to be located *Nigerians as Outsiders* and *Terminus: End Game Doctrine.* In these works which he wrote and published between 1992 and 2000, he aligned himself and the Fourth Dimension institution to the mass based, popular democratic agitation of that age, and made an eloquent contribution in the areas of the tactics and strategies of democratic struggle, the limitations of a military sponsored and driven democratization process and, in a related context, launched an inquest into military political adventure through a matchless expose of its distortions, moral atrophy and social, political and economic destabilization pyrotechnics.

The three phases in Arthur Nwankwo's intellectual growth, which reflected the essential political and ideological mindset of the mainstream tendency in the Fourth Dimension institution were the phase in which he concentrated on the location of the Igbo spirit in national development, as well as the structural and institutional limitations and handicaps set on their way; the phase in which he made a modest concession to the ability and willingness of the military to democratize society and improve the well-being of the people; and the phase in which he threw the whole Fourth Dimension institutional weight behind the mass democratic agitation of Nigerian popular classes through a systematic exposition and popularization of pro-people democratic options and strategies. Between the second and third phase, he turned his attention to continental issues by, first, writing a caustic expose on the bestiality and dehumanizing propensities of African tyrants and regime despots (African Dictators: Regime Tyranny and the Logic of Power) and, second, by celebrating the emergence of what is now heralded as the African century on the promise of the AU and NEPAD with their strategic economic, social and political platforms. This renascence epoch will be driven by regional integration and the emergence of a Union Government, and the implementation of the objects, protocols and covenants on good governance through the African Peer Review mechanism. He went on to deconstruct the prevailing, Euro-Caucasian supremacist views and ideologies propagated by Fukuyana, Nixon and others in The African Possibility.[6]

A careful reading of Arthur Nwankwo's major works on politics and a close reading of the editorial essays and opinion page comments of a very politically oriented newspaper like *New Outlook* will reveal a well articulated and robustly presented analysis of the Nigerian political process, perhaps far greater than the output, qualitatively speaking, of any other centre of learning in Nigeria during the period under review. It is thus important that this significant contribution is accorded its correct and well-earned place in national political discourses and is recognized as one of the central intellectual-strategic and political platforms that have helped in negotiating Nigerian democratic transitions.

In Arthur Nwankwo's analysis of the role of the military in Nigerian politics and political transition; and in the various discussions that shaped the Fourth Dimension institutional approach to the subject it had become abundantly clear that the key limitations and deficiencies in the military option to democracy which became a dominant political issue in the mid and late 1970s had in the late 1980s and early 1990s, been substantially investigated and pronounced upon. And here reference is being made, not to incidental intellectual productions or closet scholarly pieces in rarefied and exotic academic journals, but in over 15 book length, well-researched studies, a book length commentary and thousands of newspaper articles, interviews, reflections and opinions.

It was precisely from these efforts that the terms "negotiated withdrawal", "transfer of power", "institutional basis of elite power dynamics" and "the theoretical-paradigmatic design and Institutional-Strategic Framework of (Government of National Unity) GNU became instantly popularized, to be re-affirmed, moderated, distorted and even deconstructed by later day commentators on the subject. I know for one, being an integral member of that institution who helped with a measure of editorial work on Arthur Nwankwo's writings, as an Editorial Consultant to the *Fourth Dimension* and *New Outlook* newspapers, that a significant portion of Babangida's failed transition agenda contained distorted and vulgarized borrowings of these theses.

And later, in the 1990s, when the issue of Igbo/Eastern marginalization and the necessity of a Sovereign National Conference/Government of National Unity, became popular it was difficult for many students and observers of the Nigerian political process to locate their genetic sources within the context of Arthur Nwankwo's writings, the dialogical oriented work of members of the Fourth Dimension institution, and the theoretical - ideological and intellectual-political systematizations of the Eastern Mandate Union (EMU), particularly at the historical phase (1996-1998) when it aligned itself wholly and completely to the National Democratic Coalition.[7] Till date, the contributions of Arthur Nwankwo, the Fourth Dimension Institution and the Eastern Mandate Union (EMU) to these discourses remain matchless in their coherence, logic, scientific base and application, including the EMU-authored and NADECO submitted position paper on the idea of a Sovereign National Conference and a Government of National Unity at the CMAG Conference on Nigerian Political crisis at Edinburgh, Scotland, in July 1997. But more on this in detail in volumes 2 and 3 of the present study.[8]

Suffice it to stress here that from a close study of the Babangida regime's political transfer programme; and from a scientific examination of previous attempts by the military to democratize society, the conclusion was drawn that given that institution's colonial origins and neo-colonial outlook; given its praetorian nature and qualities; given the inter-play of centrifugal ethnic supremacist tendencies within its ranks; given the weakening of its core institutional and professional base through political contamination and moral exhaustion; given its wholesale destruction of civic sensibility, including social psychology through a commandist and militanstic mindset; given its incapacity to evolve strategic vision for social amelioration and economic development and well-being of the people; and given its poverty of ideology, perhaps with a noted sympathy toward an anti-people, pro-reactionary conservative ideological predilection, that the Nigerian military was incapable of democratizing society.[9]

To negotiate these fairly insurmountable obstacles, and to create the condition in which re-entry into politics was built into the transition agenda and arrangement it evolved a mechanistic, ahistorical and undialectical approach to the transfer of power, conceived as either "negotiated" or leisurely withdrawal, depending on the alignment of social forces, and the state, scale and operation of social contradictions it has unleashed on society. The transfer of power, now so-called, became an intra-elite game of revolving doors whereby political batons kept on changing hands between different factions of the military elite and their malleable civilian collaborators in an absurd and nauseating relay race.

It is also noted that leisurely withdrawal from power which defined the Obasanjo 1979 transition (with allowance made for the problematic of what constitutes twelve two third percent mathematical equation in a nineteen state structure whose resolution was negotiated), and the early and middle phase of the Babangida transition (the dissolution of the 13 political parties; the legislation, together with their manifestoes and constitutions, of the two parties to the left (SDP) and to the right (NRC); the dismantling of their national leaderships and the foisting on them a compliant corps of political leaders; and the subsequent disqualification and detention of more than 20 presidential aspirants), was always an accepted choice when the supervising military despotic authority was in near absolute political ascendancy and control, and when the alignment of social forces and the behaviour of social contradictions weighed in its favour. This context also defined and described the Gen Sani Abacha transition up to his death. Indeed, that regime radically redefined and re-conceptualized the strategic design and vision of leisurely withdrawal by implanting the notion and logic of instantaneous political re-entry through the life-presidency project superintended by the five political parties the regime legislated into existence.[10]

However, when there existed a balance in the forces that were mutually opposed; and when the scale and operation of social contradictions weighed somewhat against the withdrawing regime, the tendency was to negotiate the regime's safe exit out of power, but not to a degree in which it was completely overrun and overwhelmed but in the context in which it would be able to implant a new political leadership that would at least be sympathetic to its causes, ensure the security of its key personal, and safeguard their wealth and resources accumulated while in office. This situation best describes the Gen Absulsalami Abubakar regime and its relationship with the Gen Olusegun Obasanjo administration it foisted on the nation on May 29, 1999.

Happily, though, the Nigerian military has successfully re-negotiated its institutional authenticity since 1999. Driven now by the vision of younger, better trained, intellectually deep and professionally skilled officer corps; fully recognizing the obsolescence of military despotism as an African and global phenomenon; and recognizing also its institutional and moral exhaustion given its decades of meddling in state politics, the contemporary Nigerian military is constantly renewing and re-positioning itself as a professional fighting force, and has aligned itself to the democratic leadership of the day, with clear, concrete and objective signals that it would uphold and protect the constitution unconditionally. By subordinating itself to civil democratic control through executive and legislative oversight, and by its deep involvement with the global emphasis on security sector reform and even transformation, the military has shown an acute responsiveness to the political and social character of the polity, and the democratic expectations of a populace that won their struggle with toil, blood, tears and sweat.

I have gone to this extent in placing on public record empirically ascertainable facts about the contributions of

Arthur Nwankwo and the Fourth Dimension institution in the debate about the direction of the Nigerian state not only because I was a part of that institution and shared and espoused its tendencies, stand and perspectives on the national question but, more so, human memory being what it is time and space may obscure some of the facts and deny people and the ideas they either created, projected or popularized their proper historical significance. Although it may be preemptive to declare at this stage on a matter of this nature (substantial part of this declaration is to be found in volumes 2 and 3 of this work), already in extant Nigerian literature on the role of individuals, groups, entities, and institutions in the pro-democracy struggle that ushered in Nigeria's Fourth Republic, a deliberate attempt has and is being made and sustained to obfuscate reality and deny people their proper contribution and sacrifice in narratives that are partial, prejudicial and coloured with ethnic supremacist and jingoistic cant.[11]

When I made my journey of 1990 to see Arthur Nwankwo in Enugu in the company of Viktor Kalu, I was not fully aware that my destiny will be almost irreversibly altered. I had set out for myself, from my boyhood days, to pursue the study of literature to the highest possible academic level. And when I earned my M.A. degree at the University of Benin, enrolled for the PhD programme and wrote the draft of four scholarly works, I was determined to see this ambition through and become a university professor not later than 36 years of age. Indeed, I was set on this course from my first day at Abia State University, ensuring that my works became published, and becoming a Senior Research Fellow/ Senior Lecturer at the beginning of 1995 when I was 31 years.

That journey was to alter everything, and on hindsight, I would have taken it ten times over because of its results and consequences on my life. True, my academic advancement in terms of promotion (I would have probably become a professor by 1997 or 1998 when I would have been 35 if I had devoted myself completely to university research work from 1989 to that year), and put paid, though temporarily, to the completion of the researches that had reached advanced stage, on the writings of Ngugi wa Thiong'o, Tess Onwueme, as well as a materialist reading of all Chinua Achebe's novels.

Nevertheless, what I lost in this direction (I have even now reconnected to my literary calling, issued the second edition of all my works, published four new ones, and have started research on three others), I have more than been compensated in the realm of social practice. My intellectual development did not suffer one bit; rather I began to apply my modest intellectual gifts, in the context of the Fourth Dimension Institution, the Eastern Mandate Union, the National Democratic Coalition, and eventually as the Founding National Secretary of Alliance of Democracy, to the service of humanity and in the propagation of mostly, humane causes. I also gained tremendous mileage in my knowledge of the forces that shape Nigerian society and got exposed to and deeply interacted with Nigerian political elite at an age when most of my peers had not yet broken out of a narrow relationship framework made up of immediate family members and childhood and school friends. Through this connection I became a respected public figure with an instantly recognizable name. I could not have wished for more.

My tutelage under Arthur Nwankwo, Viktor Kalu, the late Engr Victor Nwankwo, and to a great extent, Hon. Ejike Nwankwo did not last long. I was a willing student and an enthusiastic follower. Many a time Viktor Kalu would rib me about my Oko Declaration, and how I, like him before me, had been seduced by Arthur's vision, creative imagination, profound intellect, deep insight into Nigerian military and civilian politics, boundless faith and incurable optimism about Nigeria's future destiny, tremendous courage and willpower, and most importantly the ability, as a wealthy entrepreneur, to commit class suicide in favour of a revolutionary-populist transformation of Nigerian society. I sharpened and honed my debating skills and would hold audiences (made up of the leading lights in Nigerian politics) spellbound with the lucidity and clarity of my thought.

At a time even, we evolved the Theory of the Fourth Dimension as a material-spiritual category, and located African liberation within its pedagogical context. We took from geometry, and by extension, the study of matter and its properties, the dimensional theory of reality. We understood that geometrically speaking, and this has found resonance in algebra, mechanics and physics, a *line* has one dimension, a *surface* two dimensions of length and breadth and a solid three dimension of length, breadth and thickness. By extension, we projected that the Fourth Dimension occupies an inscrutable realm, the realm of knowledge that cannot be captured by these geometric categoric specifications. *The Fourth Dimension Pedagogical Theory of African Liberation* then implies the harnessing of the pristine spiritual essence of African cosmology in a process that weighs heavily in favour of historicity and dialectics; de-romanticizing those spiritual ingredients on the weight of stupendous historical omissions, setbacks and tragedies; and incarnating a new idiom of African historical re-emergence as a combination of both the material (3 dimension) and spiritual (1 dimension) of African cosmogony. This somewhat exotic thought was eventually celebrated by Arthur Nwankwo in the appendices to some of his works.[12]

However, it was in my unrelenting exposure to and mastering of the Nigerian elite that my first and later sustained contact and involvement with the Fourth Dimension Institution took its initial meaning and became one of the defining phenomena in my life for a decade and more. The account of this, which forms the next chapter of this volume, covers the whole of the 1990s, though attempt will be made to separate the elite that constituted the political circles of EMU, NADECO and AD, who will be given separate treatment in the remaining two volumes, from the rest.

Overlaps occur in the narrative, as well as repetition of names and what they stand for as would be inevitable in a work of this nature that deals with segments of social reality that are sometimes dialectically fused and interdependent from one historical period to the other, and between the political formations most of them operated within.[13]

CHAPTER SEVEN
NOTES AND REFERENCES

1. From 1969 to the present time, Dr Arthur Nwankwo has steadily established himself as one of Nigeria's foremost political thinkers, historians, public intellectuals, pro-democracy activists and fervent human rights advocates. He has over 30 books to his credit some of which are: *Nigeria: The Challenge of Biafra; Biafra: The Making of a Nation; My People Suffer; The Power Dynamics of Nigerian Society; Cimilicy; Military Options to Democracy; African Dictators; Before I Die; The Retreat of Power; Nigeria: Political Transition and the Future of Democracy; The African Possibilty in Global Power Struggle; Nigerians as Outsiders;* and *Terminus.*

2. Arthur Nwankwo's viewpoint on the Nigerian Military Formation was conditioned by his radical political thought and politics. He is inherently suspicious of the capacity of the military to genuinely democratize the Nigerian society. In close analytic discourse after another, he is of the view that only when the military are overwhelmed by popular democratic forces as was the case between 1993 and 1998 that they could be compelled to make minimum concessions in any genuine democratic process.

3. Cimilicy is a novel ideological paradigm Arthur Nwankwo constructed in his analysis of the character of Nigerian society, its power dynamics and power relations. Cimilicy involves a dialectical fusing of contending political and ideological variables realized in a thesis of popular, activist based democracy in which the military are civilianized and the civilians militarized.

4. Viktor Kalu's *The Nigerian Condition: Nwankwo's*

194 ■ DEMOCRATIC TRANSFORMATION AND SOCIAL ...

Thoughts and Viewpoints on the Nigerian State is a critical appraisal of Arthur Nwankwo's writings on Nigerian politics, the essential ingredients of which are to be found in notes 1and 2 above.

5. A rash of narcissistic, self-celebratory and self-indulgent Western literature came out in the early 1990s with the collapse of the Soviet Union, the collapse of the Berlin wall, the re-unification of Germany, and the retreat of Sovietized Euro-Communism. Some of these works which either proclaimed the end of history and the cessation of procreative intellectual, ideological, political, cultural and social thought in a de-ideologized new world order or the triumph of Western liberal democracy over her ideological opponents underpinned Francis Fukuyama's highly influential but controversial work, *The End of History and the Last Man* and Richard Nixon's *Seize the Moment.*

6. *The African Possibility* was written by Arthur Nwankwo as a rejection of the thesis stated in note 6 above and a robust defence of the place of Africa in the configuration of global power dynamics.

7. The contribution of the Eastern Mandate Union (EMU) to the national discourse over the institutional and structural marginalization of the old Eastern Region as a consequence of the civil war which they lost in 1970 was enormous, deep-rooted and virtually peerless. The EMU stated its twin mission as the "de-marginalization of the East and the de-annulment of the results of the 1993 Presidential election" which was won by the late Chief M. K. O. Abiola.

The EMU was made up of radical and liberal political elite, pro-democracy and human rights advocates, labour leaders and youth and students activists. Through its conferences, press briefings, media appearances, publications, pamphleteering, leafleting and the use of handbills, EMU became the most consistent East-based pro-democracy movement in Nigeria between 1994-1998 and between 1996-1998, the principal partner of NADECO (National Democratic Coalition) in driving the democratic struggle.

EMU's contribution to the discourse on the need of a Sovereign National Conference and National Restructuring was formidable, articulate and intellectually strong. Eventually, EMU's position was adopted by NADECO as its main thesis on the subject, and its substantial presentation during the Commonwealth Ministerial Action Committee meeting (CMAG) which held at Edinbungh, Scotland, UK, in 1997. Dr Arthur Nwankwo, the Chancellor of EMU and NADECO's Deputy-Chairman, led the EMU delegation to the conference.

8.   For the full meaning of CMAG and EMU's contribution to NADECO's position paper at the conference, see note no. 7 above.

9.   The relative success of the 1999 transition programme aside (a "success" engendered in part by the robust pro-democracy resistance to military despotism, which ensured that the military's exist strategy was forced and hasty), Nigeria's historical experience has shown the incapacity of the military to effect a successful transfer of power and its sustenance: 1974-1975; (Gowon)1979-1983 (Obasanjo); 1983-1985 (Buhari); 1985-1993 (Babangida); and 1993-1998 (Late General Sani Abacha).

10.   Leisurely withdrawal from political power strongly suggests a situation whereby the retreating military

power wielders deliberately design a faulty political programme which makes leisurely re-entry into power no longer a distant possibility but a political and historical certainty. Leisurely withdrawal from power is usually effectuated in collaboration with a malleable and morally compromised wing of the civilian political elite who readily and quickly surrender political power during the next re-entry process.

11.   A large body of literature is steadily emerging on the Nigerian pro-democracy struggle, particularly the struggle to de-annul the June 12, 1993 Presidential election. Most of these works were written by activists from the South-West and Mid-West of Nigeria. As rich as the details in them are, and as helpful as their insight are in throwing light on the complex political circumstances of those years, their perspective and viewpoint remain partial, selective and limited. The need to redress this imbalance is long overdue in order to accord all the individual players and groups their rightful contribution, stature and space in the democratic struggle. One of such efforts is the present volume, which is the first of a three-volume work broadly titled "Democratic Transformation and Social Change in Nigeria". Some of the partially reflective works referred to above include:

Wale Oshun – *Clapping With One Hand and The Open Grave.*

Olatunji Dare – *Diary of a Debacle: Tracking Nigeria's Failed Democratic Transition (1984-1994)*

Omo Omoruyi – *Tale of June 12.*

12. See the Appendices to Arthur Nwankwo, *The Retreat of Power,* and *The African Possibility in Global Power Struggle* for a full examination of the historical, civilizational and ideological context and content of *The Theory of the Fourth Dimension*.

13. The political elite, or the power elite, relate to those individuals who exercise a high degree of influence in molding political behaviour and attitude of the mass of the people, and some of who are either in the ruling political coalitions or have established a close relationship with those in power.

Afterword

This first volume is coming out at a crucial juncture in the evolution of Nigeria's postcolonial Fourth Bourgeois Democratic Republic. As I indicated in the introduction, the act of 'non-recognition' of the forces worked into the nation's constructed ontology by the political elite is pushing the performance of liberal democracy to its absolute limit. The material content of the social formation and the social relations which undergird the political economy of power is increasingly under structural and institutional stress. The intra-class contradictions among the different factions of the ruling elite are sharpening and spreading at an astronomical pace and unleashing social forces that are steadily aggravating the nation's pristine and inherited faultlines. The 2015 General Elections may mark a watershed in the viability of the idea and reality of the Nigerian state, including its constitutive historicist and cultural necessity. For the optimists among the ranks of the elite who, in spite of being sufficiently embarrassed by the unpredictability of the autotelic currents buffeting the system, that process will witness the renewal of faith and belief, the deconstruction of an old power arrangement and the construction of a new, pan-national power structure capable of driving an agenda of national restoration on the basis of the equality of the nation's complex geo-political and geo-strategic spaces. For the pessimists, 2015 will magnify the exhaustion of the idea of the state, incrementalize the subversion of its sovereign hegemony, transgress the falsity of its colonial inheritance and unleash a season of centripetal dialectic along its exaggerated faultlines.

I suspect that the true picture lies in between these two theses. The strategic alliance between the nation's ruling classes and the power and finance structures and platforms of the polis, in combination with the nation's strategic location in the African region will impel a compromise solution that may well extend the frontiers of its legitimacy and continued historical possibility. Not to be overlooked also is the fact that even in the agony of the 'non-recognition' of the nature, character and essence of the nation's ontology; even in the absence of a coherent national ideology and philosophy of being; and even in the normativization of incompetence, ineptitude and social imbecility as the defining idiom of public service, a great self-preservative weapon still remains intact: the sustenance of the state is located in the sustenance of primitive accumulation, agglutination of public resources, and the buccaneering of national patrimony. So long as the social formation, its material relations and the political economy of power excrete these oddities, so long will the squabbling elite be able to overcome the deep divisions within their ranks and construct a historical trajectory whose compass will be the survival of the state, for now.

However, there is a distinct possibility that the social forces already unleashed could become unmanageable given their current anarchic and atavistic propensity, and in combination with the blind pursuit of power by those whose bellicosity and political hysteria are the effect of the trillions of oil money they believe it is their turn to inherit, could herald a season of angst and ennui capable of leading the nation along an inexorable path of political and corporate perdition. No matter which face of the tossed coin shows up, I believe that the real Nigerian possibility is not far off; that the threshold of a new dawn that will embarrass many and bemuse others is about to beckon; and that the unconcealing of the true nature of things will occur in the direction, not of the sustenance of a perfidious postcolonial bourgeois order, but the construction of a genuine national ontology undergirded by materialist dialectics and a substantially secularized material transcendence now realized as a 'materiality of ideology'.

Appendix I

WORKING PAPERS FROM THE MARXIST MOVEMENT (MYM) YEARS 1981-1984

The documents that make up this appendix are merely representative of the mass of papers dealing with the administrative, organizational and operational activities of a student society devoted to the propagation of the ideas of Karl Marx, the conscientization and mobilization of students and the wider society into appreciating the revolutionary possibilities inherent in Marxist ideology and practical preparation for what we then believed was the dawning of an inevitable socialist revolution in Nigeria. I am currently researching into radical student movements in Nigeria of the 1980s and will be incorporating the papers in this appendix into that body of work. It is important to stress that the papers dealing with disciplinary issues are presented not as a means of censuring any comrade but purely in underscoring the seriousness, commitment, passion and revolutionary zeal with which students whose average age was 18 regarded their revolutionary cause and pursued its implementation.

I have prefaced most of the papers with an explanatory comment as a way of properly situating their spatio-temporal specificity but also most crucially of establishing their wider local, national and international significance.

Let me also make a few observations about the membership base and organizational and administrative structure of the movement. The Marxist Youth Movement (MYM) was open to both undergraduate and graduate students. While the bulk of the members were undergraduate students, a number of MA and PhD students also enrolled as members. The movement's Staff Adviser and other lecturers who are comrades also participated in its activities, especially in helping to facilitate the Political Education and Ideological Studies Classes. Expectedly, the bulk of the movement's membership base was drawn from the ranks of students studying Social Sciences (Political Science, Sociology and Anthropology, Philosophy and Religion, Psychology, and Economics) and Humanities (English and Literary Studies, Linguistics, History and Archeology, Mass Communication, and Fine and Applied Arts). Interestingly, quite an appreciable number of its members were students from the Faculties of Engineering, Physical Sciences, Biological Sciences and Education.

Organizationally, the movement was unpretentious in its being loosely modeled after the Bolshevik Party of the then Soviet Union. It has a General Congress (GC), presumably its highest decision making organ but in reality its powers were exercised by the Central Committee (CC) and within the Central Committee by the Politbro (Political Bureau). The Politbro was made up of the following Principal Officers: Secretary General, Deputy Secretary General, Secretary of Publicity who is in charge of the Publicity Bureau, Secretary of Political Education who is in charge of the Political Education Bureau and oversees the Political Education Classes Programme, Secretary of Ideological Classes who is in charge of the Ideological Classes Programme and Financial Secretary who is in charge of the

Financial Bureau. These various offices have committees attached to them and members are encouraged to belong to any or some of the committees in line with their personal preferences and choices.

MARXIST YOUTH MOVEMENT

UNIVERSITY OF NIGERIA, NSUKKA, WELCOME RELEASE
THE STRUGGLE DEFINITELY CONTINUES

(It is the tradition of every serious minded student club or association to issue a release welcoming freshmen at the commencement of every academic session. This release is meant to inform the new students about the existence of such an association, to enunciate its philosophy and vision and to literally woo such students into its ranks. The Marxist Youth Movement is traditionally at the head of this kind of membership drive in order to secure the membership of as many as these new students as possible before they are 'poisoned by the decadent and obscurantist ideas of the petty bourgeois student clubs'.)

We particularly welcome our fresh students to our midst, even though belatedly while we equally wish, as the title of the release suggests, to confront them with the realities of this nation today as well as highlight a recently introduced obnoxious law.

Before we go further, we congratulate our freshmen on their admission to this university despite all the obstacles intentionally planted on their way by the neo-colonial education policy. It seems apposite therefore that we remind them that their presence here does not necessarily certify their being more academically brilliant or even more competent than our colleagues to whom the university gates were shut. It had been necessary to limit the number of students in order to preserve the class structure of our society. The proliferation of private universities e.g Afendomifiok, Pope John Paul II etc. is a justification of our assertion that the capitalist system is a discredited, exploitative one maintained only to preserve the acquisitive propensies of the ruling class.

We therefore call on you all to join us in the struggle to overthrow this oppressive and repressive system that is decidedly against the collective wishes of the hoi polloi of this great country. Join in the struggle to assert the dignity of labour; to enthrone the workers who produce for the survival of our country; to overthrow discredited politicians who can boldly declare their mission in politics as "to amass wealth and not reduce poverty"; politicians who can publicly declare they were not elected "to carry your shit" and only to turn millionaires within four years in order to buy jets and 12 inches caps.

This is the historic duty to which we are all called. You cannot afford to be indifferent.

THE OBNOXIOUS ELECTRICAL APPLIANCES BOND

A number of students have strongly expressed their views against this bond while others were satisfied with grumbling but none had gone to deeply analyze or explain what could have brought about the reactionary, retrogressive decision. It is known throughout this country that UNN symbolizes reaction at its worst in any academic society. Over the years we go to polls only to elect people into our students union either on 'Kparapo' basis or on the basis of the faction of the ruling class-political party – to which he or she belongs or even on how much booze he can declare. As a result, we have only been turning out political hoodlums, cohorts, turn-coats and hirelings whose mission is to satisfy their political pay masters.

With these firmly registered in our minds, we discover that the university authority, itself an extension of the ruling class, feels free to test the pulse of the students and see whether even a single resenting voice will be raised. In other words, the decision to clamp down that obnoxious injunction was not really an end in itself but a means to an end. Glaringly, the end was to see whether students of UNN will dare raise their voice should the government or its representative decide to increase boarding fees, the cost of each meal or even introduce tuition. We therefore call on all students to support the union's Secretary General on this issue.

NANS/NUSA

By now, we should all have heard the ignoble role of the babies of Imo Solidarity in generating confusion and fanning embers of disunity within the only symbol of student's unity in this country–the NANS. It had been the long-standing policy of the outgoing executive under Emeka Duru to do this and we call on all students of this great university to resist this by particularly charging the incoming executive to see to it that the unity of NANS is maintained.

Aluta Continua.
By Pub. Bureau MYM.

(The list below is by no means the entire membership of the movement. It is actually a sample of the movement's membership in the working papers I have and merely points to the structure of its entire membership base)

MEMBERS OF THE MARXIST YOUTH MOVEMENT

S/N	NAME	DEPT	RM/HOSTEL
1	Ahmed, O.	Pol. Sc.	B2 317, Alvan
2	Udenta O. Udenta	English	215, Okeke
3	Omonijo, M.A	Pol. Sc.	334A Akpabio
4	Iroegbunam, C.	Engineering	A1/105, Eni
5	Egini, P.I	Pol. Sc (L.G)	E5, ZFH
6	Omu, E.	Vet/Path	215A, Awo
7	Chukwukelu, C.E	H.P.E	A2/104/ ZFH
8	Aniagboso, J.O	History	B2/303
9	Umoru, J.O	Pol. Sc	A2/223, Eni
10	Okeke, Dan	Envir/Geog	B4/303 ZFH
11	Agbo Sam	Ling	432, Mbanefo
12	Okongwu B.O	Pol. Sc (LG)	E9, ZFH
13	Ejike Okonkwo	Engineering	421 Akpabio
14	Ezenwa Chike	Pol. Sc.	421 Akpabio
15	Iheanetu Mike	Psychology	421, Akpabio
16	Enemaku Alex	Pol. Sc	103 Isa
17	Obiora Moneke	Mass Comm.	B2/204 Alvan
18	Asuzu Johnny	History	115 Okeke

19	Akalonu, M.	Maths	321 Isa
20	Titilola Bayo	Pol Sc.	A1/115 Eni
21	Ezeazu Emma	History	107 Mbanefo
22	Aja Nwachukwu N.P	Vet Med	434 Mbanefo
23	Agu, K.I	Philosophy	A2/206 ZFH
24	Uwadoko Christian	Econs	C2/206 ZFH
25	Okonkwo Okey U	Soc/Anth	216, Slessor
26	Nwagu, C.C	Pol. Sc.	217B Awo
27	Onyejekwe Kele C.	Mass Comm	B2/201 Alvan
28	Agbo Chijioke		
29	Uyot Chris	Mass Comm	A5/202 ZFH
30	Morebise, Adelabu	Pol Sc	303 Okeke
31	Nwogbo, D.C	Pol Sc	B1/406 Alvan
32	Gafaru, A.O	Pol Sc	A1/214 Eni
33	Ilesanmi, K.	Religion	314 Akintola

(This clarion call for re-commitment to the ideals of the movement in the form of revolutionary admonition is a standard administrative measure in instilling discipline among members. Its exuberant nature attests to the zeal of the movement's leadership and its sufficient mastery of the historical tradition of revolutionarily enforced discipline within the ranks of revolutionary youth movements, but surely not as implacable and fanatical as the measure adopted by the anarchist Nachaev in Russia.)

MARXIST YOUTH MOVEMENT
UNIVERSITY OF NIGERIA, NSUKKA

It has become historically necessary, even though regrettable to inform members that ever since the session commenced a state of incommunicado has developed between the secretariat and members owing to lack of contact addresses. Many members change their hostels and rooms of residence without deeming it fit to relay their new contact address to the secretariat.

We are constrained to view this attitude as the highest summit of revolutionary inaction and inexactitude. Therefore, the secretariat has resolved to launch a frontal attack against this passivity that smacks of ideological bankruptcy. Members are advised to link-up before Thursday 11 November, 1982.

We make it bold to say that if the popular, just cause we stand for must not suffer unnecessarily from nonchalant approach by a handful of members then iron revolutionary discipline must not only be maintained but continually reinforced. On the strength of this, members are strongly and strictly advised to link up or face the devastating aftermath.

You can link up with the following:

Omonijo, M.	Udenta.O Udenta
33YA Akpabio	215 Okeke
Egini, P.A	Umoru, O.J
E5, 2FH	A2, 223 Eni Njoku
Emma Ezeanzu	Anyagbaoso, J.O.J
107 Mbanefo	B2303 Flats

"Every generation, out of relative obscurity, discovers its mission, betrays it or fulfils it."

....

Signed	Signed
Udenta O. Udenta	Femi Ahmed
Sec. for Publicity	Sec. General

(The following two agendas of the meetings of the CC clearly demonstrate how serious the movement took itself, the depth and breadth of its intellectual and strategic engagements and the maturity of its leading cadres. The topics listed were developed by the students without any input from their Staff Adviser(s). These topics will be assigned to various members who have the revolutionary obligation of researching into them, writing them and presenting them to audiences made up of students, lecturers and workers. The 'Kunle Adepoju' solidarity day refers to one of the most revered if not sacred students' observances in commemoration of Kunle Adepoju who was killed by the repressive state apparatus during the students' protest against the Gen. Olusegun Obasanjo's retrogressive educational policies in 1978.)

CC MEETING OF 15ᵀᴴ JANUARY, 1982

1. Kunle Adepoju's Day – Feb 1

   (Press release)

   Speeches at jointly organized solidarity rally.

   Student workshop theme: Student Unionism in the 80s

   a. Student Role in Social Development
   b. Students as Oppressed Class in Our Society: Past, Present and Prospects.
   c. Conscious Student Activism: A Challenge to the Ruling Class.
   d. Social Dislocation and Graduate Unemployment: Prospect in the 80's.
   e. Toward a Joint Student-Worker Action Committee: Experiment in the 80's
   f. Student Unionism, Activism and Partisanism
   g. Student Unionism in the 80s: What Future, What Goals?
   h. Other solidarity days in the month
   i. Orientation for new members – papers and other logistics
   j. Organic relationship between the movement and the workers, lecturers' groups and workers education programme.

CC MEETING OF 10/1/82
VENUE PAA

Agenda:

1. Meeting
2. Activities for the session
   a. Admissions
   b. Political education, cell system
   c. Ideological studies/public debate
   d. Revolutionary path
   e. Solidarity days and other commemorations
3. Organizational issues and programme for action
   a. Bureau and committees
   b. Organizational guidelines/structure
   c. Orientation of new members.
4. Organic relationship between the movement and the workers/ lecturer's groups.
5. Newsletter and *Valley Echo* Magazines
6. General.

(Typically, as is the practice in most revolutionary organizations, the GC usually comes after the meeting of the CC and traditionally ratifies most, if not all, the recommendations/decisions of the CC)

GENERAL CONGRESS OF THE MARXIST YOUTH MOVEMENT HELD ON 14 JANUARY, 1982

Agenda:

1. Activities for the session
   a. Admissions
   b. Political education
   c. Ideological studies
   d. Solidarity days and other commemorations
2. Organizational issues and programme for action
   a. Bureau and committees
   b. Organizational guidelines/structure
   c. Orientation of new members
3. Newsletter and *Valley Echo* Magazines
4. General.

(Nothing better explains the totality of the revolutionary work plan of the movement, the depth of its leadership's understanding and mastery of the key concepts in Marxism and the world revolutionary process and its mature vision about the kind of society it desires for Nigeria and Africa than this incomplete report of the Political Education Committee. Even today I marvel at the range of discourses we handled as young adults barely out of our teen years, and most regrettably the decay and collapse of radical student unionism in Nigeria under intense pressure from global late, postmodern capitalism.)

EDUCATION COMMITTEE REPORT (MYM)

Agenda:

i.   Topics
ii. Speakers
iii. Time (duration)
iv. Structure
v.   Policy
vi. Venue

The education committee, according to the Secretary General, Mr Femi Ahmed, is solely responsible for the political education class and formulating education policy.

This is so because there is the need to develop the revolutionary intelligentsia. In fact, the committee is seen as the prima-inter pars of all the committees. It is through the recommendations of the education committee that the movement can come up with some revolutionary strategies.

The topics chosen should relate to the African situation. Every member of the movement must deliver not less than one topic a year. It was finally agreed that a topic should be assigned to two persons so that every member should have the chance to express his opinion.

Both the Secretary General of the movement and the Chairman of the committee agreed that only the members of the movement should be selected to speak in order to develop the individual's awareness of the Marxist theory.

For effective development of the individual theoretically, the movement had been grouped into two. These are the main campus and the down campus. The Chairman of the Education Committee should lead the down campus side while the Secretary General, Mr Femi Ahmed, will lead those from the main campus.

Each side will present topics once a week while the first sitting will be once in two weeks.

Side A, i.e. down will present on Saturday while side B,

i.e. main campus will present on Sundays. The venue is Princess Alexandria Auditorium (P.A.A.) and the time for each is 8:30 pm.

The joint meeting which will be held once in two weeks will be on Wednesday night by 8:30 pm at P.A.A. room 102. The Education Committee Secretary should be in charge of the movement library. The present arrangement remains until further notice.

The Topics

1. Classes and Class Struggle
2. Marxist Conception of Imperialism
3. Apartheid as a Function of Imperialism
4. Failure of Socialism in Africa
5. Historical and Dialectical Materialism
6. Dialectics of Capitalist Development
7. Marxist Conception of Alienation and Social Change
8. Labour Theory of Surplus Value
9. Wage Labour and Capital
10. Marxism and Religion
11. Socialism, Scientific and Utopian
12. Multinational Corporations and the Question of Development in Africa
13. Marxist Conception of the State
14. Nigerian Educational Policy and Relevance to Society
15. The Russian Revolution
16. The Angolan revolution
17. The Cuban Revolution
18. The Portuguese Revolution
19. The Algerian Revolution
20. The Ethiopian Revolution

(This note from one of the movement's leading lights clearly illustrates not only the seriousness with which revolutionary duties are taken but also the excruciating pressure movement's activities exert on academic work. Many comrades do manage to achieve a delicate balance between these two sets of obligations but oftentimes academic work did take a back seat to revolutionary commitment with unpleasant consequences. My level of devotion was such that when the degree results came out my friends, associates, admirers and even fellow comrades were busy searching for my degree result under the Social Sciences column (the principal membership domain of the movement) rather than in the English Department's section, my course of study. They least expected that the Secretary General of the movement read English and not Political Science, Sociology or Philosophy.)

Udenta

I got your note on my return from Dept yesterday. From my point of view I think it would have been better if a CC meeting had been summoned to consider other options since it was the CC that decided that we use the other system.

In any case, since you're resolved that members of the movement be used for the registration, we may explore that angle BUT I will not be able to partake in the recruitment drive because:

1. I have two exams for which I'm ill-prepared next week. I will therefore have to concentrate on a crash programme (Monday and Wednesday).

2. I have a Pseudo-Research paper to submit on or before Monday. I'm yet to choose even the topic.

3. Also, it will be impossible for Comrades Evans and Kolade to participate since the former is sick and in addition has an exam next week (a sudden one) and the latter will have to take two exams next week in addition to other great commitments.

In view of the above, therefore, I think there are two options open: (1) that the exercise be postponed till after next week Wednesday; and (2) that other people be used for the exercise.

In any case, since Femi lives down Franco and is therefore nearer Chris than myself and since he must have been there when the decision was taken, I think it will be better if he were contacted to contact Chris for necessary action in that part of the campus. I wholeheartedly support your actions so far on the NANS issue.

— Omonijo, M. A.

(*Revolutionary Path* is the flagship publication of the movement. It is written every week and mass circulated all over the campus. Topics range from topical local issues, national issues, international issues, remembrances of great revolutionary occasions, moments and personalities to serious theoretical and ideological matters that will educate, inspire and motivate students.)

REVOLUTIONARY PATH

TO AROUSE CRITICAL CONSCIOUSNESS
NO 120782
SOCIALISM AS A HIGHER FORM OF PEOPLE'S DEMOCRACY

Capitalism and Socialism can be comparatively defined as follows:

Capitalism: A system which permits the unchecked enslavement, subjugation and exploitation of the great masses of the people of a society at the hands of the few, the tiny minority who own and control the means of production. It is also a system which maintains callousness towards the misery of the masses whose anguish under the oppression of hunger, want, ignorance, unemployment, social injustices and suppression of man by man remains unattended to. The sole emphasis under this system is the creation of capital and profit from the supplies value of the workers' sweat.

A capitalist is any person who believes in practices, condones and connives with the penetration and perpetuation of this atrocious and barbaric system.

Socialism: This is a system which sets out to emancipate the workers and peasants from the enslaving clutches and tyranny of capitalist exploitation, and gives the avenue for the fullest material, intellectual and psychological development and advancement of the masses. The economic basis of socialism is public ownership of the means of production; the social basis is the equality of all citizens. Under socialism the condition for the happiness, dignity, security and welfare of each individual is the condition for the happiness, dignity, security, and welfare for all.

Nigeria is a clientele, neo-colonial capitalist state with all the seamy and torrid manifestation of this bankruptcy nearly manifest.

Alliance of all progressive forces will surely and steadily bring the required change.

JOIN THE STRUGGLE!

Issued by the publicity bureau, Marxist Youth Movement.

(This sample invitation is interesting on several scores. It demonstrates the serious revolutionary intent of the movement in organizing a week of revolutionary activities (symposium, book fair, marches, drama sketches, etc), the degree of fraternal relationship between revolutionary student cadres and their comrade lecturers, and the maturity of topics selected by the students themselves.)

THE MARXIST YOUTH MOVEMENT
UNIVERSITY OF NIGERIA, NSUKKA

c/o Secretary General,
Room 213c, Isa Kaita.
17th September, 1982.

Professor Claude Ake,
Department of Sociology,
School of Social Sciences,
University of Port-Harcourt.

MARXIST YOUTH MOVEMENT WEEK 15TH TO 20TH OCTOBER, 1982

The above mentioned patriotic organization is organizing her first ever week scheduled below.

We will be very grateful if you will accept to deliver a paper at symposium on "Political Economy of Africa", on 20th November, 1982.

Venue will be communicated to you as soon as we receive your message of acceptance.

_____
Signed
Femi Ahmed
Secretary General

THE MARXIST YOUTH MOVEMENT
UNIVERSITY OF NIGERIA, NSUKKA

c/o Secretary General,
Room 213c, Isa Kaiter.
17th September, 1982.

Professor Segun Osoba,
Department of History,
University of Ife,
Ile-Ife.

MARXIST YOUTH MOVEMENT WEEK 15TH TO 20TH OCTOBER, 1982

The above mentioned patriotic organization is organizing her first ever week scheduled below.

We will be very grateful if you will accept to deliver a paper at the symposium/public lecture on "The Unfinished Revolution in Southern Africa" on 18th November, 1982.

Venue will be communicated to you as soon as we receive your message of acceptance.

Signed
Femi Ahmed
Secretary General

THE MARXIST YOUTH MOVEMENT
UNIVERSITY OF NIGERIA, NSUKKA

c/o Secretary General,
Room 213c, Isa Kaiter.
17th September, 1982.

Professor Ola Oni,
Department of Economics,
University of Ibadan,
Ibadan.

MARXIST YOUTH MOVEMENT WEEK 15TH TO 20TH OCTOBER, 1982

The above mentioned patriotic organization is organizing her first ever week scheduled below.

We will be very grateful if you will accept to deliver a paper at the symposium/public lecture on "Dialectics of Revolutionary Struggle in Nigeria" on 19th November, 1982.

Venue will be communicated to you as soon as we receive your message of acceptance.

_____
Signed
Femi Ahmed
Secretary General

THE MARXIST YOUTH MOVEMENT
UNIVERSITY OF NIGERIA, NSUKKA

c/o Secretary General,
Room 213c, Isa Kaiter.
17th September, 1982.

Director General,
National Institute of National Policy
and Strategic Studies
Kuru, Jos.

MARXIST YOUTH MOVEMENT WEEK 15TH TO 20TH OCTOBER, 1982

The above mentioned patriotic organization is organizing her first ever week below scheduled below.

We will be very grateful if you will accept to deliver a paper at the symposium on the "Role of The Intelligentsia in Social Development" on 20th November, 1982.

Venue will be communicated to you as soon as we receive your message of acceptance.

_____
Signed
Femi Ahmed
Secretary General

(The events marked on the dates indicated speak for themselves. They represent, in their singularity and totality, the world view and consciousness of all comrades-students, lecturers and workers alike. For members of the movement these dates have a sacredness that is almost spiritual in nature, context and content. The lives of members revolve around these observances in their contribution to the raising of consciousness, dedication to the struggle and implacable enmity with capitalism.)

BELOW ARE SOME EVENTS AND THEIR DATES, FOUND TO BE WORTHWHILE COMMEMORATING

DATE	YEAR	EVENT
Jan. 10th	1959	Cuban Revolution
Jan. 20th	1973	Amilcar Cabral's Day –Death of
Jan. 21st	1961	Patrice Lumumba's Day –Death of
Feb. 1st	1971	Students Solidarity day in Kunle Adepoju's memory
Feb. 3rd	1969	Eduado Mondlame's Day–First President of FRELIMO (assassinated).
March 8th	1910	International Women's Day
March 21st	1961	Sharpeville Massacre in South Africa
April 20th	1978	Students Ali-Must Go Massacre Day
April 26th	1980	Bakolori Massacre Day
May 1st		May Day- International Workers Day
May 10th	1973	Formation of POLISARIO–beginning of struggle
May 25th		Day of Solidarity with Palestinian Struggle
May 25th		Africa Day
June 7th	1981	Unife Massacre day
June 12th	1964	Nelson Mandela's Day
June 13th	1980	Walter Rodney's Day–Death of
June 16th	1976	Soweto Massacre Day
June 25th	1975	Mozambique Independence Day

July 1st	1970	Birth of the EPLF (Eritrean Peoples Liberation Front).
August 8th		Namibia Day
Sept. 9th	1979	Death of Chairman Mao.
Sept 11TH	1979	Dr. Agostino Neto's Death
October 1st	1949	Victory of the Chinese Revolution
October 7th	1917	Great October Revolution in Russia
Nov. 17th		International Students Day
Nov. 18th	1949	Iva Valley Massacre Day
Nov. 11th	1975	Angolan Independence Day
Dec. 6th	1961	Frantz Fanon's Day
Nov. 14th	1962	Forceful Annexation of Eritrea (abrogation of the Federation) and the forceful annexation of Eritrea by the USA backed expansionist Ethiopia Regime.
October 8th	1967	Che Guevara's Day-death of, in Bolivia

(The Great October Socialist Revolution in Russia was arguably the most important commemorative event. The reason for this is not far-fetched. Soviet Union was the birth place and spiritual abode of world socialism, the leader of the world revolutionary process, the defender of socialist internationalism while its super power status and mortal ideological combat with Western imperialism was a ready source of inspiration and pride to all Marxists. In our naivety, we assimilated all the intellectual and ideological message that flew from it without question, with religious zeal and canonical finality. Being either unaware or dismissive of the Western intellectual current critical of Sovietized Marxism, we saw in that variant the only correct path to socialism. The collapse of the Soviet Union and the retreat of EuroMarxism was devastating, to say the least, to world view of many a Third World Marxist but this is a different subject altogether.)

66TH ANNIVERSARY OF THE GREAT OCTOBER SOCIALIST REVOLUTION IN RUSS1A

Today definitely marks the 66th anniversary of the Great October Socialist Revolution in the Soviet Union. Today is a great day of remembrance by all patriotic, progressive and committed people the world over, because it is the day that the forces of reaction, oppression and bastardization were uprooted and a new egalitarian and contradiction-free social order established. In international perspective, the significance of the socialist revolution in Russia could not be over stressed. It is a source of inspiration to all repressed people, a source of courage to all revolutionary movements that for long have locked themselves in a dialectical struggle with the forces of capitalism and international imperialism.

What lessons of history is there in the "10 days that shook the world?"

One, it is that a definite time in history will come when the ruling class can as longer rule as in the old days when there was pretension to democracy and the toiling masses– proletariat and the peasantry–can also no longer live as they used to live in the old ways when life was manageable. When such objective condition has ripened and coupled with the class consciousness of the working people and their grasp of the basic revolutionary situation socialist revolution will surely occur.

Two, that the forces of repression and subjugation will learn their lesson because of their stinking desire to consolidate their class base and tighten the manacles on the people the more. For us Nigerians while we reel from the shock of our falsified history, from the drama of electoral awards, deceit, economic woes and social stupor, let us hope and strive, for the guiding influence of the Great October Socialist Revolution will definitely penetrate our being and bring the much needed dose of revolutionary injection that will be our only salvation.

Long live the Courageous Soviet Comrades!
Long live all Fighters for Justice!
Long live the Working Class Movement!
Aluta Continua!

Issued by the Solidarity Days
Committee, MYM CC:

MARXIST YOUTH MOVEMENT
UNIVERSITY OF NIGERIA, NSUKKA.
PATRICE LUMUMBA SOLIDARITY DAY–21ST JANUARY.

Today, we join progressive forces the world over in remembering our comrade who along with other close associates (Mpolo and Okito) was cruelly murdered by imperialist-colonialist Belgian forces aided by local renegades and bankrupt retrogressive elements like Joseph Kasavubu, Moise Tshombe and Mobutu Sese Seko. He is Patrice Lumumba, the first Prime Minister of Independent Congo who fought comradely against balkanization and neo-colonial incursion into the country. For this, he paid the supreme price.

The lesson imperialists have refused to learn is that the murder of one or two progressive revolutionaries cannot in any way deter the revolution. It may be true that it may be delayed but surely liberation must come. Take the case of Zaire (formerly Congo Leopoldville or Kinshasa) for example. While it is true that since Lumumba was murdered exactly 22 years ago there had been no much progress towards the Revolution, we all know that the forces of retrogression cannot hold forte for a long time again. In this, we believe the situation in Zaire today justifies us. Today, Zaire is the only Black African Country that maintains diplomatic relations with Zionist Israel in addition to being the greatest lackey of the leader of the Capitalist countries-United States of America. This is clearly depicted in the fact that Zaire could not attend the last abortive O.A.U. Summit because of some diplomatic maneuvers between her and Israel.

However, we need to mention some lessons taught us by the Congolese crises itself. Foremost among this is the fact that the United Nations Organization is still as presently constituted by the same Anti-Progress forces that collaborated with Belgian forces in denigrating Congolese sovereignty. Secondly, this reinforces the necessity for true African Unity and hence the need for Pan-African force which Nkrumah advocated for. Thirdly, we note the fact that the Bourgeois camp will always face constant feud born out of the criminal struggle among the bankrupt elements in the Bourgeois Camp. The fact that is was Mobutu who ousted Joseph Kasavubu and Tshombe in a coup d'etat on 25th November, 1965 attests to this.

We realize that this picture can be generalized and extended to cover all other conservative countries in Africa led by Kenya. Nigeria is no exception.

DO NOT PITY, MOBILISE!
JOIN THE STRUGGLE!!
ALUTA CONTINUA!!!

Issued by the Central Committee of the Marxist Youth Movement.

MARXIST YOUTH MOVEMENT CENTENARY OF MARX'S DEATH–14TH MARCH, 1983

Today, we are commemorating the 100 years anniversary of Karl Marx's death. Marx was born on May 1818 and died on March 14,1883. Karl Marx stands out among the great men of history. Not only was he, with the co-operation of his closest friend, Fredrich Engels, the originator and formulator of the blazing ideas of scientist socialism and the tactics of the great proletarian class struggle, but Marx also a great philosopher, genuine practical revolutionary and organizer of the working class movement (First Communist International).

Marx gave socialism a broad, scientific world out and took away from it utopian embellishments and speculations and developed it into the greatest, reliable, developed and advanced of the social systems starting from the band days through the instrument of dialectics. Marx enhanced the historical process of the man's development by showing the tortured and beleaguered stages of mankind's progress, the causes and courses of historical changes, contradictions in the old systems, including capitalism, through the restoration of property into public lands and the socialization of the means of production.

Marxist analysis of the capitalist accumulation of capital and the dynamics of capitalist development has a special relevance for us today, because not only has Capitalism becomes a world system, but its moribund, highest and oppressive stage, imperialism, has been used to manacle, gag, repress, exploit and dehumanize the concrete aspirations and genuine yearnings for freedom of the Third World countries of which Nigeria is one. The diction "the history of all existing societies is the history of class struggle, and all class struggle is a political struggle" shows that the interests of the working class and working people are irreconcilable and antithetical to those of the bourgeoisie.

While we commemorate this day we should realize that every progressive and class-conscious individual has a historical role and task. What is this task? To use the Marxist – Leninist teachings and revolutionary science to affect a fundamental change in our country's mode of production and political structure and the introduction of genuine independence and social organization and economic relations that are humanistic, objective and scientific.
That is what Marx fought for:
The Spirit of Marx Still Lives!
Aluta Continua!

Issued by the Solidarity Days Committee,
Marxist Youth Movement.

IN SOLIDARITY WITH OPPRESSED SOUTH AFRICANS–MARCH 21, 1982-22ND REMEMBRANCE OF THE SHARPVILLE MASSACRE, MARCH 21, 1960.

Today is exactly 22 years since the South African racist police opened fire on South Africans protesting against the introduction and ratification of the Obnoxious Pass Law; a law that condemns them to perpetual carriage of passbook, a law that irrevocably identities and singles them out for oppression, victimization, suppression and crude exploitation.

Today marks the 22 years since the guns boomed in Sharpeville and scorching shrapnel's tore the souls of the freedom fighters. It was not only a racist cum Apartheid blow and onslaught but the onslaught of international imperialism and national capitalism, the two instruments that perpetuate and consolidate the apartheid regime.

As those blacks lay writhing in the throes of agony and death on that fateful day, so is an Asian, American, El Salvadoran, and Irish worker or peasant tormented and brutalized by the forces of international exploitation. The time has come when sober reflection should be made on apartheid and racism. Both are disgusting, repressive and bloody systems directed not against a particular race, because without the embellishment, propagation, abetment and support of capitalism and imperialism its historical growth could since have been halted.

It is a regime of exploitation and violence aimed at the working people, the proletariat, the peasant and the progressive intelligentsia, the blacks inclusive.

It is a non-restrictive system with international character; a system chained to the apron string of international capitalism, local reaction and comprador bourgeois ethos.

Today marks our 22 years of solidarity and fraternal comradeship with the oppressed people of South Africa and all others, the world over. Today marks a new dimension and strategy in the course of national liberation and the emancipation of the working people and peasants of the black race in South Africa. Because the time demands resolute stand, confidence and dissemination of knowledge to the freedom fighters, the fight against apartheid does not mean war against the whole white race, against other races outside the people of black extraction. It means the systematic and methodological destruction of a class system, a system of oppression supported and aggravated by international imperialism and exploitation synonymous with most of the Western European countries, the USA, Britain, Canada, France, W. Germany and Israel prominent among them.

We also seize this opportunity of our solidarity and Remembrance Day to caution all progressives, all lovers of the working class and peasants, and sympathizers with the pathetic and tragic South African problem to watch with wariness the double dealing of most African Countries, Nigeria included. While secretly supporting imperialism and apartheid, while flirting with international capitalists and exploiters, while having shady deals with the South African regime, working closely with certain S.A companies, these governments will shamelessly and hypocritically cry "Down with apartheid, a disgraceful humanity", and "we are poised to eradicate racism, colonialism etc." These are mere bogus bourgeois insincere deceit because the class character of capitalism and apartheid is the same and these countries will not genuinely fight for its destruction.

In this commemoration of the black 21st March, 1960, in this our solidarity with the S.A peoples we state, as true Marxist and socialist, that the solution to the imbroglio is a unified action by all progressive African governments, consolidation of the popular support of the world socialist countries and march to victory not only to destroy the repressive and illegal South African regime, but that of ZAIRE, MOROCCO, NIGERIA, KENYA, EGYPT which are all dependent and client, all cesspool of international capitalism and exploitative imperialism, all entangled in the high monopoly finance capital market, all not less bloody than the South African Regime.

We finally urge all progressive peoples of South Africa of whatever race to intensity their revolutionary struggle, that the whole lovers of peace and progress are behind them.

LONG LIVE THE ANC!!!

LONG LIVE THE JUST STRUGGLE OF THE SOUTH AFRICAN PEOPLES FOR SELF-DETERMINATION!!!

LONG LIVE OUR SOLIDARITY WITH THE SOUTH AFRICAN FREEDOM FIGHTERS!!!

The struggle definitely continues:

Issued by Solidarity Days Committee, Central Committee (CC), Marxist Youth Movement.

(This short release was issued about 1982, yet all the issues raised in it still resonate in the Nigeria of the 21st century, from mass pauperization of the people, battle over minimum living wage, corruption by the political and bureaucratic elite and labour strikes. In very many respects, the nation's political, economic and social circumstances have taken a turn for the worst.)

LABOUR MOVEMENT–STRIKES GALORE

It must be admitted, even if I had not proved it so often in detail, that the Nigerian workers cannot feel happy in this condition, that theirs is not a state in which a man or a whole class of men can think, feel and live as human beings. The workers must therefore strive to escape from this brutalizing condition, to secure for themselves a better, more human position; and this they cannot do without attacking the bourgeoisie which persists in exploiting them. But the bourgeoisie defends its interests with all the power placed at its disposal, and by the wealth and the might of the state. In proportion, as the working man determines to alter the present state of things, the bourgeoisie becomes his avowed enemy.

Moreover, the working-man is made to feel at every moment that the bourgeoisie treats him as a chattel, as its property, and for this reason, if for no other, he must come forward as its enemy. "Yes, ₦300 is too much as the minimum wage for the workers, it will ruin the economy" but the fantastic salary of the legislators, their riding flashy cars, making a man an institution to cover up the misappropriation of ₦2.8 billion, the award of ₦300 million contract for efficient telephone service with no result after four years, to mention but a few, are not wreaking the economy. What a pity.

To make the bourgeoisie cough out the portion of the "national cake" they have so greedily swallowed and thereby denied the proletariats their own portion, Nigerian workers must continue to unite and go on strike which is their only weapon, as of now revolts must continue, general consciousness must be awakened. It cannot be long again, when the long-awaited Nigerian Revolution must come. Nigerian Workers Get United.

Issued by the MYM Publicity Bureau

REVOLUTIONARY PATH
Vol. 040482

THE HISTORIC ROLE OF THE PROLETARIAT:
THE AFRICAN SITUATION

A modern proletariat already exists in Africa, though it is electively small in size. This is the class base for the building of socialism, and must be seen in the context of the international working class movement from which it derives much of its strength.

The emergence of the working class in Africa is associated with colonialism and imperialism and with foreign monopoly capital. In most areas, the size of the proletariat remained small because of the lack of large scale industrialization. However, in countries with most developed economies, such as Egypt and South Africa, a strong working class emerged. It was in these countries in the 1920s, where Africa's first communist parties, consisting of intellectuals, workers and peasants, were formed. At the same time, communist parties linked with the French communist parties were founded in Algeria, Morocco and Tunisia.

African workers played an important role in national liberation struggles. By strike action they succeeded in disrupting economic life and caused great embarrassment to the colonial administration.

There were general strikes in Kenya, Nigeria, Ghana and Guinea in the years leading up to independence. In addition, there were throughout colonial Africa innumerable strikes which affected particular sectors of the economy. During these strikes of which the Rand Miners strike of 1946 and the strikes in the Tanganyika Sisal Industry between 1957-9 are typical examples, mass feeling was awakened and workers became to some extent conscious of themselves as a class.

In recent years, the working class has been increasing in

Africa, considerably. It is the task of the proletariat to win the peasantry to revolution by taking the struggle to the countryside. But once the urban proletariat and peasants joined forces in the struggle to achieve socialism, the African revolution had in effect been won.

It has been argued by bourgeois theorists that the African peasants are too ignorant that it will take centuries to raise their level of consciousness. However, history had disproved this backward assumption and myth. The Agbekoya riots of 1968 in the Western region and the Bokolori uprising of 1980 are cases in point. These particular cases show that overexploitation of peasants will get them organized.

Workers are workers, and nationality, race, tribe, and religion are irrelevant in the struggle to achieve socialism

PROLETARIAN INTERNATIONALISM!

The Working Man has no Country!

Workers, farmers and progressive intelligentsia, GET ORGANISED!
YOU HAVE NOTHING TO LOSE BUT YOUR CHAINS.

This is so because the contradictions of our moribund class system can only be resolved by the enthronement of Socialism-THE PEOPLE'S HOPE!.

Issued by the Publicity Bureau,
Marxist Youth Movement.

REVOLUTIONARY PATH
Vol. 090482

SOCIALISM AND SOCIETY

Society's development today is characterized by the great role played in it by political factors. This makes it necessary to subject the political organization of society and the objective laws of its development to an all round examination.

Real socialism provides for the most equitable organization of society in the interest of the working people. Socialism is a society of real humanism. It values above all, the working man, everything for the sake of man, for the benefit of man. In it is the most profound meaning of the coming socialist reconstruction, culture and way of life.

Socialism is a society of emancipated labour, of genuine democracy, of people's participation in decision-making and policy implementation, of real individual freedom, and of most highly advanced science and norms. It abolishes oppression and destroys all relationships of exploitation, naked subjugation and repression that have reduced the working masses and the peasantry to the state and class of sub-human beings.

Socialism ensures full employment and provision of the real prerequisites for all round creative growth of all its citizens. Socialism is a society of social optimism, it assures and guarantees the proletariat and the peasantry continued creative development and welfare, believing in the maxim of "from each according to his ability, to all according to his needs".

It is the harbinger of peace, progress, respect of sovereignty of nations, equal co-operation between countries and sincere yearning for the betterment of the human lot. It, invariably, is a pillar of strength and succor, abode of refuge for all people fighting for their independence, to freedom fighters and national liberators.

Above all, socialism leads to the emergence of a classless society where all contradictions between man and man, mental and physical labour, have been totally annihilated.

In the face of bellicose aggression and intimidatory onslaught launched by the imperialists, their comprador bourgeois partners in the periphery and their witch-hunting local reactionary collaborators, we stand firm and resolute. In the face of repressive measures meted against the proletariat and the peasants, they remain stubborn in the struggle because THEY KNOW THAT THEY HAVE NOTHING

TO LOSE BUT THEIR CHAINS.

DARE TO STRUGGLE!

Issued by the Publicity Bureau,
Marxist Youth Movement.

REVOLUTIONARY PATH
Vol.1 No.1: 10382

TO AROUSE CRITICAL CONSCIOUSNESS
VICIOUS CIRCLE OF CONTRADICTION

Capitalism is inherently contradictory. If it is not intent, as a social system, indulging in the brutal exploitation and oppression of the proletariat and the peasantry, it finds this solace in the willful destruction and repression of its class agents. National bourgeoisie slugs it out with the agents of imperialism and multinational corporations.

Local reactionary comprador bourgeoisie enters into unholy battle with diehard feudal lords and the bureaucratic bourgeoisie. Individual and class interest move in a perilous dynamic of egoism and aggrandizement to swamp their ultimate class goals: domination and perpetuation of their class rule. Nigeria is no exception. The capitalists are at their mischief again.

Yesterday it was the burning of the independence building to cover up the culprit in the multimillion hemp deal involving Nigerian British embassy and diplomatic bags. Today it is the scandal of the House of Representatives Committee on Foreign Affairs trip to Switzerland totaling some millions of Naira.

Yesterday, the Airways building will have to go up in flames to cover the millions of national and international debt owed to the corporation. Yesterday Chief MKO Abiola will donate N1million at NPN launching and today one worker's child will die because of lack of medical centre.

Yesterday, Saraki, Nwankwu and Dantata will acquire contracts totaling billions, today a peasant lost his landholding for some non-existence comprador bourgeois government Agric Project.

- Like the Bakolori Massacre
- Like the Ife Massacre of students
- The progressive (or retrogressive) alliance vs NPN=ALL ONE CLASS.
- Like PARTY STALWART VS PARTY JUGGERNAUT

The circle widens but solidifies, it takes shape, the noose becomes thin.

Workers of Nigeria arise and seek for your right and freedom!

It is destined that you rule as you produce, that you control production as labour leads, it is your historic duty, you have nothing to lose but your chains.

Workers of all countries, unite!

Issued by the Publicity Bureau, Marxist Youth Movement.

REVOLUTIONARY PATH
NO. 050782
TO AROUSE CRITICAL CONSCIOUSNESS

THE NIGERIAN WORKING CLASS

The working class of Nigeria, like any other class society, constitutes a significant section of the oppressed and exploited. Through their daily sweat the continued existence of mankind is ensured, but the ruling class have consciously denied them a commensurate share of the fruits of their toil.

For Nigerian workers the experience has been hell. Their democracy has only meant going to vote for people who then turn around to use their legal power to brutally subjugate workers to poverty and misery. This year could be rightly described as the year of mass dismissal of workers. Thousands of workers have been retrenched by various companies because they want to maximize profit. The same holds true of the public sector.

While the meager allowances and salaries of the workers are delayed for as much as 3 months or even frozen as an austerity measure the exorbitant amounts used to pay the allowances and emolument of the legislators, executives, ministers, Plos', political, economic, water, fuel, air and food advisers and agents are provided promptly. As a result of the 'squandamania' and siphoning of public money to private coffers by the various state and federal governments the workers are once again stripped of their bare existence.

What Nigeria really needs is the intervention of the organized working class and farmers to democratize, nationalize and industrialize the nation, and the commanding heights of its economy. But the seeds of such a movement are already being planted and it will be the terrorism, swindling and treachery of the ruling class itself in the next years that will fertilize these seeds by teaching the working class just how useless and brutal the ruling class is and what great reserve of power and initiative the workers, farmers and students of Nigeria have.

ALUTA CONTINUA!

VICTORY IS CERTAIN!

Issued by the Publicity Bureau, MARXIST YOUTH MOVEMENT.

REVOLUTIONARY PATH
No: 040582

FUNERAL REQIUEM FOR IMPERIALISM?

Imperialism, we know, is the highest, most aggressive and violent stage of capitalism. Imperialism through its multidimensional and varied sources – high finance capital, international monopoly, multinationals, local comprador and bureaucratic bourgeoisie in the periphery, ruthlessly exploits nations and keeps the working class and the peasantry in a state of perpetual misery, exploitation, suppression and deprivation.

But lately imperialism's vicious sway and dominance especially in the developing countries has come under serious and systematic challenge by the deprived working class, peasants and the progressive intelligentsia. In this vein one must grasp the basic tenets of Lenin's definition of a revolutionary situation that can lead to the destruction of capitalism and imperialism. The objective factors have really matured and developed, the internal contradictions inherent in capitalism– cyclical crisis, depression, inflation– are now more apparent, and in some countries the subjective factor-workers' and peasants' consciousness of their class positions- is already manifest.

From far flung Asia, the working masses and the peasants, with the communist party vanguard, have buried once and for all the bastion of imperialist domination in Vietnam, Laos, Cambodia (Kampuchea) N. Korea, Mongolia, Albania, etc – and are busy reconstructing their societies along scientific socialist lines.

In Latin America – that wretched area of vicious oppression, feudo-capitalist entrenchment and foreign imperialist meddling– came the cheering news that Nicaragua, under Sandinista, has succeeded in destroying a local despot, Somoza, who was propped up by imperialism, and are already advancing steady towards the path of socialism, progress, peace and victory. El Salvador is in turmoil, Guatemala in confusion, Honduras, Bolivia and Chile are all quaking because of the rising force of the people to shatter a better course for themselves.

In Africa, the Polisarion, Eriterian, South African and Namibian struggle is increasing taking a class and anti-imperialist dimension. But is imperialism dead? No. No. Not until the last inch of the world is freed of its ugly and cold clutch. In this light we charge – "that the future will have no pity for those men who, possessing the exceptional privilege, of being able to speak words of truth to their oppressors, have taken refuge in an attitude of passivity, of mute indifference and sometime of cold complicity."

F. Fanon.

TAKE UP THE STRUGGLE, ALUTA CONTINUA! VICTORIA ASCERTA!

Issued by the Publicity Bureau,
MARXIST YOUTH MOVEMENT.

(The International Women's Day, celebrated every 8 March, is one of the most important solidarity events commemorated by the movement and indeed by all progressive associations and groups the world over. Reproduced below is the list of topics of the talks to be delivered by students and faculty alike in a seminar organized by the movement in commemoration of the Women's Day.)

INTERNATIONAL WOMEN'S DAY

(1) International Women's Day: Origin and its Significance in Contemporary Nigerian Society

(2) Sex Inequality: Myth or Reality.

(3) The Place of Women in the Struggle for an Egalitarian Society.

(4) A Comparative Study of the Place of Women in a Socialist and Capitalist / Neo-Colonial Society.

(5) Assessment of the Position of Women in Pre-Colonial and Post-Colonial Nigeria.

(6) Educated Women and the Problem of Social Acceptance in a Developing Country: Nigeria as a Case Study.

(This is is a sample copy of the cover of the magazine published by a fraternal student organization based at the University of Ilorin, Nigeria. The magazine is called *Struggle: The Theoretical and Organizational Journal of the MLMN* (Marxist Liberation Movement of Nigeria.)

MONTHLY PUBLICATION VOL. 2 NOS 9 & 10 SEPT. & OCT. 1980

MOTTO: GET ORGANIZED

IN THIS ISSUE:-

• The Exit of Paul Unongo: An Indictment of the Nigerian Ruling Class.

• Wahala or Independence: A Commentary on the 20th

Anniversary of Nigeria's Political Independence.
- The Minimum Wage Issue.
- New Style Pilgrimage: The Rush To America.
- The Question of National Unity and Sports.
- Yusuf Bala Usman and The Liberation of Nigeria: An Unaccomplished Task.

Address: Editorial workers,
c/o Hall D.,
University of Ilorin,
Ilorin, Kwara State,
Nigeria.

(When I joined the Marxist Youth Movement I was looking forward to a cohesive, united and disciplined entity. I was pained to be exposed to a fractious, disunited and disorganized structure, rent by ideological indirection, squabbling, opportunism and a measure of careerism. The movement was split right down the middle between a faction that favoured a less rigid application of doctrines, enforcement of rigorous ideological and political education demands on members, and a more diluted form of organization that opened its doors to 'petite bourgeois' elements, and a tendency that subscribed to a puristic interpretation of dialectical and historical materialism, the political and ideological tasks the movement must execute and the strategies for realizing them. I was essentially caught between these two tendencies, in part because of my relative newness to the fraternity and also as a consequence of my limited knowledge of Marxism. I was eventually selected as the Secretary of the Fact-Finding/Disciplinary Committee set up by the GC to get to the root causes of the conflict bedeviling the movement and recommend appropriate sanctions against erring members.

Even though I eventually threw in my lot with the puritanical tendency led by Femi Ahmed that emerged as the dominant force within the movement at the conclusion of the tasks set before the committee which led to the purging of its ranks, when I became the Secretary General in 1982, I adopted a more moderate, centrist ideological perspective that opened up the ranks of the movement to wider followership and made it become arguably the most formidable and respected group on campus.

The following minutes, reports, recommendations, etc of the committee demonstrate, as nothing else would, the ideological maturity of the movement, the commitment of its membership to its principled ideological and political causes and the dialectical process that led to the construction of a new synthesis within its organizational domain. Beyond these objectives, my intention is not to impugn on the character of any comrade regardless of the ideological tendency he/she purveyed; if anything, I held and still hold all my comrades in the movement to the highest possible esteem and respect.)

MARXIST YOUTH MOVEMENT
INVESTIGATION COMMITTEE,
U.N.N
25 – 1 – 82

"Sample"

....
....
....
....

Sir,

INVITATION TO MEET THE ABOVE COMMITTEE

We will like to choose this opportunity in inviting you to appear before the above committee on Friday 29 – 1 – 82, 8 pm at the Princess Alexandria Auditorium.

After the General Congress of the Movement sat on Thursday 21 Jan, 1982, it was resolved that the above committee should be set up to investigate and clarify certain unwarranted happenings in the movement, especially the subject of Nkem Abonta's untimely resignation as the Secretary General.

It is the sincere hope of the committee that your attendance and subsequent contributions will help in no small a way in the settling of these anomalies. Endeavour to be punctual.

Sincerely Yours,

Udenta O. Udenta
Secretary

Cc
Femi Ahmed
Joe Anyanwu
Innocent Akenuwa
Nkem Abonta

MARXIST YOUTH MOVEMENT
INVESTIGATION COMMITTEE

Sitting on 12 – 2 – 82
Members: Antifon, R, Enemaku, A and Udenta O. Udenta
Guest: Joe Anyanwu

The meeting started about 8.03 pm

The chairman of the committee, Antifon, R, began by stressing that the invitee's duty is to give the Committee necessary information that will help it in its investigation.

Joe Anyanwu thanked the members and started by saying that as a member of the movement and the past CC, that the movement's interest should be paramount. His information, he said, will be unemotional and objective.

On sabotage charges leveled against Abonta, he said he has not much to say. The area he is very much concerned with is the resignation – not the resignation in itself, but the manner it was carried out. He said that the manner of

Abonta's resignation as the Secretary General of the movement smarts of complicity and sabotage against the movement. He maintained that Abonta had manifested this in his actions since a long time on the specific areas he sited

(a) That Abonta treated the issue of scheduling meetings in a lukewarm attitude. He was reluctant to summon CC meetings in September.

(b) During his discussion with Abonta in December, Abonta said that he is going to resign, that he is now a Social Democrat and that he is going on philosophical incubation.

(c) That on the Jan. account giving meeting where Abonta tendered in his resignation paper, that he objected on the following grounds:

    (i) That the resignation is untimely

    (ii) That the CC meeting is not the right place to do it

    (iii) Joe maintained that as the giving of account should be the last CC meeting for the session that Abonta's tenure of office is ending so it is improper for him (Abonta) to resign at that time as he did.

Joe made it known to the committee that he challenged Abonta on the reasons for his resignation – because the philosophical reason Abonta gave is very vague – to this Abonta did not explain.

ON MISCONDUCT
Joe said that Abonta is a real and inspiring figure in the movement but as from September 1981, he started seeing new changes in Abonta – behavior which is capable of damaging the image of the movement.

At this point Alex said, on the question of resignation, that Abonta did it near the end of the CC – but Joe still maintained that the manner of the resignation is still not clear.

Antifon wanted Joe to tell the committee how the CC received the resignation.

Joe said that the CC was divided – that the question should

be taken to the congress for revaluation, but the CC verbally accepted the resignation.

On Abonta's stand that no objection was raised by his resignation in the CC – Joe was against it and pointed out that there was objection and that Abonta's resignation as the Sec. General should go hand in hand with his resignation from the movement.

    (a)   Joe further said that on the first congress for the session Abonta did not come

    (b)   The second one he did not come.

    (c)   The congress that set-up this committee – he was absent

On Antifon's suggestion as to whether the CC wrote any letter to Abonta after the resignation, Joe and Alex maintained that the time was short and the Congress meeting is already at hand.

When Antifon wanted to know if Abonta had at any time told him that he never believed in Marxism, Joe said that Abonta had never told him.

On Abonta's statement that nobody can even tell the number of files in his possession and there is no record whatsoever to show it, Joe said that it goes at length to amplify Abonta's complicity and sabotage.

Joe still said that when he told Abonta that as he was resigning as the Secretary General, he should handover the files – Abonta said that Joe should come and collect it or when the new Secretary General gets elected he should come and collect it.

Further Joe said that Abonta sorted out the movement's documents and those of Awareness – 1 Club together in their presence, (he and Femi Ahmed) – for 3 hours. So he, Abonta, could still have exchanged some documents. Joe wanted to know why Abonta should mix the Marxist Movement files with those of Awareness – 1 Club.

At the meeting scheduled at Femi's room, Joe said that he got an invitation inviting him to a meeting at 213c Isa Kaita Hostel–Femi's room–signed by Femi. When he asked

Abonta whether he has got any circular, Abonta said no, that Ogbaji said that it is an improper meeting but Joe said that they should attend.

(a) Joe said that first question he put to Femi was why he scheduled a meeting without inviting Abonta. Femi said that Abonta got the circular and was instrumental in the scheduling of the meeting.

(b) Joe asked him (Femi) if it is his constitutional right to summon a meeting. He wanted to know if Femi met with the Secretary for Publicity. To this Femi had no answer.

Antifon concluded by saying that he is satisfied with Joe's answers and that if the committee is in need of his help again he would not hesitate in inviting him. Joe said he would respond in any way.

On this note the meeting was adjourned about 9 pm till 14 – 2 – 82

MARXIST YOUTH MOVEMENT
INVESTIGATION COMMITTEE

Sitting on 14 – 2 – 82
Members; Antifon, R, Ememaku, A, and Udenta O. Udenta
Guests: FEMI AHMED and NKEM ABONTA

The meeting began about 11:15 pm

The chairman, Antifon, R, began by thanking the guest, Ahmed, F, for appearing before the committee and urged him to start from treating the question of Abonta's role in the retrogression of the MYM and his abrupt resignation.

Femi started by saying that the question of Abonta's resignation would be seen together with the general progress of the movement and its redundancy. He apologized for his inability to appear before the committee before now. He said that it was due to certain unavoidable circumstances, but he said any indictment charge against him for laxity would be accepted.

He said that the problem of the MYM could be traced to Abonta's conscious effort to retard the progress of the movement. This can be seen during:

(a) PYM Congress where he was seriously discredited on the question of religion

(b) In political education classes where Abonta appeared directionless and lax.

(c) He said that in any progressive and revolutionary movement, the theoretical level is necessary for praxis. But the movement lacks direction and dynamism because of Abonta's concerted effort not to make things move – Abonta's lack of zeal and laxity had reached a stage in his intellectual development when he started to be anti-Marxist. He also stressed that Abonta was unable to apply his theoretical knowledge of Marxism on practical issues, hence his ideological confusion.

(d) He said that Abonta's resignation came as a result of pressure from the progressives when he (Abonta) knew that he was washed up as a Marxist. Femi maintained that Abonta was isolated by the PYM, they do not correspond with him anymore and the PYM said they would stop corresponding with the movement if we do not eject him from the movement.

(e) Abonta said that he would use every pint of his blood to fight Marxism and would set up a counter-revolutionary journal to combat Marxism.

(f) That from the whole of 1980 – when Abonta resigned – Abonta never summoned any CC or General Congress meeting – CC meetings were not summoned through his initiative.

ABONTA BECAME THE SECRETARY GENERAL ON THE 6TH OF MAY 1980

On Antifon's question on how many CC meetings have been summoned and who initiated the meetings – Femi said that CC meetings came as and when due. He said that they constantly pressed Abonta on the need to have CC meetings.

On forces forcing Abonta to resign Femi said that when the PYM met on March 1980, Abonta as Sec. Gen. presided. but during emergency meeting preceding the G.C – some comrades from Zaria were skeptical about Abonta's commitment and said that the PYM G.C should be cancelled.

On the Annual Congress the comrades said that any religious subjective views should be indicated and Abonta was exposed.

Concerning the Struggle Magazine – since a year now it has not been sent through Abonta – but through the student union.

Femi further said that Abonta is alienated from some progressive movements in the country, like:

1. Anti-Imperialist Youth Front (AYF)–Bayero University, Kano.
2. Movement for Progressive Nigeria (MPN)–Ahmadu Bello University, Zaria
3. Movement for Advanced Socialist Society (MASS)– University of Jos
4. Alliance of the Progressive Students (APS)–University of Ife (now Obafemi Awolowo University, Ife)

He is also alienated by some powerful comrades like:

1. Comrade Rauf
2. Comrade Chom Bagu
3. Comrade Bavar Zimir
4. Comrade Tom Adambara
5. Comrade 'Dapo Oluyomi
6. Comrade Biodun Shofunke
7. Comrade Huzzein Abdulrahman

On financial account and general summary of his tenure of office, Abonta said that he has sufficiently said much about it during CC meeting that there is no need repeating it here.

On the issue concerning the movement's file – Antifon wanted to know why he refused to hand over the file during the CC meeting. When Abonta said that he informed Joe Anyanwu to come and collect them in his room, Antifon was against it because it was irregular and somehow out of conformity with the laws guiding such matters. Antifon continued that the congress was made to understand that he, Abonta, was reluctant in handing over the files.

Alex in support said that Abonta agreed only to hand the files to the new Secretary General. This he said was further buttressed when he (Abonta) met Joe Anyanwu on the Akintola Hostel stairway. Joe said he wanted the files – but Abonta refused, saying that when the new Sec.Gen gets elected he can come and collect the files.

Abonta was of the contrary view, maintaining that he was never reluctant in handling over the files – this he said could be seen by the way he gave the files to Joe. He continued that had he wanted to withhold the files, he would have done so.

On subversive activities – Antifon, reading from the committee's terms of reference, said that on 22nd Dec, 1981, Abonta and Femi agreed to summon a meeting on the first Sunday of January being 3rd. The meeting was deferred to 5 Jan, 1982. When the meeting convened, he, Abonta, denied categorically ever telling Femi to summon a meeting.

In defence Abonta said that he gave Femi no directive to summon a meeting and that Femi has no right to summon CC meeting. The right, he said, rests with the Sec.Gen and that when Femi returned on 3rd January evening he could not have come for the meeting. He maintained that Femi summoned an illegal meeting and made a release with the Sec.Gen's signature, which is impersonation and unconstitutional.

That the GC meeting was summoned for Zaria, and probably because of Abonta's inability to communicate this information and lack of zeal as the Sec.Gen of the movement, the PYM's files are now in Ife – to be confirmed later.

Femi said.

(a) On Abonta's pledge to fight Marxism and that he never believed in it, Femi said that Abonta told him one evening in September 1981, December at Ekpo Refectory that he is no longer a Marxist and is conscience-stricken to lead a movement he never believed in. And Abonta called him. Abonta said he was contemplating resigning from the movement and as the Sec.Gen. When Joe Anyanwu asked him why resign when the handing over is near, he said that he wanted to make it symbolic, that he is no longer a Marxist and that he never believed in it, and would feel a prick of conscience for leading a movement he never believed in.

(b) The day he went to produce the Welcome Release, he met Abonta and Akenuwa in front of ANSA Building on the first week of January and Akenuwa was telling Femi what he discussed with Abonta about not believing in Marxism.

ON SUMMONING OF CC MEETING IN JANUARY 1982

Antifon asked whether Femi has the constitutional right to summon a meeting – Femi said that because of the situation of the movement he was correct.

Antifon asked whether Abonta's denial was due to lack of unconstitutionality of the meeting summoned by Femi but Femi said that he was given the power by Abonta but Abonta's denial was to further his sabotage against the movement.

Femi said that the unconstitutionality of the meeting was not upheld by Comrades Akenuwa, Phenson, UE and Femi.

Abonta even denied receiving any circular for the meeting and this was false.

On Alex's suggestion that Femi's apprehension is that Abonta said that he is no longer a Marxist, Abonta argued that he told Femi and Joe this many a time, one of which Femi told him that he is very lucky, that he has already singled him out for dismissal from the movement.

On whether he is still a member of the movement, Udenta pointed to Abonta that as he has decided to part ways with Marxism on philosophical grounds, that he should resign his membership of the movement.

Abonta disagreed with the view and maintained that he is still interested in the movement and would still remain there. He specifically said that his continued stay in the movement is that he is still a student of Marx and that he still wants to help the movement thrive and progress. He pointed out that never a time has he said that he would use all the powers within his command to fight Marxism.

(a) Abonta said that Femi told him in his (Abonta's) room that he would suspend certain portions of the constitution to dismiss him (Abonta) from the movement.

(b) That Alex is in the committee to guard Antifon, R and Udenta to toe the line prescribed by Femi during its sittings.

(c) That he, Femi, has singled out certain members like Abonta, Joe and Ogbati for dismissal.

On this note the meeting ended and was adjourned till Thursday 4 – 2 – 82 for further hearing of evidence from other witnesses.

NB: Abonta maintained that the CC never queried his resignation and a letter of clarification was not given him to write.

(NB 2: This less than elegant report is a combination of the presentations made to the committee by Femi Ahmed and

Nkem Abonta.

NB 3: PYMN is the acronym for Patriotic Youth Movement of Nigeria, the umbrella platform for the leadership of all the Marxist/Progressive Movements in Nigerian universities and the near 'invisible' 'unseen' and 'shadowy' power behind the National Association of Nigerian Students (NANS). The PYMN was a virtual underground movement that charted the revolutionary, political and ideological path for its affiliate organizations, coordinates inter-organizational agenda and initiatives and resolves theoretical and operational disputes in the application of Marxism in the Nigerian context. Most crucially, the PYMN decides which affiliate organization will produce the NANS leadership and works assiduously towards its realization. It is thus not surprising that in the whole of the 1980s up to the mid-1990s the leadership of NANS was made up of committed Marxists and radical, left-leaning progressives).

RECOMMENDATIONS SUBMMITTED
BY
THE MARXIST YOUTH MOVEMENT
INVESTIGATION COMMITTEE

The committee was set up by the General Congress of the movement when it sat sometime in 1982. It has Antifon, R as its chairman, Udenta O. Udenta as Secretary and Alex Enemaku.

The committee has as its terms of reference – the following issues to determine.

1.a. Concerning Nkem Abonta's resignation as the Secretary General of the movement.

1b. Account of His Stewardship
    ii. Allegations of certain misdeeds leveled against Abonta that
    (a) He, Abonta, has on many occasions said that he never believed in Marxism
    (b) That he will use all the resources available to him to fight marxism.
    (c) Meeting Scheduling – His reluctance to summon CC meetings of the movement.
    (d) Reluctance in handing over the movement's properties e.g. files

In determining the above issues, the committee decided to invite some members of the movement who could help it in its investigation and deliberation. Invitations were dispatched to those concerned such as Nkem Abonta, Joe Anyanwu, Olufemi Ahmed and Innocent Akenwa to appear before the committee on 29 – 1 – 82. Of all the invitees only Nkem Abonta appeared on the first day of the committee's sitting.

During the committee's discussion with him, he said that on the reason for resigning as the Secretary General of the movement, he has the following points to make:

(a) That he would not do any forced labour or work: that is, that he would not work unwillingly.
(b) That he has changed his philosophical stand i.e. he stopped being a Marxist – especially from December. So his resignation should be seen from the philosophical angle.
(c) He maintained that the CC never queried his resignation.

On the issue concerning the movement's files, he said that he has never been reluctant in handing them over. That he told Joe Anyanwu to come and collect them from his room. That had he wanted to withhold the files, he would have done that without any person questioning him, more so, now that no member of the movement knew the correct number of files in his possession.

On summoning of the controversial Jan. 5th CC meeting by Femi, which he (Femi) claimed Abonta gave him directive to do, Abonta said that:

(a) He never told Femi to summon any CC meeting
(b) That Femi summoned an illegal meeting because the prerogative to summon CC meetings lies with the Sec. Gen
(c) That Femi issued a release with the Sec. Gen's signature which is tantamount to impersonation.

On the committee's suggestion that he should part ways with the movement now that he is no longer a Marxist, he maintained he is still interested in Marxism and the movement and would like to see it thrive and progress – hence his continued stay.

On this note, the committee adjourned sitting for the day pending the development and progress of its findings.

After the committee's discussion with Abonta, 12 – 2 – 82 was fixed as the day it will see the other invitees. Out of the remaining invitees only one of them came. That is Joe Anyanwu.

Joe Anyamou said that on allegations of misdeed leveled against Abonta, he has not much to say, that the area in which he is greatly interested is the question of Abonta's resignation as the Sec. General of the movement. Nevertheless, he said that:

(a) That Abonta treated the issue of scheduling CC meetings with disdain and with a lukewarm attitude. Also, that he was reluctant to summon CC meetings in September
(b) That during his discussion with Abonta in December, Abonta said that he is going on philosophical incubation.

On the question of Abonta's resignation, Joe said that it was during the CC meeting of January that he handed over the letter of resignation. He said he was against the whole exercise because:

(a) The resignation is untimely
(b) That the CC meeting is not the right place to resign.
(c) That Abonta's tenure of office is ending so it is improper for him to resign at the time he did.
(d) He said he seriously challenged it and that the philosophical reason given by Abonta is vague and unclear.

Joe further said that Abonta failed to attend two consecutive meetings during the term but said that Abonta never told him that he had at no time believed in Marxism.

On Abonta's statement that no member of the movement knew the number of files with him, Joe said that it would go to lengths to prove Abonta's complicity and sabotage. He maintained that when he asked Abonta to hand over the files now that he is resigning, Abonta said:

(a) That he should come and collect it from his (Abonta's) room
(b) Or that he would give it to the new Secretary General when he gets elected.

Joe said that Abonta sorted out the movement's documents from that of the Awareness – 1 Club for over two hours and was present during the exercise. He was of the opinion that Abonta could have misplaced the movement's documents in the process.

On the meeting scheduled by Femi, Joe said that he asked Femi:

(i)   If it is his constitutional right to schedule meetings – to which Femi has no answer

(ii) Whether it was the directive of the Secretary General that the meeting be scheduled to which he answered in the affirmative.

On the next committee sitting of 14 – 2 – 82 Femi Ahmed attended. Femi said that the question of Abonta's resignation should be viewed in conjuction with his role in the movement especially since 1981. He said that because of Abonta's lack of commitment to the movement he was indicted

a)   By the PYMN congress held in the campus last year on the question of religion.

b)   In political education class Abonta appeared directionless and lax.

c)   He said that Abonta was unable to apply his theoretical knowledge of Marxism on practical issues hence his ideological confusion.

d)   That Abonta's resignation came as a result of pressure from the progressive, when he (Abonta) found that he was swabbed up as a Marxist. Femi maintained that Abonta was isolated by the PYMN, they do not correspond with him any longer.

e)   He maintained that Abonta said he would fight Marxism with all means available to him like setting up a counter – revolutary journal.

f)   That since Abonta's election in 1980 he has never taken any initiative in summoning CC meetings.

g) That the Struggle magazine sent to the movement through Abonta's hands since last year has been sent through the student union.

After going through the evidence put before it by those invited, those contacted individually and separately and using its discretion, the committee, on its final sitting on 20-2-82 resolved that:

1. Abonta's resignation was detrimental to the progress of the movement because the movement has not been functioning very well under his leadership and that the resignation will not argur well for the progress of the movement. That Abonta's tenure of office was just ending and that the reason he gave for resigning at that time is unacceptable.

2. That the manner Abonta handed over the movement's properties smacks of arrogance and irresponsibility and therefore not logically tenable.

3. That between Sept. 28 – 14 Oct. and 14 Dec. to 24 Dec. a meeting could have been convened and that the committee believes that the failure to convene the meeting was due to the ideological conflict he experienced and renunciation of Marxism which he admitted. On this basis the committee believes that his resignation as the Secretary General should have gone hand in hand with his resignation as a member since the movement is purely for Marxists and not for students of Marx.

4. Philosophically, a non-Marxist who still retains the leadership or membership of a Marxist movement will be guilty of ideological sabotage, opportunism and philosophical contradiction.

On the basis of the controversy generated by a meeting summoned by one of the members of the CC without using the proper constitutional channels, in view of the fact that the constitution was not very clear on the proper method of resignation of offices, Secretary General, etc the committee recommends that the constitution of the movement be reviewed.

On Resignation:

In compliance with the provisions of the movement's constitution, Article 4, Section E, Sub-section vii designated EXPULSION, the committee recommends that Abonta, the erstwhile Secretary General of the movement, be asked to RESIGN from the movement.

This is because:

(a) The experience of the movement as regards expulsion of important officers has not been in its best interest;

(b) That Abonta's activities before his ideological confusion has much to commend him;

(c) That immediately he resigns, his fee should be refunded from the time the resignation takes effect, and finally

(d) That the committee feels that if Abonta fails to tender his resignation letter within one month of receiving the letter, that the congress through the CC should send a formal letter of EXPULSION to him and inform the university community accordingly.

Appendix II

(This essay is one of several I wrote as an undergraduate. This mass of essays, particularly those influenced by Marxist aesthetic thinking, are being processed as part of my research into revolutionary student movements of the 1980s and the political, ideological, cultural and aesthetic ideas that shaped our thinking.)

WRITERS, AESTHETICS, POLITICS AND SOCIAL COMMITMENT

In discussing this topic, the first thing one has to bear in mind is to define its scope and dimension. Writers' involvement of politics in their writing could be approached from varying perspectives or viewpoints depending on the discussant's bias. The same applies to social commitment. Does it imply, one may ask, the reflection of political trends, movements and thoughts in a writer's work, or participating actively like other interest parties in the struggle for the control of state power?

As for the writer's social commitment, does it imply the role of the writer as the protector of the corporate will and collective solidarity of his people and whatever pertains to their morals, values and societal norms, in short, their cosmology?

Aesthetics, artistic beauty and the evaluation of the literary worth of a creative and imaginative writing has been the predominant issue, hence the question is, can political discussion in a writer's work and his vision of himself as a humanist who has some special responsibilities for his community (reflected in his work and elsewhere) undermine his recognition and acceptance as a master of creative literature based on aesthetic judgment?

I say NO. First, a writer has an important message for his people. No matter what people may think, politics cannot be divorced from other spheres of societal life. No single aspect of human life can be treated in isolation of others. Every political topic involves issues of economic, social and cultural growth; has religious implication, reflects tradition, belief-systems and values the society holds dear. "Arts for art's sake" (whatever it means) is a dying phenomenon in the field of creative literature. Almost all great writers' works consciously or indeliberately abound with the problems of society, government and social changes. Check: Achebe's *Arrow of God,* Armah's *Fragments,* Dostoyevsky's *The Devils, The Brothers Karamazov* and Soyinka's *Season of Anomy*.

To isolate writers from politics is tantamount to depriving their numerous readers the writer's welcome comments on the politics of the day and destroying one of the most influential writer's commitment to his society. Writers are the watchdogs of the nation. With their gift of imagination and creativity they can satirize and criticize any political situation, check the excesses of the powers that be and bring home to "the man in the street" the goings-on in his country.

Here, I will pause to take situations from our own African experience. Leopold S. Senghor said that "there can never be true political liberation without cultural liberation." The two go hand in hand. Ezekiel Mphalele commented that "African Writers are product of a common history; that of colonialism, independence and new awareness; while non-independent communities share a common yoke. Chinweizu and co dedicated their book, *Toward the Decolonization of African Literature* to Pan African Writers, "The great voices of the Black world calling us to liberation ... exemplary inciters against toleration of our oppressed situation ... raisers of consciousness who, through long centuries, have nursed our Pan-African will to freedom." Numerous other instances abound.

These critics have recognized the great role played by African writers in both cultural and political liberation, roles which they are still playing to see the last vestige of imperialism, racism and apartheid unshackled and unyoked. African writers disseminate progressive and rational pan-African political ideas, raise the level of consciousness of our people, of their need to be free, and in the face of oppression and victimization, continue undaunted in their search for pan–African Unity. Check Ngugi's influence through *A Grain of Wheat, Petals of Blood,* and *Trials of Dedan Kimathi*–influence which led to his detention even under Nzee Jomo Kenyatta– Oyono's *Houseboy,* Beti's *The Poor Christ of Bomba,* and Okot's *Song of Lawino,* and *Song of a Prisoner,* among other examples.

This so-called "protest literature" has helped immensely in the cultural and political freedom of many countries.

The Writer and the System

It was Chairman Mao Tse-Tung who said, and I quote: "in the world of today all culture, all literature and art belong to definite classes and are geared to definite political lines." There is no such thing as "art's for art's sake," art that stands above classes or art that is detatched from, or independent of politics. Proletarian literature and art are part of the whole proletarian revolutionary cause. They are as Lenin said "cogs and wheels in the whole revolutionary machine." This is also true of communal, slave, feudal or bourgeois literature.

Again, in the Afro-Asian Writers' emergency meeting of

Peking (Beijing) June 27,1966, the Secretary General of the association, Ratne Deshapri Ya said, among other things, "as writers dedicated to the revolutionary cause of the people of the two continents, our duty and task is to turn our pen into a mighty weapon. All dark forces endangering the cause of revolution of the Asian and African peoples must be exposed, and all revolutionary struggles which give impetus to their advance must be eulogized. This is the sacred duty cast upon us, the progressive Asian and African Writers"

These two quotations summarize the general current sweeping across the literary landscape of the world today. Formalized or informal, oral or written, all literary genres are nothing but the expression of the system operational when they are written. Literature serves the interest of the class in power or the dominant material force in society as its mouthpiece except protest or revolutionary literature which, while rejecting the existing class structure, serves the interest of the class it postulates.

1. In traditional African society, during the communal era, the proverbs, fables, allegories and folk tales are replete with communal ethos, politics and social life.
2. In feudal society, literature is full of songs of praise of the feudal lords, knights, sultans, emirs – Hausaland in pre-colonial times and Europe during the feudal era.
3. In Anglo-Saxon Britain-heroism, devotion, duty and service were held dear in society, for example, "Beowulf", "Battle of Maldon", "Wanderer", "Seafarer" etc.

In capitalist societies, literature reflects the politics and economics of the system, generates debates and discussions about its plausibility and comments about its acceptance. This equally applies to a greater degree to the socialist and communist countries.

So considering the above, one can see that African and other world writers; imperialist or anti-imperialist, protest or acceptance, revolutionary or reactionary, are all satisfying the yearning and aspiration of their people and the system they uphold or condemn.

Aesthetic qualities of judgment imbued in literature as the communication of significant ideas has a genuine and concrete function to perform. We do not communicate beauty and abstract experience for their sake. We communicate significant and important experience existing in a physical realm, political and social commitment included, through beautiful language, captivating imagery, irony, paradox, allegory, fable, symbols, extended metaphors, coherent and realistic plot and rounded or flat characters, all of which are the writer's tool of creativity.

Udenta O. Udenta
Dept of English
U.N.N.

Appendix III A

EASTERN MANDATE UNION

BASIC PRINCIPLES

Progress in Justice and Equity

Preamble

This is the moment of truth for Nigeria. The nation is passing through a critical and crucial phase in its evolution as a modern state. Over thirty years of misrule, planlessness, greed and squander mania by those in authority, visionless dictatorial military juntas, and the reckless abortion of the principles of fair play, equity, social justice and civilized conduct have made a tragic nightmare out of a once proud dream.

The indices abound everywhere. They exist in the misery and material destitution of our peoples. They exist in the sorry state of the national economy. They are to be seen in the political paralysis which has gripped the nation for long and which has led to the dismemberment of existing political institutions and structures. There has been no sustainable framework for the revitalization and re-affirmation of developmental objectives, and no workable national ideological strategy which will actualize the aspirations of our diverse peoples under a common national weal.

The debilitating crisis of national identity coupled with a contemporary generational fatalism knows no ethnic boundaries, geo-political frontiers, and creed or sex differentials. Nigerians are tired of the mess the nation has been led into. They know that the federal structure is unbalanced. They know that revenue generative and mobilizational capacities and potentialities are not matched with allocation of resources. They know that power is overly concentrated in the centre, and in that centre in the hands of a few people who perceive political domination as a fact of life; indeed as a theocratic necessity.

But more than any other people in the country, Eastern Nigerians know more about this untoward reality; they hear it neither in the popular press nor as rumour; they live in it every day of their lives, through their sleeping and waking moments. Having contributed immensely to the struggle for political independence and modernization of the polity; having fought a civil war; and being the primary producers of the nation's wealth, we of the East have come to the end of the road. We are, simply put, sick and tired of the state of the nation.

Marginalized politically and deprived economically, Eastern Nigerians have begun to ask themselves painful questions about the dream of our founding fathers, and about the promise of greater tomorrow, and they are beginning to wonder if the struggle is still worth the effort and labour. Common on the lips of her children, and silent in their subconscious minds are the perennial questions of their identity and their place in the polity and in the economy.

These questions need urgent solutions, if we must grapple with the fundamental issues affecting our destiny. They need the imperative responses of those who care, those who feel the pain, the anguish and the lament of the injured. They need the attention of practical men and women who are determined to exorcise the ghost of inertia and the tyranny of sadism. They need a new generation of leaders who will anchor the idiom of their struggle in the collective consciousness of their race, plan and provide for life, liberty, security and happiness of the people.

Such new leaders must be forged from the smithery of anger tempered with reason knowing, as they do, that exclusivist prejudices breed centrifugal ruptures. Such leaders must, therefore, have the capacity of combining the best in their people with the concrete possibility of a greater national affirmation. They must be guided by the truth in the adage, "Live and Let Live".

Such new leaders are now born, and the era in which we are readily provides for them the opportunity of testing their intelligence, individual and collective endowments, moral power and practical experience on the contemporary arena in such a way that the East, and indeed, the nation will never be the same again. Not anymore. Guided by the noblest of sentiments and principles, and driven by the will to redress socio-historical injustices to the best of their ability, they have decided to come together in the pursuit of a common cause and equity.

We, of the EMU, constitute the flagship for the struggle against injustice, inequality, and the suppression of fair play. We are not opposed to any group, leadership or otherwise in the East, nor do we compete with any, so long as such groups or leaderships are **NOT** opposed to our objectives, strategy, fight for justice, equality and fair play in Nigeria.

Because the **EAST** has borne the brunt of injustice, inequality, lack of fair play, civil war, marginalization, with all their luciferous concomitants, we of the **East** believe that we can show the **Light** of justice, handle the **Candle of Liberty,** and navigate the **Ship** of happiness throughout Nigeria.

And to this end, we founded the **EMU,** determined to forge ahead and with like-minded persons, groups or leaderships anywhere in Nigeria, Africa, and elsewhere in the world.

To this end, we make our **DECLARATION:**

Whereas there are fundamental distortions in the structure and character of the Nigerian State which are injurious to the survival of the people of Eastern Nigeria and their struggle to humanize their environment; whereas, these omissions which are both political, economic, cultural, social and spiritual have been allowed to fester for long; whereas the government of the day seems incapacitated in its efforts to genuinely ameliorate the grievances of our people; whereas also there is the urgent need to address these burning issues before they get out of hand; and whereas there are men and women of Eastern Nigeria, consciously realizing the historical and moral burden they are placing on their shoulders, are committed, intellectually and practically, to grapple with these stated problems.

Be it be resolved, and it is hereby resolved that we establish for ourselves an organization which will serve as the platform for the pursuit of this common cause.

Name

The organization shall be called **EASTERN MANDATE UNION** (hereinafter called the **EMU**).

Motto

The Motto of the **EMU** shall be *Progress in Justice and Equity.*

Symbol

The Symbol of the **EMU** shall be "Light"

Aims and Objectives

The **EMU** shall have the following aims and objectives:

(a) Create awareness among the entire peoples of Eastern Nigeria about deliberate policies and programmes of the federal governments which are injurious to their dignity and survival as a people;

(b) Mobilize the entire peoples of Eastern Nigeria, through practical political strategy and popular education, about the need to redress existing injustice, especially their marginalization;

(c) Forge a common bond of unity and fraternal solidarity among all the peoples of Eastern Nigeria as the concrete basis of actualizing our aspirations;

(d) Seek to exterminate division, in whatever shape, character or form, among the entire peoples of Eastern Nigeria in the larger interests of group affirmation and empowerment;

(e) Commit ourselves to a Pan-Eastern Identity and thereby take up issues at whatever level, and as may crop up in the federation;

(f) Establish linkages with other regional, zonal and geo-political units in the country who appreciate the peculiar problems of the EAST as a *sine qua non* for the survival and prosperity of Nigeria as one real, corporate entity;

(g) Commit ourselves to practical and principled political action, within the limits of the Laws of the Fatherland, as we move towards the actualization of our Eastern ideals, hopes, and needs; and

(h) Engage in other related, ancillary, corollary and dependent actions that will further the overall group interests of the peoples of Eastern Nigeria.

Membership
Membership shall be open to all progressive-minded men and women of Eastern region who cherish the idea of group solidarity; who uphold the principles of equity and social justice in words, deed and conduct; who reject the idea of discrimination based on ethnic identity, sex or creed; and who are resolutely mobilized to deal with the challenges posed by marginalization, inequitable distribution of wealth and resources and imbalance of federal structures.

Because the **EMU** shall, among its objects, be a cadre-building one, with emphasis on group political affirmation and material and spiritual empowerment, members of the **EMU** shall be men and women of enlightened political consciousness who must, at all times, be prepared to participate actively and decisively in the struggle for regional survival, progress and prosperity, in a truly federal Nigeria.

(i) An intending member shall obtain membership form with a non-refundable deposit of N100.00 (one hundred naira) and shall complete the form accordingly.

(ii) He/She shall receive a membership card, if his/her application is successful.

(iii) There shall be an annual membership due of N5.00 (five naira) only.

Honorary Members
Honorary members shall be appointed by the Steering Committee on the recommendation of the General Assembly from amongst men and women who symbolize the ideals of the EMU. Honorary members shall exercise all rights of membership except that they shall not vote or be voted for.

Patrons
There shall be patrons, not less than 7, appointed by the Steering Committee. The chairman may invite patrons as he deems it from time to time, to meetings of the Steering Committee.

Structures/Organs
The EMU shall have the following structural levels:
(i) Ward
(ii) Local Government
(iii) State
(iv) Regional/Zonal

A. **Officers of the EMU**
The **EMU** shall have the following officers:

(i)   Chairman
(ii)   Chancellor
(iii)   Deputy Chairman
(iv)   Secretary
(v)   Assistant Secretary
(vi)   Director of Publicity and Strategy
(vii)   Financial Secretary
(viii) Internal Auditor
(ix)   Four Ex-officio members

B.   **State Officers**
The **EMU** shall have the following state officers:
(i)   Vice-Chairman
(ii)   Secretary
(iii)   Publicity Secretary
(iv)   Financial Secretary
(v)   Two Ex-officio members

C.   **Local Government/Ward Officers**
The **EMU** shall have the following Local Government/Ward
        Officers:
(i)   Coordinator   (Ward or Local Government Area)
(ii)   Secretary   -   ditto
(iii)   Publicity Secretary -   ditto
(iv)   Financial Secretary -   ditto
(v)   Two Ex-officio members

D.   **The Chancery**
The Chancery shall be based at Enugu, the capital of the
        East.

E.   **Bureaus and Directorates**
The following Bureaus and Directorates shall be established
in the Chancery as part of the union's regional offices:
(i)   Directorate of Research and Planning, to be headed
        by a Director;
(ii)   Directorate of Operations to be headed by a Director;

(iii)   Directorate of Publicity to be headed by a Director;
(iv)   Bureau of Political Strategy to be headed by a Bureau Chief;
(v)   Bureau of National Liaison with not less three (3) Bureau Chiefs, under one Director;
(vi)   Financial Bureau to be headed by a Bureau Chief;
(vii) Youth and Women Mobilization Bureau to be headed by a Bureau Chief
(viii) Any other Directorate or Bureau as the Steering Committee might wish to establish.

F.   **Steering Committee**
The following officers shall be members of the Steering Committee of the EMU:
(i)   Chairman
(j)   Chairman
(ii)   Chancellor
(iii) Deputy Chairman
(iv)   Secretary
(v)   Assistant Secretary
(vi)   Director of Publicity and Strategy
(vii) One Vice-Chairman coordinating each State
(viii) Directors of Directorates and Bureau Chiefs
(ix)   Financial Secretary
(x)   Internal Auditor
(xi)   Four Ex-officio members

G.   **Consultative Forum**
Between meetings of the General Assembly and the Steering Committee, there shall be a consultative forum convened by the chairman. The Forum shall be made up of members of the Steering Committee, and other Invitees from across the EMU States.

The General Assembly
The General Assembly is the highest organ of the EMU. Its decision(s) is (are) binding on all other organs/offices of

the EMU. The General Assembly shall be composed of all duly registered members of the union who are financially up to date in their obligations to the EMU.

Functions of Officers

The following officers shall have the specified functions given below:

Chairman
i.   The chairman presides over all meetings of the General Assembly and the Steering Committee
ii. The chairman shall direct the execution of the programmes and objectives of the EMU
iii. The chairman shall be an executive member of the State Steering Committees of the EMU
iv. The chairman shall be a signatory to the account of the EMU
v.   The chairman shall have a casting vote in the event of a voting tie in the meetings of the Steering Committee and General Assembly of the EMU
vi. The chairman shall be the Chief Executive and Accounting Officer of the EMU
vii. The chairman shall perform any such other functions as may be assigned him by the Steering Committee and the General Assembly.

Deputy Chairman

i.   The Deputy Chairman shall preside over the meetings of the Steering Committee and General Assembly in the absence of the Chairman
ii. The Deputy Chairman shall be an executive member of States Steering Committees of the EMU
iii. The Deputy Chairman shall be the Head of Bureau of Political Strategy
iv. The Deputy Chairman shall exercise such other functions as may be assigned to him, from time to time, by the chairman, the Steering Committee and

the General Assembly.

Chancellor

i.   The Chancellor shall see to the overall co-ordination of activities at the secretariat
ii.   He shall generate ideas and strategies which the institutional set-up in the Chancery would actualize
iii. He shall be the Chairman of all the Directorates and Bureaus in the Chancery
iv.   The Chancellor shall inform the chairman about the need to establish directorates and bureaus which shall further the aims and objectives of the EMU
v.   The Chancellor shall be a signatory to the account of the EMU
vi.   The Chancellor shall perform such other functions as the Steering Committee and the General Assembly shall assign to him from time to time.

The Secretary

i.   The Secretary shall take the minutes of all meetings of the Steering Committee and the General Assembly
ii.   The Secretary shall be incharge of all documents of the EMU in the Chancery which deal with the activities of the Steering Committee and the General Assembly
iii. The Secretary shall issue the circular for all meetings of the Steering Committee and the General Assembly on the chairman's directive
iv.   The Secretary shall be the coordinating secretary of the State Steering Committees
v.   The Secretary shall perform such functions as the Chairman, Steering Committee or the General Assembly may assign to him from time to time

Assistant Secretary

i.   The Assistant Secretary shall take the minutes of all meetings of the Steering Committees and the General Assembly in the absence of the Secretary

ii.   The Assistant Secretary shall issue the circular for all meetings of the Steering Committee and the General Assembly in the absence of the Secretary

iii.   The Assistant Secretary shall be the Co-ordinating Assistant Secretary of the State Steering Committees

iv.   The Assistant Secretary shall perform such other functions as the chairman, Steering Committee or the General Assembly may assign to him from time to time

Director of Publicity and Strategy

i.   The Director of Publicity and Strategy shall be in charge of the public relations between the EMU and other institutions, e.g. the media.

ii.   The Director of Publicity and Strategy shall oversee all ventures that aim at popularising the EMU; e.g. organising press conference, issuing press releases and organising public enlightenment programmes

iii. The Director of Publicity and Strategy shall be in charge of the Operations Directorate of the EMU

iv.   The Director of Publicity and Strategy shall be a member of the Bureau Of National Liaison

v.   The Director of Publicity and Strategy shall perform any other function as the Chairman, Steering Committee or General Assembly may assign him.

Financial Secretary

i.   The Financial Secretary shall be a signatory of all the accounts of the EMU

ii.   The Financial Secretary shall map out strategies for the financial viability of the EMU

iii. The Financial Secretary shall be the Chief of the Financial Bureau in the Chancery

iv.   The Financial Secretary shall pay all monies of the EMU to any of its accounts not later than 24 hours after the receipt of such monies

v.   The Financial Secretary shall prepare the balance sheet of the EMU's account at the end of each financial year

vi. The Financial Secretary shall perform any other function the chairman, Steering Committee or general assembly shall assign to him

Internal Auditor

i. The Internal Auditor shall audit the account of the EMU at the end of each financial year
ii. The Internal Auditor shall present such audited account to the General Assembly of the EMU before the commencement of another financial year
iii. The Internal Auditor shall perform any other function as the Steering Committee or the General Assembly may assign to him

State Vice-Chairman

i. The State Vice-Chairman shall be members of the Steering Committee
ii. They shall be the chairman of the State Steering Committees of the EMU
iii. They shall preside over the meetings of the State Steering Committees and General Assemblies of the EMU
iv. They shall co-ordinate the activities of the union at the state level, popularize its programmes and enlighten the public about its aims and objectives
v. They shall perform such other functions as the chairman, Steering Committee or General Assembly may assign to them

The State Steering Committee shall work out the functions of the local government and ward committees of the EMU, and the functions of the other State officers of the EMU.

Directors of Directorates/Bureau Chiefs

Apart from engaging in the specific functions of their directorates/bureaus (e.g. the Director of Publicity publishing the activities of the EMU, including sending out circulars for meetings; the Bureau Chief of Political Strategy mapping out practical political strategies and tactics of struggle; the Liaison Officers engaging in national linkage jobs and the Director of Research and Planning articulating the essential ideas that will facilitate the operation of the union), the Directors and Bureau Chiefs shall perform such other functions as may be assigned them by the Chancellor, the Steering Committee and the General Assembly.

Meetings/Elections/Voting at Meeting

(i)   The General Assembly shall meet once every 3 months, or at such other times as the situation may warrant

(ii)   The Steering Committee shall meet once every month or at such other time as the situation may arise

(iii) The time frame for the meetings of the State Steering Committee and General Assemblies shall be determined by the State Vice-Chairman

(iv)   Motions, issues and resolutions at all meetings of the Steering Committee and the General Assembly shall be by acclamation, but where not possible through casting of votes by members of the EMU present and voting.

(v)   All officers of the EMU shall hold office for 2 years. They shall only be eligible to contest for another term of 2 years.

Adoption and Amendment

Once adopted, this body of rules can only be amended by two-third of the General Assembly of the EMU present at a duly constituted meeting and voting, if the process of acclamation fails.

Appendix III B

EASTERN MANDATE UNION

The Stand of the EASTERN MANDATE UNION
(EMU)
ON
FUNDAMENTAL NATIONAL ISSUES

Progress in Justice and Equality

Dr Dele P Cole
(Chairman)

Dr Arthur A Nwankwo
(Chancellor)

Dr Chuba Okadigbo
(Deputy Chairman)

Hon. Dubem Onyia
(Secretary)

Vice-Chairman

Foreword

Nigeria is in urgent need of renegotiation and restructuring. The essential elements of this idea relate to the character and structure of the federation, the establishment and sustenance of a workable democratic system of government and the enactment of equity, justice and fair play in the new Nigerian charter.

The **Eastern Mandate Union** believes that the Nigerian project is in distress because of the distortion of these noble ideals. Now is the right time for every patriotic Nigerian to start thinking and acting positively for the salvation and prosperity of the fatherland. In highlighting the fundamental national issues, the **EASTERN MANDATE UNION** is quite conscious of the enormous obligations imposed on Nigerians for proper articulation of all the key issues. We have only tried to summarize some of those elements which have been contentious in evolving the general weal, from the Eastern standpoint. In doing this, we want to re-state our commitment to the basic principles of the **EASTERN MANDATE UNION** (**EMU**):

i.   Demarginalization of the East;
ii. The restoration of democratic structures;
iii. The validation of electoral mandates;
iv. The construction of a democratic government of national unity based on electoral mandates and interest groups participation; and
v.   The immediate convening of a sovereign national conference.

We stand resolutely on these patriotic platforms which we know to be the true way of progress for our dear nation.

The Military Question

The **Eastern Mandate Union** (**EMU**) has thoroughly deliberated on all the salient facts relating to the intervention/participation of the Armed Forces in the political leadership of the country. Based on available data and contemporary political tradition, the **EMU** is overwhelmingly persuaded that military rule is an embarrassing anachronism. The **EMU** is thus of the view that the most urgent task facing Nigerians today is the immediate termination of military rule, a stop to further military intervention in politics and the quick evolution of a democratic and just social order.

(i) Excuse for Military Intervention

Experience has shown that the excuses for military intervention on politics which include saving the nation from disintegration and collapse; arbitration in times of acute political crisis; and curbing the corrupt excesses and incompetence of the civil political class have not been borne out in practice. The military have rather compounded these crises and problems as the 1966-1967; 1975; 1976; 1983; 1985; and 1993 experiences have clearly demonstrated.

(ii) Performance of the Military in Government

The woeful performance of the military in the nation's political life is seen in the following: The first serious threat to the corporate existence of Nigeria (1966-1967) was caused by the military which unleashed the civil war of 1967-1970; in the same way that the military have plunged the nation into an unending political, social and economic crisis from 1993 till date. The military have not solved the problem of power succession, if all the coups they organize against themselves are anything to go by. The Nigerian military have proven to be more corrupt, inept, visionless and planless than the politicians they accuse of these misdeeds; and the military have failed to evolve a sustainable democratic culture. They have retarded the nation's political development and stultified the evolution of a democratic, just, equitable and demarginalized social order.

(iii) Restructuring the Military/Insulating the Military from Politics

The **EASTERN MANDATE UNION** feels that there are a number of ways these can be achieved:

(a) Professionalizing the Armed Forces through retirements, re-training and the accelerated re-tooling of the course content and curricula of military schools, including the command and staff college, and the Military University/NDA at Kaduna. Apart from retirement, there should be redeployment of military personnel to civil sectors as one way of pruning down the size of the Armed Forces;

(b) The political and ideological mobilization of Nigerians through political education so that they can always use the tactics of comprehensive civil disobedience to forestall the junta syndrome which has become pervasive in Nigeria;

(c) The Nigerian Armed Forces should be decentralized and regional commands established in line with the number of federating units;

(d) Each regional command should recruit indigenes of the region and perform tasks that shall be assigned to it by the constitution of the land;

(e) Each ethnic group in a region must be adequately represented in each unit of the regional command;

(f) The National/Centre Force should be used to settle inter-regional conflicts;

(g) Each region must maintain its Armed Forces and must contribute men and materials in time of war; and

(h) There should be a Central Military Command Headquarters whose membership shall include all the Regional Defence Commanders and a few senior staff officers drawn from the regions in the proposed headquarters.

The **EMU** further specifies that the functions of the Central Military Command should include the following: the command and control of the regional forces in time of war; the central procurement of arms and ammunitions and the offer of military advice to the National Apex Council which in turn shall set standards for the training and appointment of regional commanders and shall also decide on the mode of exchange programmes for military officers.

The **EMU** believes that the question of the command structure of the Armed Forces is very central to the continued existence of Nigeria.

Revenue Generation Mobilization/Allocation

The **Eastern Mandate Union** believes that revenue generation, mobilization and allocation have very serious political implications for Nigeria, particularly in relation to the search for an acceptable model of nation development and efforts to create a new, just, equitable, democratic and demarginalized social order. There is no doubt, that proper harnessing and mobilization of national revenue, including its optimal utilization, determines the sovereign character of any state, and this, notwithstanding the laudable political vision of its leadership.

Nigeria is still a developing society where ethnic identity, religious persuasion and geo-political or zonal affinity determine the allocation of revenue. The idea of *making the centre less competitive politically, administratively and militarily* must be matched with making the centre less domineering, financially and economically. The sure way of doing this is by correspondingly downgrading the financial potential and revenue allocation to the central government in a decentralized federal structure. If political military authority is decentralized without corresponding decentralization of economic power-potential, new states, zones, regions (or whatever new federal arrangement that may be adopted) will still be dependent on the central government for financial survival.

A NEW REVENUE ALLOCATION FORMULA FOR NIGERIA

The **Eastern Mandate Union** believes that the present revenue allocation formula in Nigeria needs to be reformed because it has not answered the political question of who gets what, why and how. The present formula is used to consolidate political domination and the corrupt and selfish acquisition of power. The formula also does not take into consideration the issue of derivation and special needs, and unless and until this is done, Nigeria will remain an unequitable and unjust state.

Therefore, the **EMU** calls for the following steps to be taken immediately:

(i)   Basing the allocation of revenue on the *principle of derivation* – what one keeps is dependent on what one can give the nation. This will help stimulate economic growth, healthy competition and optimum utilization of production inputs. The oil-producing communities, for example, demand more share of the national revenue because they suffer peculiar disabilities from the wealth they generate (ecological and environmental disasters, strange diseases, poverty etc);

(ii) The percent share of the national revenue accruable to the central government should not be more than 25% of the total revenue since such revenue should be enough to maintain national law and order, carry on the nation's foreign policy, oversee the customs, immigration, citizenship, and such like:

(iii) Constitutive units (states, regions or local governments, etc) should retain 55% of their internally generated revenue, while the rest goes to the central government and a Central National Emergency Fund;

(iv) In the existing three-tier structure, the following revenue formula is advocated:

    a)   Central Government 25%
    b)   State Government 15%
    c)   Local Government 45%
    d)   National Emergency Fund   ... 15%

(v) The revenue kept in the National Emergency Fund should be used for the following purposes: the demarginalization of the East (industrially, infrastructurally, commercially and bureaucratically); national emergencies, e.g. relief, erosion menace, desertification threats, Nigeria's participation in peace-keeping operations around the world; and grants/aid to needy nations in times of national emergencies;

(vii) Points I-V above should be provided for in the new federal constitution.

As in the case of the military question, the **EMU** believes that this new revenue formula is very central to the continued existence of Nigeria.

The Marginalization of the East

That the East has been marginalized from 1970 till date is no longer an academic question. It has now become an undeniable part of the national life. The government of the day knows it. Every sincere Nigerian knows it too. The **Eastern Mandate Union** has articulated this issue in one of its committee reports. The report should be read as a companion guide to this summary. It contains most of the details and a number of the more obvious data/facts.

The real understanding of marginalization relates to the sense of loss and alienation experienced by a group in its relationship with other groups that make-up the polity. The

East knows this, having experienced marginalization at the hands of other groups in Nigeria for over 24 years now. Some aspects of the marginalization of the East include the following:

(i)   Power-sharing mechanism (structure, composition and core personnel in the presidency);

(ii)   Revenue sharing formula (in view of the revenue-generational and mobilizational capacities of the East, and the issue of special needs);

(iii) Lack of federal presence in the East in the form of well-maintained grade 'A' highways, bridges, industries, federal owned hospitals, petro-chemical and steel complexes, etc;

(iv)   Under representation in the officer-corps and high ranking cadres in the Armed Forces and security agencies: Army, Navy, Air Force, Police, State Security Service, Directorate of Military intelligence, Immigration, National Intelligence Agency, Prisons Service, Customs, etc;

(v)   Lowly presence in the administrative structure and headship of federal ministries in terms of ministers, Director-Generals, parastatals under ministries, e.g. Nigeria Airways, Airports Authority, Ports Authority, NITEL, Steel Rolling Mills, Petro-Chemical industries, NAFCON, condensate factories, Security and Minting Corporation, Defence Industries, etc; and headship of other extra-ministerial departments.

(vi)   Lack of failure to enforce Legislations, Acts, Statutes, and Laws on national citizenship, and Residency Laws of the federation and the various states; tax differentials, discrimination in school enrolment, appointment into civil service, etc;

(vii) Selective application of the federal character clause in bridging the relative disadvantage of other groups (e.g. educationally disadvantaged groups), while retaining the post-1970 status quo with regard to the integration of the East in the Armed Forces, the police, other security and intelligence agencies, etc; and

(viii) Socio-psychological marginalization expressed through scorn, contempt and derision of Easterners throughout the country; sporadic looting of houses, shops, business premises and markets owned by Easterners; and maiming, and killing of Easterners in sponsored religious and civil violence. This is by far not an exhaustive list of the aspects of marginalization of the East in Nigeria. The above merely serve as pointers to the enormity of this problem.

De-Marginalizing the East

The following are the urgent steps that must be taken:

(a) Immediate declaration by the government or its organs that the East is marginalized;

(b) Setting up a panel to study the various aspects of the marginalization of the East;

(c) Taking concrete and realizable steps to attenuate the effects of marginalization of the East by the government through the equitable and just re-composition of the Provisional Ruling Council (PRC) and the Federal Executive Council or whatever names hereafter employed;

(d) Drawing up a government blueprint on the **DE-MARGINALIZATION OF THE EAST** from the report of the panel in point (b) above and setting up an implementation committee to effect immediate and long-term solutions;

(e) Expunging any discriminatory law, statute, legislation and act which restricts individuals from exercising their rights and privileges, and the fulfilment of their obligations to society, no matter where they reside in the country; and

(f) Making the **DEMARGINALIZATION** of the East a

fundamental aspect of national discourse in the National Conference and a pre-condition for a successful *re-negotiation* of Nigeria and the resolution of the national question.

New Federal Structure/State/Zone Re-composition

The **Eastern Mandate Union** believes that the best system for Nigeria is the federal system but this must be *true*, just and fair. Federation has been distorted in Nigeria to the extent that what is being practised today is a unitary form of government.

The two main factors which have contributed to the distortion of true federalism in Nigeria are:

(i) The long period of military rule (over 24 years out of 34 years of independence): and
(ii) The attempt by a section of the country to use the unitary form of government to consolidate their political domination, and through that, the control and distribution of national wealth.

These two factors need a brief explanation. The military tradition is that of a centralized command structure where power and authority flow from top to the bottom. The operational idiom is obedience to superior officers. Military rulers run Nigeria as their battalions, regiments or divisions. The exercise of this authority could only be guaranteed if they centralize the structure, organization and management of the state apparatus. Therein lies the military's remarkable success in destroying the federal structure of the nation.

The second point is that those who want to dominate and control political power need not bother with the federating units. They only seek to control the apparatus of the central government. To achieve this, they seek a very strong centre, weak federating units, centralized Armed Forces and federally collected revenue. If the centre were to be made sufficiently unattractive, their hold on power will become meaningless. So, the domination of power has to go hand in hand with the centralization of authority. This harms federalism in the long run.

Nigeria must be a federal state because of the diverse nature of its peoples. Socio-cultural, ethnic, linguistic and religious differences demand the right of people to pursue their happiness within the greater whole. This is the essence of the idea of unity in diversity, and the essential meaning of true federalism. Nigeria started as a federal state but was eventually transformed into a unitary state. The **Eastern Mandate Union** is one with the rest of Nigerians in demanding a return to true federalism.

Urgent Steps to be Taken

(i)   Making the federating units more viable, through the constitutionally guaranteed enhancement of its powers, functions and authority potentials (The technical details of this must be worked out);

(ii) Decentralizing the command structure of the Armed Forces and Police in such a way and to such an extent that the federating units will retain some measures of control over them; and

(iii) Applying the principle of derivation in revenue allocation; abrogating the idea of federally-collected revenue; and reposing in the central government a share of the total national revenue not exceeding 25%.

The main zest of a new federal structure has to do with the powers exercised by every federating unit in relation to the central government; the structure and character of the Armed Forces; and revenue accruable to each tier in the new federal arrangement. It is noteworthy that the character or essence of the re-composed units-whether statist in orientation, ethno-linguistic in outlook or zonal/regional in content must be achieved through a consensus.

If power is overly concentrated in the centre, the expression of which is the will of **DOMINATORS** from specific geo-political blocs, thousands of new states/zones or the re-composition of existing ones will not ease the pains of injustice and neglect. In the same way, if the present revenue-sharing formula is retained, no amount of zonal re-composition will be worth the effort because such new zones may end up becoming unviable zones which could be financially strangulated through unjust and revenue-sharing mechanism.

Thus, while it may be necessary to re-compose the Federation through the creation of new zones/states based on regional, geo-political, cultural and social affinities (structure), it is very much imperative to re-define and re-negotiate the character of the Federation.

Creation of States

With respect to the present states' structure, Nigeria remains imbalanced.

The East is marginalized. The oil-producing states in the East are marginalized, especially in consideration of their contribution to the national economy. The Igbos are marginalized. In Delta State, there seems to be some consensus among their ethnic formations against the continuing membership therein of the Igbos, otherwise of the existence of the Delta State Capital at Asaba. Should and can anybody or group so ostracized reject himself/herself? The emphatic answer is NO!

However, if Nigeria were to continue with the prevalent approach to state creation, it is mandatory to redress the imbalance, thereby instituting Parity and Justice. Thus, it should be a just exercise in demarginalization to create more states in the East as follows:

(i)   Anioma State
(ii) Ebonyi State
(iii) More states from minority states in the East, viz., Cross River, Akwa Ibom and Rivers States, in accordance with

the consensus of the ethnic nationalities of those states.

With respect to the states and the awkward manner of their creation with military fiat, it must be borne in mind that many of the existing states are very dependent on federal grants. Many of them exist on their own, and many of the requests for new states today will fissle out the moment it is made evident that states will have to be self-reliant. The same goes for many of the extant local governments and the demands for new local governments.

The real key to the revision of the states structure is revenue allocation in accordance with the *principle of derivation*. We suspect that if this principle is set in motion, some of the existing states will seek accommodation with neighbouring but viable states or simply self-dissolve. Accordingly, many agitators for more states will seek other pastimes or manufacture alternative propaganda points.

Creation of Local Governments

The arguments heretofore advanced with regard to the creation of new states apply, *mutatis mutandi,* to local governments. Nevertheless, it must be noted that the explosion of local governments from 301 to 589 under the Babangida Administration is atrocious. For example, this led to a House of Representatives with a bizarre number of 589 members. In this House, representations were so bloated that the population factor was rendered meaningless. Under such regime, some local government areas, each with a federal house member, consisted merely 50,000 persons, while others, each with a federal house member, had populations ranging from 150,000 to 500,000. What a farce; what disproportion; what imbalance!

From the above follows the argument that the present local governments' structure and the attendant representations in the (federal) House of Representatives and even some State Assemblies cry out for radical redress and rational re-adjustments. Here again, the factor of derivation as a principle of revenue allocation comes in quite handy, if only as a most useful empirical razor. Still on this factor, local government can serve as instruments for assuaging the many ethnic and sub-ethnic nationalities. Clearly, such exercise can be stupendous or thorough-going and therefore seems to fall outside the ambit of a constitutional conference, sovereign or national, free or fettered.

Therefore, the **EMU** recommends

(i)   the establishment of a local government commission which shall rationalize the local government areas in the country;
(ii) trim or increase their number, in accordance with the principle of revenue allocation, as predicated on *derivation;*
(iii) establish the criteria for local governments' existence or creation;
(iv) establish modalities for fiscal accountability, management, self-reliance; and
(v)   set the mechanism for their freedom from overt or irresponsible intervention by state/federal governments. In this connection, the **EMU** maintains that the abolition of the (so-called) federal ministry of state and local governments is a desideratum.

Local Government Reform

No matter the new general structure that may be introduced, the fact still remains that the local government has a lot to contribute in the task of nation-building and social development.

It is the view of the **Eastern Mandate Union** that

(i)   The first task of local government reform in the immediate post independence years and right up to the

1970s was the harmonization and centralization of local government administration in order to create uniform local authority councils. This task was achieved to a large extent in 1976 with the first major local government reform effort.

(ii) The second rationale is the creation of a developed local authority system that will complement the central and state administrations; develop a workable local government autonomy and administrative independence in its relation to the other two tiers; and expand the responsibilities of the local councils so that the grassroots will also feel the impact of national development.

(iii) The third rationale is the enactment of statutes designed to guarantee the financial viability and survival of the local councils– an imperative requirement for a meaningful autonomous local government administration.

Present State of Local Government Reform

Local government reforms from the mid-1980s to the early 1990s tried to systemize and professionalize the local government administrative structure. Financial regulations, conditions of service, including recruitment and retirement, separation of powers through the creation of the executive and legislative arms of government and the financial autonomy of the local councils, are some of the areas these reforms addressed.

However, the Abacha administration has tended to reverse the grains in local government reforms. This reversal is seen in the dissolution of the local government councils, unilateral appointment of caretaker committees, establishment of the Local Government Service Commissions; and investiture of the state governments with supervisory, administrative and financial control over the local governments.

Local Government and the Future Federal Structure

It is the view of the **Eastern Mandate Union** that no matter what shape the new federal structure may take, the local government councils must be made to benefit in the areas of:

(a) More political and administrative autonomy to the local councils as a way of strengthening their powers.

(b) Rationalization of the number of local governments such that no state/zonal region has more local governments in contrast to others of relatively equal or larger population. Thus, Kano State cannot have 36 local governments while Lagos (with a larger population!) has only 15. Similarly, Kogi State cannot have 15 local governments, while the much more populous Anambra State has only 16. And so on.

(c) Better still, local governments must not be controlled by the federal government, over the head of the states in which they are locally located. As such, the existence of a Federal Ministry of State and Local Government not only offends the *Federal Principle* but also makes a mockery of state governments and the local governments themselves.

(d) Another way of guaranteeing the autonomy and competence of local governments is to insist on self-sufficiency of each. It is indeed questionable why local and/or state governments should exist or be created so as to foster parasitism. As such, uniform emoluments for local government executives, councilors and staff are reputable. The operating maxim should be to each according to its revenue base and ability and from each according to its revenue generational reality.

(e) The federal government should only concern itself with *criteria,* as constitutionally provided, specified operational standards and financial disbursements, as constitutionally provided, for local governments, so as to check recklessness and prevent overt state government interventions.

(f) Increase the local government' share in the federation account; some percent of the constituent revenue of which shall repose with such councils before the rest shall be channeled to other tiers of government.

The Judiciary

The **Eastern Mandate Union** holds that a strong, independent and socially responsible Judiciary is a *sine quo non* for social justice, equity and democracy. The **EMU** is disturbed by the politicization and consequent manipulation of the Judiciary by governments and other interest groups. The **EMU** therefore considers that the following are some of the steps that must be taken:

(a) Insulate the Judiciary from political interference; and
(b) Strengthen it in its discharge of its statutory responsibilities.

> (i) The independence of the judiciary must be provided for in no uncertain terms in the Constitution such that encroachment thereon by any other arm of government shall be punishable and devoid of any immunity by a Chief Executive, federal, state or local.
>
> (ii) The appointment of the Chief Justice of the Federation should cease to be an executive prerogative. Such appointment should be made by a Federal Judiciary Council whose composition should be provided for in the Constitution;
>
> (iii) The Chief Justice should be appointed from among the judges of the Supreme Court whose membership shall be four from the East, four from the West, four from the North and four from Middle-Belt. Such units shall send an equal number of judges to the Supreme Court, and a judge so appointed must be the most senior in the Supreme Court from the unit supplying the Chief Justice.

(iv) The Chief Justice should serve a constitutionally specified term of office after which another judge shall be appointed from another zone/region. Such appointments will be made until all the zone/regions have produced a Chief Justice of the Federation;

(v) At no time shall any zone/region have more judges than others in the Supreme Court; and

(vi) The composition of the Federal Appeal Courts and High Courts should follow the pattern already enumerated in iii-v above.

Citizenship

The **Eastern Mandate Union** is of the view that being a citizen of Nigeria shall not be in name alone. Actions must be taken to protect the rights, obligations and privileges of citizens. The **Eastern Mandate Union** believes that every citizen of Nigeria must be and feel like a Nigerian with all the rights, etc, irrespective of place of origin, class, sex, creed or place of residence. All matters relating to the above issues must be constitutionally provided for.

In order to achieve true citizenship for every Nigerian, the **EMU** proposes the following guidelines:

(i) Every Nigerian shall have the right to dwell in any part of the country of his/her choice, irrespective of the zone/region he/she hails from, sex, class or creed;

(ii) Every Nigerian shall have the rights and privileges of any other person, in whatever place he may reside, provided that he has satisfied the obligations of residency;

(iii) The obligations of residency shall only include the performance of legitimate trade, business, profession or work and the payment of taxes, levies or other special impositions by the authorities in the place of residency for at least three years;

(iv) Any form of discrimination against a citizen on the basis of sex, federating unit, ethnic identity or creed shall be an offence punishable with five years prison sentence on every count;
(v) While the idea and practice of true federalism is expressed in the concept of federating units and the devolution of powers from the top to bottom, the principles of citizenship shall be the weapon of unity and oneness to which every Nigerian must be obligated.

Nigeria is a pluralistic society. Therefore, the democratic structures which fit such a society must be necessarily pluralistic. Committed as **EMU** is to a single federal Nigeria, with adequate powers and resources devolving to the states/regions/local government areas the **EMU** is not necessarily opposed to any other arrangement which guarantees safety and survival of the people within their own ethnic nationalities – albeit in some acceptable form of association.

The **EMU** will provide the necessary economic policies and implementation plans for the recovery of Nigerian economy, the safety of the people and the beginning of a disciplined and corrupt-free Nigeria. The **EMU** invites all like-minded patriots to join us in this pressing and notable exercise.

Appendix III C

🙰

Response of the Eastern Mandate Union to the Federal Military Government's Ultimatum of 26th May, 1994.

This response was a by-product of the ultimatum given the **Eastern Mandate Union** by the Federal Military Government through the Chief of General Staff, Lt. General Oladipo Diya, on 26th May, 1994, as reported on the NTA 9 o'clock National Network News. The ultimatum followed the wide press coverage of the resolution of the **EMU** confabulation 20th May, 1994. That resolution contained among other things the following:

1. That the **Eastern Mandate Union** believes strongly that the military junta has nothing to offer Nigerians, and should therefore quit office on 30th June,1994;
2. That the **EMU**, while adopting the tactics and strategies of legitimate political struggle, shall liaise with other patriotic and democratic-oriented national organizations for the enthronement of democracy, equity and justice in Nigeria.
3. That the **EMU** wants the restoration of all electoral

mandates, including that of June 12, 1993, provided that such an exercise will address once and for all time, the marginalization of the East; and

4. That the **EMU**, being a grassroots-based, mass democratic organization, is working towards the establishment of a national political organization, PEOPLE'S MANDATE PARTY, at the appropriate stage in the democratization process.

RESPONSE OF THE EASTERN MANDATE UNION (EMU) TO THE ULTIMATUM GIVEN TO THE UNION ON 26TH MAY, 1994, BY THE FEDERAL MILITARY GOVERNMENT

The attention of the **Eastern Mandate Union (EMU)** has been drawn to a news item in the 9 pm News Bulletin of the Nigerian Television Authority (NTA), on Thursday, 26 May, 1994, in which the Chief of General Staff (CGSS), Lt-General Oladipo Diya, speaking on behalf of the Head of State, General Sani Abacha, gave the EMU 48hours to clarify its status in relation to its recent press releases. The releases which were widely carried in the national dailies of Wednesday, 25 May, 1994, and Thursday, 26 May, 1994, dealt with the following substantial issues:

1. That the EMU is strongly persuaded that only a sovereign national conference can address and resolve the urgent political, social and economic problems facing the country.
2. That the EMU has advised the present military regime to quit office on 30 June,1994, after putting in place a broad-based, democratically-oriented government of national unity.
3. That the EMU feels strongly that the restoration of the electoral mandate delivered by the people of Nigeria on 12 June, 1993 must be matched with the restoration of other legitimate but dissolved political structures and institutions, and the resolution, once and for all, of the

marginalization of the East; and

4. That the EMU has the plan to establish a political party which it intends to call the "People's Mandate Party" at such an auspicious time in the democratization process. No congress or meeting of such a party-in-waiting has been envisaged because of the obvious enactments of the present regime on the matter. We make this clarification, bearing in mind that a measure of difference exists between objective intention and the actualization of intent.

The Eastern Mandate Union is an organization made up of citizens of the seven Eastern states of the Federal Republic of Nigeria who are deeply and patriotically concerned about the plight and marginalization of Eastern Nigeria in the institutional set-up of the country; who are disturbed about the erosion of democratic values and cultures crafted over 8 years of a transition to civil rule programme that cost the nation hundreds of billions of Naira it can ill-afford; and who are compelled to aggregate together on the fundamental and universally acclaimed premise that people can gather together to discuss their problems once their aims and objectives are noble, patriotic and worthy.

The EMU is proud to say that its aims and objectives are noble, patriotic and worthy, for it has set for itself, using the tactics and strategies of legitimate political struggle, the goals of:

a) Achieving true, popular democracy in Nigeria;
b) Alerting the nation of the dangers inherent in the continued marginalization of Eastern Nigeria and indeed other sections of Nigerian society, and seeking ways of resolving it; and
c) Advancing the cause of good government, equity, fair play and justice-worthy ideals which we can bequeath to our children and generations yet unborn.

All the meetings of the Eastern Mandate Union (EMU) have been held in the open, at the Chancery in Enugu, and its resolutions have always been made available to the press, most of which have readily highlighted them in their publications, believing them to be noble, patriotic and worthy in our collective struggle to build a better society for our people.

The status of the Eastern Mandate Union (EMU) is thus clear in relation to the resolutions of its meeting of 20 May, 1994, because it is a status derived from the union's concern with the general state of affairs in our society; with the curtailment of democratic values; and with the general state of political, economic and social trauma which successive regimes (1960-1994) have thrown the nation into. It has the same status with the following organizations and other institutional establishments in the country which have advanced the following causes:

1. The Campaign for Democracy (CD) which called out the entire Nigerian populace to observe a day of civil disobedience in May 1994; which has called on Nigerians to boycott the Constitutional Conference delegates' elections; and which has called on the present regime to quit office.

2. The National Democratic Coalition (NADECO) which has demanded that the present regime should quit office on 31 May, 1994; that thereafter a government of National Unity will be formed by the acclaimed winner of the June 12, 1993 Presidential election, Bashorun M.K.O. Abiola; and that Nigerians should boycott the government organized constitutional conference delegates' election. NADECO has not only reaffirmed its election, but has also informed Nigerians that after 31 May, 1994, they will put in place legitimate political programme of action to make its ultimatum effective. NADECO's calls have been widely reported by the nation's media, more than even the EMU's resolution.

3. The call made by the traditional rulers of the South-Western states on Thursday, 19 May, 1994, affirming their support of NADECO's position, and calling on Chief M.K.O. Abiola to form his government without delay.
4. The cover story in *The News* edition of May 1994 captioned "Abiola tackles Abacha", with the sub-heads:
   - Forms government
   - Cabinet list out soon
   - Abacha Pack and Go

That news report even contained the expected speech the President-Elect, Chief M.K.O. Abiola, would read to the nation.

5. *The News* edition of 30 May, 1994 with the following cover choice: "All Set for Abacha's Overthrow", which included the steps progressive and pro-democracy forces would take to force.
6. The *African Concord* edition of 30 May, 1994 with the following cover choice: Showdown Over June 12th, with the subtitle: Democratic Forces Set to Unseat Abacha".
7. The *Tell* edition of 30 May, 1994 with the cover choice of: Abacha's Days Are Numbered" with detailed reports of the grand strategy of democratic and progressive forces to terminate the tenure of the present regime.
8. A news item in *The Guardian* of Wednesday, 25 May, 1994 with the following caption: "Govt, Politicians Harden Stances on Conference" which, in addition to containing comments by notable democratic figures about their opposition to the Constitutional Conference delegates election, equally contained the following statement: "Simultaneously, Chief Moshood Abiola, the acclaimed but unofficial winner of the controversially annulled June 12 election of last year, pressed his threats to form a parallel government.
9. The various statements by Chief M.K.O. Abiola, widely believed to have won the June 12 election of 1993, that

his mandate is intact; that Nigerians must resist the present government; and that he is set to claim the mandate delivered by the people of Nigeria on June 12, 1993; and

10. The various press interviews granted by the avowed human rights crusader and notable pro-democracy figure, Chief Gani Fawehinmi, that if the present regime refuses to quit office before the end of September 1994, he will float a political party and canvass for political power from the people of Nigeria. In fact, in one of his recent press statements he said categorically: "I want to rule". Already, advertisements soliciting for membership of his organization have started to appear in the print media.

All these are just a tip of the iceberg regarding the feeling, and vision of progressive and democratically-minded individuals and organizations in the country. The EMU is one such organization claiming a mandate and a status not over or beyond that are already claimed by these persons and organizations before it. The EMU is not disturbed in the least about the decision of the federal military government to single it out from among numerous others to issue the network news ultimatum. After all, the reaction of the federal military government to the news of the South-Western traditional rulers' ultimatum was to dispatch the Chief of General Staff to discuss with them; in the same way that a section of the military held series of meetings with certain progressive and pro-democracy activists and organizations before it struck on November 17, 1993. All these are nothing but eloquent testimonies to the unbalanced structure of the federation, the perennial issue of marginalization and the unjust character of the polity which sets different standards for different peoples, depending on their geo-political and ethno-cultural axis.

While the EMU has neither set for itself the objective of forming a parallel government nor claimed any mandate, it is fortified in the belief that its vision is patriotic, its goal legitimate and its agenda democratic and progressive. The ranks of democratic and progressive forces in the country, as experienced in South Africa and elsewhere have amply demonstrated, must be made more binding and resolute in order that we achieve for our society a measure of decency, peace, equity and the fulfillment of popular mandate.

The Eastern Mandate Union (EMU) recognizes the geo-political and territorial expression called Nigeria and is prepared to fight for it provided that equity, fair play and justice prevail. The EMU, while abhorring all forms and measures of dictatorship, military or civil, recognizes that there is a government still in place, and has thus resolved to pursue the enthronement of democracy and fair play through legitimate political means; while at least adopting the means, instrumentalities, tactics and strategies others have already advanced and canvassed for, as the present response has objectively demonstrated.

Finally, we reaffirm our commitment to the Nigerian dream and the vision of our founding fathers, provided that we pursue this in an environment characterized by tolerance, good judgement, decorum and love for one another.

Signed: **Dr Arthur A Nwankwo**
CHANCELLOR

Appendix IV

Arthur Agwuncha Nwankwo: Icon of Democracy@ 70

On Sunday 19th August, Arthur Agwuncha Nwankwo, founder of the Fourth Dimension Publishing Company Ltd, Chancellor of Eastern Mandate Union (EMU), Deputy Chairman, National Democratic Coalition (NADECO), founder and leader of People's Mandate Party (PMP), pro-democracy and human rights activist, quintessential Pan-Africanist publisher and educationist, author, historian, Political Scientist, radical scholar and neo-Marxist theoretician will turn 70 years. And for those of us whose ideas he shaped; whose thoughts he crystallized; whose lives he molded; whose destiny he nurtured; and who see him from the prism of a mentor, a guide and a teacher, what epistemic resource can we call upon to capture such a subject whose birth was posthumous in nature and essence? What cognitive or apprehensible schema can unfold a life so diverse and complex, a mind so fecund and capacious, and a social practice so profound and coherent?

I will but try.

Arthur Nwankwo's forceful emergence on the Nigerian public scene was signaled with the publication of his ground-breaking polemic on the Nigerian war titled *Nigeria: The Challenge of Biafra, Together with Biafra: The Making of a Nation, Nigeria: My People Suffer* and other seminal materials on the Igbo question in the Nigerian state. He constructed a coherent thesis of a people caught between the haunting dialectics of identity-formation and social becoming in a plural nation-state, and problematized the strategic framework with which they must negotiate and balance the complexities of structural and institutional disequilibria in an unfair and unjust social formation that has termed his people into decentred historical objects. Yet, his pan-Nigerian identity and ideals are near peerless; unsurpassable too are his urgings for a new national patriotic ethos founded on egalitarian principles for the Self and the Other.

With the establishment of Fourth Dimension Publishing Company Ltd in 1976–which in itself grew out of the Nwankwo-Ifejika and Nwamife publishing enterprises–he redefined publishing as an art of cultural hermeneutics and the reproduction of knowledge in the Nigerian context; shattered the myth of African strategic, technical, and intellectual incapacity in initiating and sustaining a publishing outlet with global best practices and reach, especially given the spatialization of humanistic referents under late, postmodern capitalism; re-drew the Nigerian publishing geographic and ethno-strategic space and constructed an interventionist paradigm of knowledge reproducibility that produced a generation of scholars.

Arthur Nwankwo gave us the concept of "cimilicy" a grand thesis or metanarrative on Nigerian democratic possibility whose dialectical organism stems from militarizing civilians and civilianizing the military. In formulating extensive and expansive master discourses on the place and role of the military in Nigeria's democratization process, he radically demythologized such concepts as "retreat of power", "negotiated withdrawal and leisurely withdrawal from power" and "intra-elite contradictions and the game of revolving doors," the problematic of which still haunts a nation already embarrassed by the conceptual and paradigmatic deficiencies of the 1999 political transitional pyrotechnics.

With the birth of the Eastern Mandate Union (EMU) in 1994, and Arthur Nwankwo's selection as its chancellor – a position that made him the movement's ideological guide and moral conscience – the Eastern flank of the pro-democracy agitation was significantly radicalized with the subsumption of the question of the marginalization of the East (an idea it popularized and foregrounded on the national discourse space) to the restoration of the presidential mandate of late Chief M.K.O. Abiola as a perquisite of national cohesion, stability and sustainable development.

Arthur Nwankwo is an example of an individual who deliberately elected to commit class suicide; who had all the opportunities to expand his wealth and build the typical Nigerian financial empire; but who cast his lot with the people by first, theorizing about their imbecilized condition in a series of neo-Marxist scholarly works as all organic intellectuals should in the Gramscian sense of the term, and ended up privileging a vibrant participation in their democratic practice. Arthur Nwankwo suffered series of detentions, intimidations, harassment and ruin of his businesses between 1990-1998 because of his involvement in the pro-democracy struggle against regime tyranny and obscurantist power posturing. He invested his personal fortune in the struggle and literally turned his private residence– already a more than contingent national centre of intellectual illumination, inter-subjective communicative rationality and spirited social dialogics – into a sanctuary for the oppressed and the hunted.

This analysis brings me to that rare quality which the chancellor possesses in exaggerated proportions–COURAGE– and in saying this, I want to recount three instances that remarkably demonstrated this. On 24th May, 1994, the Eastern Mandate Union (EMU),during its special confabulation, issued a 30th June, 1994 proclamation to Gen Sani Abacha to quit office after putting in place a Government of National Unity (GNU) which Chief M.K.O. Abiola would lead. It also incarnated the first version of People's Mandate Party (PMP), with the full complement of registration cards, musically scored party song and anthem, emblem and slogan. Thereafter, on 26th May, 1994 Arthur Nwankwo and I received a tip-off that a detachment of State Security Service and Nigerian Police personnel would literally "invade" the house and effect out arrest. The chancellor calmly asked me to prepare myself physically, intellectually and psychologically for the ordeal, as he had already done so himself. When, eventually, an over 30-man security squad stormed the house, they met us sitting calmly in the upper floor sitting room. The chancellor collected his prescription drugs and food supplement bag, stood up and calmly told the leader of the invading army, "let's go". The officer was clearly baffled and visibly taken aback. He immediately collected his wits together, saluted him, and off we marched to our first detention.

Again, a few weeks to the Commonwealth Ministerial Action Group (CMAG) meeting on Nigeria which held at Edinburgh, Scotland, about July, 1997, the Eastern Mandate Union received an invitation from NADECO to partner with it and adopt a common position at the conference. Upon the receipt of what could possibly be classified as an explosive invitation – a singular act that would further cement EMU's standing as a leading national pro-democracy platform– Arthur Nwankwo embarked upon wide-ranging consultations among Igbo political leaders on what his reaction to the invitation should be. Without exception, all those he consulted counseled him to decline the offer to participate. They were alarmed about the over-exposure and its likely negative consequences without a thought for the national subalterns who desperately needed an agency for the re-mobilization of their humanity.

Arthur Nwankwo was able to locate this Igbo elite mindset as a derivative of extant historicized nuances of negational politics that was founded on a romantic self-redemptive idiom: a bitter, internecine, and increasingly bloody competition between two triumphalist ethno-strategic enclaves that instrumentalized their corporate decentring, and a contest they wished would consequent in their mutual annihilation. He however saw through this limited, and somewhat irrational historical logic through an ideological deconstruction of its inherent subjective spirit, and rather settled for a materialist mode of reasoning and intervention that would not only recuperate his people's emancipatory instincts and possibilities but those of the Other as well.

The pressure was so fierce that I was elected to reply on his behalf to late Senator Abraham Adesanya who signed the letter of invitation and politely declined it. I was already seated in the study of the Chancery struggling on how to proceed when the Chancellor stormed in and commanded me to change the letter to one of robust, unequivocal acceptance, declaring thus: "At times like this, men and women of courage must stand up to be counted. In the absence of heroism, our people are lost forever. We must attend that meeting". In spite of all the threats to his person, he led the EMU delegation to the conference, and thereafter embarked upon a blistering international campaign against military despotism in the USA and several European countries.

The internationalization of EMU's pro-democracy agitation, particularly in the USA, resulted in a deeper, more entrenched and strategic penetration of the American governmental space and civil society sphere by the Nigerian Diasporic and exile community and its self-constructed platforms. Inevitably, this decisive thrust that widened the pan-Nigerian character of the democratic struggle beyond its putative regionalist presencing (a de-legitimating weapon in the hands of the Nigerian praetorian junta) led to the establishment of EMU-ABROAD. Built around the highly focused Nigerian Democratic Awareness Committee (NDAC), it had as its chairman Prof. Eddy Oparaoji and such other staunch pro-democracy activists as Dr Innocent Chima, Lawrence Onyekwere, Tochukwu Ezukanma, Vincent Erondu, Nwakuba, Ugo Harris, and several others.

Shortly after the CMAG conference, the entire South-West leadership made up of late Sen. Abraham Adesanya, late Chief Bola Ige, late Chief Solanke Onasanya, Chief Ayo Adebanjo, Chief Olanihun Ajayi, Sen. Kofo Akerele-Bucknor, Chief (Mrs) Ayoka Lawani, Sen Femi Okorunmu and several others took a night bus to the Chancery of the EMU for a strategic meeting with its leadership. The highlight of the meeting was the re-construction of NADECO's leadership as follows: Late Anthony Enahoro (Chairman); late Sen. Abraham Adesanya (Chairman-Nigeria); Dr Arthur Nwankwo (Deputy Chairman,); Air Commodore Dan Suleman (Vice Chairman); and Chief Ayo Opadokun (Secretary). The Chancellor brushed aside the fear and anxiety of the EMU leadership present about his selection and announced his acceptance of not only the offer but also the urgency of the EMU's institutional purchase into and full application of its intellectual, ideological and strategic resources towards the successful prosecution of the pro-democracy struggle.

Throughout all the periods of our detention at various points between 1994 and 1998, particularly in May 1998 when over seventy military, police and SSS personnel came to arrest just seven or so pro-democracy activists with over 20 vehicles, the Chancellor and I inclusive, his spirit was always buoyant, his wit as sharp and caustic as ever. He never lost hope that potent ideas in the margin would one day become immanent national categories, that the struggle would triumph over inhuman odds, or that the oppressed and the dehumanized, the bestialized and the traumatized, would inherit a new Nigeria.

What I cannot speak of now is whether the Chancellor's

incurably optimistic spirit about the enormous Nigerian possibilities has flagged given the present reign of perfumed unreason, insolent simulacrum and fickle-minded idiocy that fester in the land, barely able to deodorize the putrescent spectacle that the contemporary Nigerian conduction has become: the sheer kleptomania of the ruling elite; the weakening of the nation's historicist consciousness and bonds of fraternal inter-group solidarity; and the inexorable national drift into political, economic, social, cultural and spiritual perdition, collective immolation and irredeemable angst, in short, into a state of non-being.

I can only conclude this very modest assessment of the Chancellor by quoting from my thoughts about him with specific regard to the formulation of the Fourth Dimension Pedagogy of African Liberation in the first of a three-volume study I have tentatively titled: *Democratic Transformation and Social Change in Nigeria: From Intellectual Conscience to Praxis*:

Arthur Nwankwo evolved the theory of the Fourth Dimension as a Materialist-Spiritual Category, and located African liberation within its pedagogical context. He took from geometry, and by extension, the study of matter and its properties, the dimensional theory of reality. He understood that geometrically speaking, and this has found resonance in algebra, mechanics and physics, a line has one dimension, a surface two dimensions of length and breadth, and a solid three dimensions of length, breadth and thickness. By extension, he projected that the Fourth Dimension occupies an inscrutable realm, the realm of knowledge that cannot be captured by these geometric categoric specifications. The Fourth Dimension Pedagogical Theory of African Liberation then implies the harnessing of the pristine spiritual essence of African cosmology in a process that weighs heavily in favour of historicity and dialectics; de-romanticizing those spiritual ingredients on the weight of stupendous historical evidence, omissions, setbacks and tragedies; and incarnating a new idiom of African historical re-emergence as a combination of both the material (3 dimensions) and spiritual (1 dimension) of African cosmogony. This liberationist theorizing was eventually celebrated by him in the appendices to his *The African Possibility in Global Power Struggle*.

Bibliography

Achebe, Chinua. *Things Fall Apart.* London: Heinemann, 1959.

──────. *Arrow of God.* London: Heinemann, 1964, 1974.

──────. *A Man of the People.* London: Heinemann, 1966.

──────. *There Was a Country: A Personal History of Biafra.* London: Penguin Books, 2012.

Adorno, Theodor and Hokheimer, Max. *Dialectic of Enlightenment.* London: Verso, 1944, 1997, 2010.

Agbagha, Mma. *Pressure Group Politics.* Ibadan: Spectrum Books, 2003.

Agbaje, Adigun AB. Ed. *Nigeria's Struggle for Democracy and Good Governance.* Ibadan: University of Ibadan Press, 2004.

Ahmad, Aijaz. *In Theory: Nations, Classes, Literatures.* London: Verso, 1992, 2008.

──────. *Lineages of the Present: Political Essays.* New Delhi: Tulika, 1996.

Alkali, M. N. ed. *Nigeria in the Transition Years* (1993-1999). *Presidential Advisory Committee*/NIPPS, 1999.

Alozieuwa, Simeon H. O. *From Parliamentarism to Militocracy and Presidentialism: Nigeria in Quest for Stable Political Order.* Abuja: Authentic Media Networks, 2008.

Althusser, Louis. *For Marx.* London: Verso, 1965, 2005.

——————. *On Ideology.* London: Verso, 1971, 2008.

Amuta, Chidi. *Toward the Sociology of African Literature.* Oguta: Zim Press, 1986.

Badiou, Alain. *Being and Event.* London: Continuum Books, 2006, 2010.

——————. *Second Manifesto For Philosophy.* Cambridge: Polity and Blackwell, 2011.

Baudrillard, Jean. *Selected Writings,* ed by Mark Poster. Cambridge: Polity and Blackwell, 1988, 2004.

Benjamin, Walter. *The Arcades Project,* trans. Howard Eiland & Kevin McLaughlin. Cambridge, MA. & London: Belknap Press, 1999.

——————. and Theodor Adorno. *The Complete Correspondences* 1928-1940, ed. Henri Lonitz. Cambridge: Polity Press, 1999.

——————. *One-Way Street and Other Writings,* trans. J. A. Underwood. Harmondsworth: Penguin, 2009.

Bhabha, Homi. *The Location of Culture.* Oxford: Routledge Press, 1994. (Special Indian Edition 2004).

Boguslavsky, *et al. ABC of Dialectical and Historical Materialism.* Moscow: Progress Publishers, 1975, 1978.

Chinweizu, *et al. Toward The Decolonization of African Literature.* Enugu: Fourth Dimension Publishers, 1980.

Chu, Amy. *World on Fire: How Exporting Free Market Democracy Breeds Ethnic Hatred and Global Instability.* London: Arrow Books, 2003.

Cook, David and Okenimkpe, Michael. *Ngugi Wa Thiong'o: An Exploration of His Writings.* London: Heinemann, 1983.

Cook, Deborah, ed. *Theodor Adorno: Key Concepts.* Stocksfield: Acumen Publishing Ltd, 2008.

Derrida, Jacques. *Specters of Marx.* New York: Routledge, 1994, 2006.

Dolgov, K. M, *et al. Marxist-Leninist Aesthetics and the Arts.* Moscow: Progress Publishers, 1980.

Eagleton, Terry. *Criticism and Ideology.* London: Verso, 1976.

—————. *Walter Benjamin, or Toward a Revolutionary Criticism.* London: Verso, 1981, 2009.

—————. *Literary Theory: An Introduction.* Oxford: Basil Blackwell Publishers, 1983, 2008.

—————. *The Illusions of Postmodernism.* Oxford: Blackwell Publishing, 1996.

—————. *After Theory.* London: Penguin Books. 2003

—————. *The Idea of Culture.* Oxford: Blackwell Publishing, 2000.

—————. *Sweet Violence: The Idea of the Tragic.* Oxford. Blackwell Publishing, 2003.

—————. *Trouble With Strangers: A Study of Ethics.* Oxford: Willey-Blackwell, 2009.

—————. *Why Marx Was Right.* New Haven and London: Yale University Press, 2011.

—————. and Matthew Beaumont. *The Task of the Critic: Terry Eagleton in Dialogue.* London: Verso, 2009.

—————. and Walker, Brain, ed. *From Culture to Revolution.* London: Verso, 1968.

Ego-Alowes, Jimanze. *Minorities as Competitive Overlords.* Lagos: The Stone Press, 2013.

Ezeagu, Benedict Chuks O. *Chief M. K. O. Abiola and June 12: The Immortal Phenomena (A Record for Posterity).* Enugu: Ndubest Productions, 2001.

Fanon, Frantz. *The Wretched of the Earth.* London: Penguin

Books, 1965, 1980.

Fatunde, Tunde. *No More Oil Boom and Blood and Sweat.* Benin: Adena Publishers, 1984.

——————. *No Food No Country,* Benin: Adena, 1985.

——————. *Oga Na Tief Man.* Benin: Adena, 1986.

Fishcher, Ernest. *The Necessity of Art.* Harmondsworth: Penguin Books, 1963.

Frolov, I. ed. *Dictionary of Philosophy.* Moscow: Progress Publishers, 1980.

Galeano, Eduardo. *Open Veins of Latin America: Five Centuries of the Pillage of a Continent.* New York. Monthly Review Press, 1973, 1997.

Gbilekaa, Saint. *Radical Theatre in Nigeria.* Ibadan: Caltop Publications Ltd, 1997.

Goldmann, Lucien. *Method in the Sociology of Literature.* Oxford: Basil Blackwell, 1981.

——————. *Towards the Sociology of the Novel.* St. Louis: Telos Press, 1976.

——————. *Lukacs and Heidegger.* London: Routledge and Kegan Paul, 1977.

Golwa, Joseph H. P. & Ochinya O. Ojiji, ed. *Dialogue on Citizenship in Nigeria.* Abuja: IPCR, 2008.

Grant, Damian. *Realism.* Bristol: Methean, 1970.

Habermas, Jurgen. *The Structural Transformation of the Public Sphere.* 1962; trans. Thomas Burger. Cambridge: MIT Press, 1989.

——————. *The Philosophical Discourse of Modernity.* Cambridge: MIT Press, 1987.

——————. *Legitimation Crisis.* Boston: Beacon Press, 1975.

Hauster, Arnold. *The Social History of Art.* Vol. 4. London. Routledge and Kegan Paul, 1951.

Heywood, Christopher. Ed. *Perspectives on African Literature.* London: Heinemann, 1971.

Holman, Hugh C. *A Handbook to Literature.* 3rd ed. Indianapolis, Indiana: Bobbs-Merril Educational Publishing, 1978.

Howe, Irving, ed. *The Idea of the Modern in Literature and the Arts.* New York: Horizon Press, 1967.

Igbokwe, Joe. *Heroes of Democracy.* Clear Vision Ltd, 1999.

Ihonvbere, Julius O. Nigeria: *The Politics of Adjustment and Democracy.* Transaction Publishers, 1994.

Irele, Abiola. *The African Experience in Literature and Ideology.* London: Heinemann, 1981.

Iyayi, Festus. *Violence.* London: Longman, 1979.

——————. *The Contract.* London: Longman, 1982.

Jameson, Fredric (afterword). *Aesthetics and Politics: Adorno, Benjamin, Bloch, Brecht, Lukacs.* London: Verso, 1977, 2007.

——————. *Postmodernism, Or, The Cultural Logic of Late Capitalism.* Durham: Duke University Press, 1991.

——————. *The Cultural Turn: Selected Writings on the Postmodern,* 1983-1998. London: Verso, 1998, 2009.

——————. *A Singular Modernity: Essays on the Ontology of the Present.* London: Verso, 2002.

——————. *Brecht and Method.* London: Verso, 1998, 2011.

Jega, Attahiru. *Democracy, Good Governance and Development in Nigeria.* Ibadan: Spectrum Books, 2007.

Jones, Eldred. Ed. *African Literature Today,* No. 10. London: Heinemann, 1979.

——————. *African Literature Today,* ed. No. 12, London: Heinemann, 1982.

Jones, Gareth Stedman, *et al.* Western Marxism: A Critical

Reader. London: New Left Review, 1977.

Juan, E. San Jr. *Beyond Postcolonial Theory*. New York: St. Martin's Press, 1998.

—————————. *Working Through the Contradictions: From Cultural Theory to Critical Practice*. Lewisburg: Bucknell UP, 2004.

—————————. *Racism and Cultural Studies: Critiques of Multiculturalist Ideology and the Politics of Difference*. Durham & London: Duke University Press, 2002.

Kant, Immanuel. *Critique of Judgment*. Indianapolis: Hackett, 1987.

—————————. *Critique of Pure Reason*. Indianapolis: Hackett, 1996.

Ker, David. *The African Novel and the Modernist Tradition*. Ibadan: Mosuro Publishers, 2003.

Kuka, Matthew Hassan. *Democracy and Civil Society in Nigeria*. Ibadan: Spectrum Books, 2002.

Lenin, V. I. *On Literature and Art,* Moscow: Progress Publishers, 1967.

—————————. *Collected Works,* Vol. 20. Moscow: Progress 1965.

Lindfors, Bernth. *Early Nigerian Literature*. Ibadan: Caltop Publications Ltd, 1982.

—————————. *Early Achebe*. Trenton, NJ: Africa World Press, 2009.

Lukacs, Geog. *Studies in European Realism*. London: Merlin Press, 1972.

—————————. *The Meaning of Contemporary Realism*. London: Merlin Press, 1963.

—————————. *History and Class Consciousness: Studies in Marxist Dialectics*. London: Merlin Press, 1971, 2010.

Lyotard, Jean-Francois. *The Postmodern Condition: A Report on Knowledge*. Trans. Geoffrey Bennington and Brian Massumi. Minneapolis: University of Minneapolis Press, 1984.

Magubane, Zine. ed. *Postmodernism, Postcoloniality, and African Studies*. Trenton, NJ: Africa World Press, 2011.

Markov, Dmitry. *Socialist Literatures: Problems of Development*. Moscow: Raduga Press, 1984.

Marx, K. and Engels. F. *On Literature and Art*. Moscow: Progress, 1976.

Mwangi, Meja. *Going Down River Road*. London: Heinemann, 1976.

─────────. *Kill Me Quick*. London: Heinemann, 1978.

Nasidi, Yakubu. *Beyond the Experience of Limits*. Ibadan: Caltop Publications Ltd, 2002.

Ngara, Emmanuel. *Art and Ideology in the African Novel*. London: Heinemann, 1985.

Ngugi Wa Thiong'o. *Petals of Blood*. London: Heinemann, 1977.

─────────. *A Writer's Prison Diary*. London: Heinemann, 1981.

─────────. *Detained: Writers in Politics*. London: Heinemann, 1981.

─────────. *Barrel of a Pen*. London: New Beacon Books, 1983.

─────────. *Devil on the Cross*. London: Heinemann, 1982.

─────────. *Moving the Centre: The Struggle for Cultural Freedoms*. London: James Curry, 1993.

Nnoli, Okwudiba. *Ethnic Politics in Nigeria*. Enugu: Fourth Dimension Publishers, 1980.

Novikov, Vassily. *Artistic Truth and the Dialectics of Creative Work*. Moscow: Progress Publishers, 1981.

Nwankwo, Arthur Agwuncha. *Nigeria: The Political Transition And The Future Of Democracy.* Enugu: Fourth Dimension Publishers, 1993.

——————. *Nigerians As Outsiders: Military Dictatorship and Nigeria's Destiny.* Enugu: Fourth Dimension Publishers, 1996.

——————. *The Retreat of Power: The Military in Nigeria's Third Republic.* Enugu: Fourth Dimension Publishers, 1992.

——————. *Terminus: Endgame Doctrine.* Enugu: Fourth Dimension Publishers, 1997.

——————. *African Dictators: The Logic of Power and Regime Violence.* Enugu: Fourth Dimension Publishers, 1990.

Nwoga, D. I. ed. *Literature and Modern West African Culture.* Benin: Ethiope Publishers, 1978.

Obiechina, Emmanuel. ed. *Onitsha Market Literature.* London: Heinemann, 1972.

——————. *An African Popular Literature: A Study of the Onitsha Market Pamphlets.* Cambridge. Cambridge University Press, 1973.

Obi, Amanze. *Delicate Matters: An Interpreter's Account of the Nigerian Dilemma.* Stirling-Horden Publishers, 2013.

Ogbuefi, J. U. *The Time Between.* Enugu: Cecta Publishers, 1986.

Oko, Okechukwu. *Key Problems for Democracy in Nigeria.* London: Edwin Mellen, 2010.

Omoruyi, Omo. *The Tale of June 12: The Betrayal of the Democratic Rights of Nigerians* (1993). London: Press Alliance Network Ltd, 1999.

Omotoso, Kole. *The Form of the African Novel.* Akure: Fagbamighe Publishers, 1979.

Onukaogu, Allwell Abalogu and Onyerionwu, Ezechi. *21st*

Century Nigerian Literature: An Introductory Text. Ibadan: Kraft Books, 2009.

Onwueme, Tess. *The Desert Encroaches.* Owerri: Heins Publishers, 1985.

——————. *The Broken Calabash.* Ibadan: Heinemann Nigerian Publishers, 1988.

——————. *The Reign of Wazobia.* Ibadan: Heinemann Nigerian Publishers, 1988.

Oshun, Olawale. *The Open Grave: NADECO and the Struggle for Democracy.* London: Josel Publishers, 2002.

——————. *Clapping With One Hand: June 12 and the Crisis of a State Nation.* London: Josel Publishers, 1999.

Otite, Onigu. *Ethnic Pluralism, Ethnicity and Ethnic Conflicts in Nigeria.* Ibadan: Shaneson Ltd, 1990, 2000.

Ousmane, Sembene. *God's Bits of Wood.* London: Heinemann, 1960.

Ovcharenko, Alexander. *Socialist Realism and The Modern Literary Process.* Moscow: Raduga Publishers, 1978.

Palmer, Eustace. *The Growth of the African Novel.* London: Heinemann, 1979.

——————. *Languages, Literature and the Arts of War and Women, Oppression and Optimism: New Essays on the African Novel.* Trenton, NJ: Africa World Press, 2008.

Roscoe, Adrian. *Uhuru's Fire: African Literature East to South:* London: Cambridge University Press, 1977.

Roxburgh, Angus, tr. *Marxism, Aesthetics and the Arts.* Moscow: Progress Publishers, 1980.

Said, Edward. *Orientalism.* London: Penguin Books, 1985, 2003.

——————. *Culture and Imperialism.* London: Vintage Books, 1993, 1994.

——————. *Humanism and Democratic Criticism.*

Basingstoke: Palgrave Macmillan, 2004.

——————. *Reflections on Exile and Other Literary and Cultural Essays.* London: Granta Books, 2001.

Slaughter, Cliff. *Marxism, Ideology and Literature.* London: Macmillan, 1980.

Spivak, Gayatri Chakravorty. *In Other Worlds: Essays in Cultural Politics.* New York and London: Routledge Classics, 1987, 2006.

Sprinker, Michael, ed. *Ghostly Demarcations: Derrida, Eagleton, Jameson, Negri, et al.* London: Verso, 199, 2008.

Suberu, Rotimi. *Federalism and Ethnic Conflict in Nigeria.* Washington, DC: USIP, 2001.

Thometz, Kurt, ed. *Life Turns Man Upside Down: African Market Literature.* New York: Pantheon Books, 2001.

Ushie, Joseph and Abdullahi, Denja, ed. *Themes Fall Apart But the Centre Holds.* Ibadan: Kraft Books, 2009.

Willet, John, tr. 2nd ed. *Brecht on Theatre.* London: Eyre Methuen, 1974.

Williams, Raymond. *Culture and Society.* London: Harmondsworth, 1963.

——————. *The Culture and the City.* St. Albans: Paladin, 1975.

——————. *Marxism and Literature.* Oxford: Oxford University Press, 1977.

——————. *The Long Revolution.* London: Penguin Publishers 1965.

Witte, B. *Walter Benjamin: An Intellectual Biography.* Detroit: Wayne University Press, 1991.

Wizisla, E. *Walter Benjamin and Bertolt Brecht: The Story of a Friendship.* London: Libris Press, 2009.

ZIS, A compl. *Problems of Contemporary Aesthetics.* Moscos: Raduga Publishers, 1984.

Zizek, Slavoj. *For They Know Not What They do.* London: Verso, 1991, 2008.

——————. *The Ticklish Subject: The Absent Centre of Political Ontology.* London: Verso, 1999, 2008.

——————. *Revolution at the Gates: Selected Writings of Lenin from 1917.* London: Verso, 2002.

——————. *In Defense of Lost Causes.* London: Verso, 2008, 2009.

——————. *First As Tragedy, Then As Farce.* London: Verso, 2009.

——————. *The Parallax View.* Cambridge, Massachusetts: MIT Press, 2006, 2009.

——————. *Living in End Times.* London: Verso, 2010, 2011.

.

www.ingramcontent.com/pod-product-compliance
Lightning Source LLC
Chambersburg PA
CBHW022138020426
42334CB00015B/950